The Sohbat Series

The Sohbat Series

This series captures the intensely personal journey of the spiritual wayfarer's path to wisdom and enlightenment. Encompassing everything from edifying lessons to powerful love poetry, these books explore the most intimate reflections and experiences of disciples at the hands of their spiritual masters.

Each volume is distinct in structure and form, mirroring the unique, extraordinary bond that exists between novice and sage. These personal recollections of both one-to-one and collective experiences will enable you, the reader, to savour the presence of the Sheikh who so enraptured the heart of the disciple.

Other books in the series:

Servant of the Loving One
Paul Abdul Wadud Sutherland
(Sheikh Nazim al-Haqqani)

~

The Merciful Door: Living with a Sufi Teacher in India
Scott Siraj al-Haqq Kugle
(Pir Rasheed Kaleemi)

THE SCHOOL OF Celestial Fire

A SUFI MASTER TEACHES

THE SCHOOL OF Celestial Fire

A SUFI MASTER TEACHES

John Lindsay

BEACON BOOKS

Published in the UK by Beacon Books and Media Ltd
Earl Business Centre, Dowry Street, Oldham, OL8 2PF, UK.

Copyright © John Lindsay 2021

The right of John Lindsay to be identified as the author of this work has been asserted in accordance with the Copyright, Designs and Patents Act 1988. All rights reserved. This book may not be reproduced, scanned, transmitted or distributed in any printed or electronic form or by any means without the prior written permission from the copyright owners, except in the case of brief quotations embedded in critical reviews and other non-commercial uses permitted by copyright law.

First published in 2017 by the author
This edition first published 2021
Reprinted with corrections 2022

www.beaconbooks.net

ISBN: 978-1-912356-69-0 Paperback
ISBN: 978-1-912356-70-6 Hardback
ISBN: 978-1-912356-71-3 eBook

Cataloging-in-Publication record for this book is available from the British Library

Every effort has been made to identify material quoted from other publications and to acknowledge its sources in the text. The publishers will be glad to do likewise for any other such quotations brought to their attention.

Illustrations by Elliot Flynn

In the Name of God, the Most Compassionate, the Most Merciful, this book is dedicated to Sheikh Abdullah Sirr-Dan al-Jamal, may God be well pleased with him.

Above is a rendering in Arabic calligraphy of the Sheikh's name, Abdullah Sirr-Dan al-Jamal. Underneath it he wrote: 'Let this be a doorway to my presence so that your thoughts can be with me and my thoughts, in turn, can be with you.'

Below that he wrote the following:

'Behold with awe the Majesty of the Name within this name,
And remember with each heartbeat to repeat it always with love
And true devotion.
Thus ecstasy, in harmony with that state
Where all is absolutely still, will flood your being
To drown both time and distance with all your senses,
    in the Ocean of His Mercy
Where that Love which lies behind the Beauty of His Majesty
Is Truth and Truth alone.'

Contents

Editorial Note	xi
PROLOGUE	1
RAW	11
COOKED	63
BURNT	147
EPILOGUE	169
NINE DISCOURSES by Sheikh Abdullah Sirr-Dan al-Jamal	177
To the Seeker	289

Editorial Note

EXPLORING any field of human endeavour means encountering unfamiliar names and technical terms. In Sufism these are often in Arabic and other foreign languages. We have tried to minimise both their number and any obstacle they may pose, especially by omitting the 'diacritical marks' used by scholars in transliteration from the original script.

Foreign words including names are given as spelt and pronounced by Sheikh Abdullah Sirr-Dan al-Jamal himself, or by the person concerned, or in the way most easily grasped by English speakers, or in the way established by custom and practice, or some combination of those four.

All pupils who remained with the Sheikh during the period covered by this book converted to Islam, and after about 1980 their Muslim names were normally used, as was his. Accordingly we have used Muslim names throughout, but in most cases they have been changed (as have English ones) for reasons of privacy.

The main body of this work is based mostly on interviews and memory. Speech quoted at second hand is given to the best of the hearers' recollection, but all quoted speech has been edited (as have diary entries and the like), sometimes extensively. Numerous passages have been taken from pupils' notes of the Sheikh's lectures where we believe they are verbatim or nearly so, and amended slightly where necessary for publication. The nine discourses by the Sheikh himself are reproduced word-for-word, though edited in respect of minor details.

Of those pupils who were especially close to him, two had died before this work was begun, and others have not made their recollections available, which has also meant that their insights could not be brought to bear on the task of compilation. We extend heartfelt thanks to those others who have contributed their time and their often intimate memories in the service of his legacy.

Sheikh Abdullah had a high regard for the sonnet that forms the epigraph to this book. It has no title apart from the first line, and is Charles Causley's translation of the French inscription on a crucifix of 1632 in Bayeux Cathedral.

The Sheikh also thought highly of Thomas Gray's 'Elegy Written in a Country Churchyard', from which we have borrowed the reflection that even a humble grave may hold 'some heart once pregnant with celestial fire' that could have been kindled into life.

This second edition incorporates many corrections and amendments, and includes an additional lecture ('The Journey to Redemption').

Koranic quotations are taken from various translations.

Lastly, it is worth emphasising that the question of whether any disciple can rightly be called 'devoted' is a matter for the sheikh, and for him alone.

I am the great sun, but you do not see me,
I am your husband, but you turn away.
I am the captive, but you do not free me.
I am the captain you will not obey.

I am the truth, but you will not believe me,
I am the city where you will not stay.
I am your wife, your child, but you will leave me.
I am that God to whom you will not pray.

I am your counsel, but you will not hear me,
I am your lover whom you will betray.
I am the victor, but you do not cheer me,
I am the holy dove whom you will slay.

I am your life, but if you will not name me,
Seal up your soul with tears, and never blame me.

THIS MAN, this great teacher, is not always easy to find—and even when you meet him he is not going to be what you think.

You may sit with him while he interprets your dreams, without knowing he can appear in them if he chooses.

You may visit him on a winter's evening in his modest London room without realising you are not alone, for he also receives callers you cannot see: guests both welcome and unwelcome, from other worlds parallel to this.

Whether you know it or not, he is a beacon for voyagers in a sea of darkness: an enchanted island where you will meet both danger and succour. Having stumbled ashore despite yourself, you will find that he is a land whose interior you cannot map.

Yet he is also an ocean in his own right, containing terror and wonder and infinite depths. 'Just unfathomable,' said a pupil.

Another pupil put the question in verse: 'Who, tell me, is this man of light?'

So leave your expectations behind. You may see him in the dignity of a master's robe and turban, without having felt his irresistible laugh or having seen him attack a black tiger snake with a shovel. You may be engrossed by his discourse without having seen him at a Turkish wedding in London, dancing to the band as if his life depended on it.

'I am only a meaning,' he declared: and before you look for him, you must want to hunt that meaning down.

1

PROLOGUE

AT SOME TIME or other, even if only when you were a child, you have gazed upwards on a clear summer night in the open air, and seen the same as everyone else.

Not only star upon star. Galaxy upon galaxy—inescapable arrays of galaxies in the blackness: and beyond the limit of your sight are further squadrons. Astronomers say there are complexes and walls and sheets of galaxies. They say our little Milky Way holds 400 billion stars; that 170 billion more galaxies surround it, and innumerable others emit light that has not even reached us yet. It will only reach us, or the place where we used once to be, aeons after we have died and our world itself has disappeared.

Stars beyond counting. Galaxies without end. Vastness beyond understanding. How can your life amount to anything against this reality that stares back at you from the sky?

It's a fair question, although many have never asked it. Of those who do ponder the purpose of their existing, most dismiss the riddle quickly enough for lack of an answer. Many mock the very idea of asking. Still others find a semblance of purpose, whether avowedly or thoughtlessly, in the thousand tasks and pleasures of life, which will all vanish away at death.

A very few seek the true purpose which will eclipse those false purposes as the sun eclipses the pathetic beam of a torch. You may be one of them.

The Sufis, the mystics of Islam, affirm that there truly is such a purpose, and that it can be attained. In the often repeated words of Sheikh Abdullah

Sirr-Dan al-Jamal, 'The whole of life is on a journey. Humankind has the opportunity to complete that journey.'

The Sheikh, whose English name was John Ross, stands among Sufism's greatest masters. Like all his peers, he went far beyond merely stating the challenge of existence. He wrote that the Sufi saints are the custodians of the knowledge of the eternal reality of the universe; and that, as such, they pursue a mission to awaken the rest of humanity 'to experience and appreciate the inner reality of life pulsating at one and the same time at the heart and throughout the essence of all creation'.

Therefore he not only confirmed each seeker in his or her quest; he would try to lead that person to the goal by the best available route.

This book, compiled by one of his pupils with the cooperation of many more, testifies to his life's endeavour of bringing others to the all-consuming realisation of eternal peace that he himself knew—of taking men and women, as he said, back to the source of their own being.

'People are searching for the deep mysteries of life. They want the solution. This is something that's deeply rooted in every human being. We believe, in Sufism, that we have these answers. We don't offer dogmatism. We say, "Come, taste and experience for yourselves."'

The Sheikh never wrote for publication himself, and as a reader you must never forget his warning: 'Intellectual pursuits are absolutely worthless. Real understanding has to be grafted on to our instincts.' Nevertheless, the enlightenment of which you may here catch a glint is utterly real, and the quest for it is more urgent than you can imagine.

He warned that in order to come to real consciousness, to understand your true purpose on earth, you must strip yourself entirely of what he once called falsities—and you must do it before you die, because if your quest is not complete by then, it will become far more difficult afterwards.

As one of his pupils declared, 'We are alive in order to prepare ourselves to die: to be dead. And I didn't know that before [I met him].

'He enabled me to understand not only that I have something in me which is eternal, but that that's the important thing: everything else is just ephemeral. He gave me a sense of purpose. Not even just what that purpose was, but that I could *have* a purpose—and that everything else in life is pale by comparison to the colour of Sufism. That's the real thing; that's what being human is all about. Nothing else matters in comparison to that.'

The riddle posed by the immense universe is real enough. You, your little body, your daily doings, your family, our shared landscape of earth—they really will all be extinguished as if they had never been. They really are an atom in the void. There's nothing at all you can hold on to that will change that. There is no answer out there.

Yet there is an answer in here: and when the Sheikh spoke the words 'in here!' he would strike his hand against his breast. The solution, your true purpose, is within you.

Many centuries ago one of the saints, the master who gave his name to the Sufi order to which Sheikh Abdullah and his pupils belong, answered a question from his son-in-law by simply placing his foot on that of the younger man, who afterwards described that moment:[1] 'I experienced a great exaltation, in which it was as if I witnessed the entire universe within myself. When I returned to my ordinary state, he said, "That is the heart—the central point of connection. To know the heart is to know one's purpose, and to find the heart is to find one's purpose."'

Our Sheikh more than once communicated the same exaltation to his own pupils in the same way. Far more importantly, he taught the process of physiological as well as psychological development through which a pupil can attain that purpose for himself or herself, and thus realise what he called 'our ultimate hope for each one of you': the condition in which, as another master put it, 'the whole universe has been ripened in the heart'. Or to put it another way, the heart has been developed as a bridge between this world and others.

In an essay he used different terms to describe the same destination. 'Eventually a relationship with the Divine Presence is constantly enjoyed in which there is continuous peace of mind, coupled with the bliss described as the love of God. The state of peace and ecstatic bliss [produces] eternal pleasure in which God is seen in all things and all things are seen to flow from God. This everlasting pleasure is a direct experience derived from feeling the love of God in practical terms through the pursuit of the spiritual science imparted by the master as knowledge of his energy and emulation of his actions and mode of life.'

Those last few words provide a signpost to the route that any seeker must follow—the route that he himself taught with meticulous care. It is a journey of experience, not belief.

Born of Scottish ancestry between the two world wars, Sheikh Abdullah sought the Sufi path as a young man, and was perhaps unique as a Westerner in travelling it to its ultimate goal. When asked at one of his lectures to talk about his own training, he described how he had known clairvoyants in his youth, having himself given clairvoyant readings in public when as young as thirteen, but had never been able to understand how people with such marked intuitive

---

1 A fuller account is on pp. 161–2.

powers could often possess unpleasant, hypocritical, cynical characters. It had been a riddle that greatly disturbed him.

Then he said: 'Eventually I found Sufi sheikhs who had the answers. I was subjected to courses of discipline that would make you people curl up with fear, and I performed them all as a slave performs the commands of his master. Eventually I was authorised to teach.'

Although that was almost all he ever said on the matter, he associated with, and was treated with esteem by, several other Sufi masters, and like all of his peers he stood as the latest in a line of spiritual succession stretching back to the Prophet Muhammad himself.[2] He passed from this world on 17 September 2000 after having taught publicly in England and privately in Australia for more than thirty years, in three main ways. For much of the 1970s and half the 1980s he gave weekly public lectures in London, numbering several hundred. Most if not all of these were recorded, but the recordings are privately owned, and only three transcripts are printed here. Secondly, he prescribed certain exercises for his pupils, laying great emphasis on their continual and correct performance: his instructions were to perform them 'in the way someone wants air when drowning'.

Thirdly, he taught by means of personal contact, and for the most part that is the province of this book. In fact he said that his pupils were his book; and it is they who speak here along with him. Although the tales we recount allow a mere sampling of the individual and collective experiences of scores of people over decades, they offer a glimpse of immediacy and a taste of relationship, and without those two elements there is no teaching at all. The group which he built around him provided not only a vehicle for learning but a school of companionship and a family of fellow-travellers.

Besides the three lecture transcripts, we have appended three essays and some other writings by Sheikh Abdullah. You will find that those nine discourses greatly illuminate, reinforce and expand on what now follows. In many cases they repeat it, overlap with it or shed another light on it. If they appear to contradict it, please rest assured that the contradiction is only apparent.

But because he cautioned that 'people who want a teaching figure may be unable to accept the changes in circumstances and attitudes the Sufi way demands', a moment's orientation may be useful.

---

2 It is customary in Islam to add *'Salla-llahu alaihi wa salaam'*, 'May God honour him and grant him peace', or a similar benediction, whenever the name of the Prophet Muhammad is spoken or written. This was almost always Sheikh Abdullah's own practice, and these words should be understood as included when appropriate throughout the main text of this book. They have been retained in the nine discourses reprinted at the end.

PROLOGUE

To begin with—and stepping inescapably into the present tense—when you are with the Sheikh, nothing is trivial. Everything matters. In the world of this book, a world he created, his slightest comment or the tone of his voice can provoke intense reflection among his pupils: who, it bears mentioning, are intelligent men and women in professions ranging from carpentry to psychiatry and from architecture to nursing.

As he explained, 'When students have gone beyond the stage of needing to be praised, they will adopt an attitude of cooperation with the master to make sure they remember the finer points. Such intensity of effort may look abnormal to an outsider, but once teacher and student are working together . . . they have a very special relationship which cannot be judged from outside.'

To quote another Sufi of modern times, Javad Nurbakhsh, 'because [the pupil] knows with certainty that the master speaks by the inspiration of God and not by the promptings of the self's desires, [he or she] constantly strives to understand the relationship between his [or her] own state and the words of the master'.

If, reading on, you become acclimatised to this world, you will realise that it does not centre on otherworldly ecstasies (which in any case cannot truly be described), because in the Sheikh's words, 'If you don't change your habit patterns and attitudes to life, you obtain the experience of mental states only: you do not progress. It's like tuning in to your own television set, just looking at visions. You have to change the content of the programmes.'

It was a critical part of his teaching that until you have disengaged from all those patterns and attitudes—from 'pushiness, self-orientation, emotional self-obsession'—your inner and intuitive experience will be distorted; your dreams and visions will not reflect reality. By the same token, if you succeed in changing, you will enter what he called the true dream. If you dream of meeting people, 'they will communicate information usually of a factual kind, and verifiable in terms of your attitude, or of events which may come about, *et cetera*'. En route to that remarkable stage, the reader will hopefully taste rigour and realism. This is a path on which, as the Sheikh stated on his group's letterhead, 'in seeking the perfect knowledge of Absolute Being, [pupils] strive to improve the imperfect in themselves and in their surroundings'.

If you have read about other Sufis you will already have encountered that path, for it is the way of the masters, plural. Not only do many thousands follow it today, as members of Sufi orders and circles across the world; every Sufi sheikh, or teacher, operates by authority of his or her own sheikh, and the heart of the teaching has never changed. At every turn Sheikh Abdullah's teaching echoes and is echoed by the Sufi saints and poets of history—by Rumi, Hafiz, Ibn Arabi and countless others. Not a hair separates their testimony from his.

Yet the piercing sharpness, or sweetness, and often strangeness of the encounter with Sufism are one thing to read about in old tales and verse, and quite another to feel in your own flesh. 'We say that you have to make a ruin in order to find a treasure,' the Sheikh said. 'You have to destroy all the identifications within your being, relating to your ego relationship and your personality relationship with life.'

In the service of this task, 'the sheikh has the function of pointing out your patterns: and if you become exceedingly angry at something he says, you may be sure it touches a part of you you do not wish to accept at all. Similarly he may make you very embarrassed.' He cited bewilderment as another one of his tools, and remarked that in Sufism an aspirant would often find the master's teaching incomprehensible.

An even more fundamental challenge must be faced, too. 'You can't say what a teacher would look like. We can only point in certain directions. Sufis refuse to stick to one particular mode or to projecting a certain appearance. A Sufi divine may not look, talk or act like a mystical master at all.'

As a reader, you will find that advice worth remembering.

'We say you can only teach by the method applicable to each pupil. There is a time and place and a certain company. Synchronicity, so that the penny drops at the right time, is essential. When we work through very banal things we have to do it in just that way. Failure to appreciate this can prevent you from learning more, and leave you attached to the externals loved by hypocrites.'

One pupil remarked, though overstating the case, that there was practically nothing he had heard the Sheikh say of which he hadn't also heard him say the opposite. The Sheikh did not disagree, saying, 'There is only a time, a place, a situation.'

He also cautioned, 'A lot of people have tried to keep me as a pet. They find that I don't make a very good pet.' Indeed Sufis have a long-established reputation for unpredictability and non-conformity. Do not therefore be surprised if you get bitten.

Or to put it another way, if you come looking for nourishment here, you will have to trust the cook, and not be shocked if you are served something you consider unpalatable. In his words, 'a crude yokel wouldn't accept lumpless soup, because he had never seen it before: all peasants' soup is coarse and thick, and constitutes their only meal. If you've never seen clear soup before, it's not soup—it's water.

'That's how people relate to the world. You take your yardstick, which is built in by society, and measure against it all new experience, so you are drugged by society. You can only be cured by experience of a different kind: but before you can even gain that, you must be able to conceive the possibility of such experience.

'Then you have to be exposed to it for a while, since in most intellectual learning processes one telling isn't enough. The real way to learn is a repetitive method, but we are so impatient that we think we take in intellectual content. Any book and technical content really has to be read many times to sink in, and more often than not the thing has to be experienced before any hope of understanding can come about.'

So the essence of the matter is not book learning at all. Sheikh Abdullah called Sufism 'the science of re-orientating the whole inner life of a human being', and a development of the central nervous system—certainly not the intellect, and not even the ordinary senses. He frequently spoke of changes at cell level during which energy is raised and inner experience unfolds as a series of subtle plexuses are opened up in the body. No doubt that is one meaning of his words: 'In mysticism we go up and down Jacob's ladder into the white light and even into the darkest pit. Even there, there is white light.

'Jacob's ladder is within you. You can go up or down that ladder any time. You don't have to wait until you are discarnate [i.e. have left your body at death]. It is entirely up to you. It's the same energy that motivates everything on earth and comes from the sun. It is energy of a positive kind.'

As he often declared, 'The energy within you is the same energy that burns in the heart of a star.' The physical means of raising and distributing such energy are not detailed in this book because they are strong medicine which should not be taken without prescription, but the reader must at least entertain conceptions that lead far beyond those commonly accepted when it comes to the existence, nature and role of that energy, and to the ultimate scope of consciousness.

'No intellectual knowledge from your background can help you understand the processes of Sufism,' he warned. 'You have to put yourself in the hands of the Sheikh and submit completely.'

That particular injunction is very hard for many people to accept. You may even be shocked by the expectation of obedience in this world you are entering. And yet there is no getting away from it. You cannot learn from a Sufi sheikh unless you accept, or at least try to accept, that his word is law—or again, more precisely, like a doctor's prescription. The doctor has qualified in medicine. You haven't, and you may not even understand what he says, but you need to comply with it if you want to be cured. As our Sheikh would often say, 'the pupil must be in the hands of his sheikh like a corpse in the hands of the public washer' (who washes a deceased Muslim before burial). This attitude cuts across just about every tenet of modern Western culture, but it means what it says, and it is a condition of entry to the world of the Sufis.

A famous Koranic story tells how Moses meets and seeks discipleship with a vastly wise personage, who is unnamed in the story but always known as Khidr, the Green One. Khidr warns, 'You will never be able to bear with me patiently! How can you bear with something outside your experience?' But Moses swears he will do so, and what ensues can be paraphrased as follows.

Khidr replies, 'Very well. Just don't ask me about anything until I mention it myself.'

Proceeding, they board a ship, but Khidr makes a hole in it. Unable to contain himself, Moses remonstrates with him.

Khidr replies, 'What did I tell you?'

'Don't be angry with me,' begs Moses.

But then Khidr kills a boy. Moses is horrified and says so. Khidr repeats: 'What did I tell you?'

A shame-faced Moses replies, 'Get rid of me if I do it again.' Finally they reach a village whose inhabitants refuse them hospitality, yet where Khidr repairs a collapsing wall. 'You could have got paid for that!' exclaims Moses.

Khidr tells him, 'Enough is enough.' But before they part, he discloses the reality. The ship would have been seized by a king had it not been damaged. The boy's parents were true believers and there was every chance he would have grieved them with his wickedness. The wall belonged to two orphans of a righteous father, and stood on top of a treasure which they would inherit when they grew up.

'And I did not do any of this of my own accord,' Khidr concludes.

Moses, the Sheikh said, couldn't stop criticising. 'You can't do two things at once. If you are preoccupied with criticising you can't learn.'

His pupil Ahmed relates: 'When we got to Australia the new house had a big lawn around it, full of weeds. The Sheikh set Abdul-Barr and me to dig them up one by one. We made a start with little trowels, and soon we'd made a big mess. It looked as if drunken moles had run amok. We couldn't get the hang of digging the weeds up neatly, and in any case we told each other the job was impossible. There were just too many of them. When the Sheikh saw our efforts, he put a stop to them—not only blasting us for the mess but saying that, when given a task, "You must accept my assessment of it, not your assessment." The ladies ended up doing the job instead, and after some weeks or months the lawn was flawless.'

The two men should have known far better. Long before that, the Sheikh had given all his pupils a small card bearing a quotation from the renowned medieval Sufi al-Ghazali (1058–1111): 'The disciple must cling to his sheikh as a blind man on the edge of a river clings to his leader. Let him know that the advantage he gains from the error of his sheikh, if he should err, is greater than the advantage he gains from his own rightness, if he should be right.'

That will also explain, if you find yourself wondering, why there is no criticism of the Sheikh in this book.

We take our cue from him in another respect too. A reporter who had interviewed him for the *Radio Times* wrote in 1981 of the 'stern' response she had received to most of her questions about his personal history: 'He has no intention of talking about himself. [He says:] "Sufis are not terribly into ego and personality games. If I tell you, this will form a disproportionate part of your article."'

So this is not a biography either. Instead we hope the attentive reader may catch sight of something infinitely more precious: not only the overwhelming presence of the man, but the reality he taught.

In holding out that hope, we cannot rely on the recollections of his pupils themselves, however generously shared. A pupil is only a camera, capturing what lies within his or her field of perception. Although we have tried to combine all those mental images into a panorama, we are far from perfect either; therefore you too must work to discern the picture's meaning. To paraphrase the Sheikh, you are seeking an inner completeness, not an outward coherence. 'Few things are what they seem in the universe': and the outer way leads to the inner.

As he told a pupil in 1980: 'My teaching is not understood even at the most basic level. I am trying to give you capacity.'

MAKING LANDFALL on the enchanted island and falling under the sway of its magus, Shakespeare's party of miscreants in *The Tempest* were subjected to all manner of sorcery to bewilder and beguile them.

The Sheikh had been in a Cairo hotel as a young man when someone sitting on the opposite side of the lounge had caught his eye. It was one of the hully-gully men: street magicians—'but most of them were dervishes,'[3] he said.

The man had gazed at him intently and pulled a dove out of his clothing, at chest height, and then another; and then another. It was an invitation; and telling the story, the Sheikh added: 'So you see, I have been with the real masters.'

Yet only he knows exactly what he underwent on his own quest, or by what route he travelled.

His eagerness to join the Sufis once compelled him to dive off a yacht into the Golden Horn at Istanbul. The female owner wanted him for herself, but he had escaped her by swimming ashore. Then he endured a three-hour search of his luggage by customs men whom she had told, in revenge, that he was a drug smuggler. They found nothing, and at last he made his way to the dervishes.

The destination is everything. Many years after that adventure and who knows how many others, he spoke of the goal at which he had long ago arrived:

'Reality is beyond all the heavens and all the hells; the complete abnegation of self. . . . You can merge with the divine ocean and time and space far away. You can see clearly for ever and ever: no past, no present, only the now.'

That was only one description, among innumerable others, of the capacity he was trying to instil.

---

3 The term 'dervish' (always pronounced 'darvish' by Sheikh Abdullah) applies to any Sufi, not only to the 'whirling dervishes' of the Mevlevi Order.

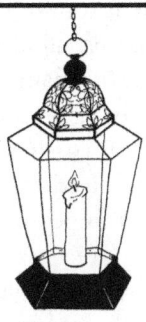

2

RAW

> The stars are setting and the caravan
> Starts for the dawn of nothing—Oh, make haste!
>
> – *The Rubaiyat of Omar Khayyam,* by Edward FitzGerald

THIS BUSINESS is a journey. Like us—the forty or fifty of us or more—you have to set out on it very deliberately, and you have to keep going until you arrive, if you can.

It bears saying at the outset that there is not much time. At least eight of our companions have already died along the way.

This is the notebook of our trip, and please understand that every part of it is true. Please also think that you are one of us. You will meet many of us by name, starting a few sentences from now, and you will soon see that your travelling companions are just like yourself.

So who will be our guide? 'That man of light will be your guide', one of us wrote:

> though he seems close to you,
> he is far-removed indeed.

Or in the Sheikh's own words: 'You may think he is very different from you. You would be wrong. You may think he is very like you. You would be wrong.'

The personal journey is different for everyone, but much of it unfolds in a common setting. With few exceptions, all of us became the Sheikh's pupils in London during the 1970s and 1980s, maintaining weekly or even daily contact with him, and in some cases living with him. Although many left sooner or later, some stayed with him till his passing. We attended his lectures, we sat with him, we ate with him, we received his guidance, we worked under his supervision; and that continual, unforgettable association is the thread from which our stories—even our lives—are woven.

The resulting tale unfolds mostly in England and latterly in Australia, but we also savoured powerful impressions when we travelled with him elsewhere, visiting both France and Turkey more than once. An excellent place to start happens to be a particular day in September 1981 when a party of us were in Istanbul.

We were a dozen or two Londoners mostly in our twenties, with Sheikh Abdullah at our head. By that time most of his pupils, including all of this party, had become Muslims, and we used our Muslim names when we were together. Hopefully the reason for our conversion will become fully evident.

We had travelled in minibuses to a small park in a nondescript old area on the Asian side of the city in which stood a small polygonal building—the tomb of a Sufi saint whose name none of us can remember. To our disappointment it was locked, and we left; but then a message arrived that we would be allowed in after all (it later turned out that we were the first to gain entry in twenty years). With some reluctance we went back, to find waiting for us not only the elusive tomb keeper but also a group of well-dressed middle-aged women whom we'd never seen before. They had just arrived in great haste. One kissed the Sheikh's hand and exclaimed, 'Ah, you are the cause of my coming! You're the one that's been in my dreams ever since I was a girl!'

Like many Turks she spoke some German, and one of our group translated. The woman had been hosting a lunch party for forty or fifty friends in an upmarket district on the other side of town when she had suddenly realised she must drop everything. Something had told her she must hurry to the tomb. She had arrived to find no one at first: but on our return the reason for her irresistible urge had become clear.

The Sheikh would say that pupils are drawn to a sheikh, as that woman had been drawn, like moths to the flame. They cannot help themselves. Even his pupil Amira's cats wanted to sit near him, although he didn't like cats; and then there was Oiseau, the little canary that belonged to Aziza, a Frenchwoman. It became known as Poo-Poo because of the Sheikh's endearments: 'You're a sweetie-poo-poo!' he would tell it. He clipped its tiny claws when they grew too long, and he was dreadfully upset once when he nicked its flesh in doing so. This bird would fly across the room and land on his hand; it would sit on his shoulder and peck at his beard.

In fact the moth is actually in love with the flame.

In 1982 or 1983 Samira was seven or eight. She was the daughter of a female pupil and had joined the adults for the evening prayer one night during the month-long fast of Ramadan. Ramadan[4] was the only time we went to the local mosque, a converted cinema in the Kingsland Road in Stoke Newington. Afterwards someone encouraged Samira to go up to the Sheikh and kiss the ring he wore on his left hand. Although it was an odd suggestion, the little girl didn't argue.

'I remember feeling a bit nervous,' she says. 'He was standing beside the car, ready to open the door for the ladies. You know in *Star Trek*, where those little ships get to the mother ship, and once they get into that field, that's it: it just takes you in? You're on autopilot, it just does it for you. There was no looking left or right, it was just shoom! straight toward him. He opened his arms and just gave me a hug, so I didn't have to kiss his ring—and I remember his energy: it was like being beamed in.'

If you embark on this journey you are on course to discover, even despite yourself, the power of attraction; and to experience the fate of the moth. 'We lead you to your own death', said the Sheikh, 'through curiosity.' He had no need to conjure doves from his garments to keep his pupils enthralled.

He had first taught in Britain in the 1960s. By the late 1970s he was giving a public lecture every Thursday evening, almost without fail, in a series of hired halls in London. The talks were promoted by fly-posting and later in *Time Out*, for a long time with the phrase 'The Journey to Expanded Consciousness'. By the early 1980s they were attracting more than 100 people. He charged an entry fee, noting that people might not value something they did not have to pay for, and saying, 'I believe the labourer is worthy of his hire.'

His lectures drew on an immense range of material from many different cultures. They served as both as an essential introduction for newcomers—an explanation, as he said, of 'what we are trying to do for you'—and further guidance for existing pupils, who it was expected would attend regularly. Although he brought a few books from his library, bookmarked to serve as source material and memory-joggers, most of the time he spoke entirely off the cuff. His pupil Sakina calls it 'the most astonishing virtuoso performance: he spoke

---

4 Observant Muslims abstain from all food, all liquids and all sexual activity between dawn and sunset during this lunar month.

spontaneously and in a careful, even way for about two hours, but he had no notes'. Afterwards he would invite questions, and if there were none he might read out one of the comical teaching stories about the Mullah Nasruddin.

Ishaq first came one week when the Sheikh was away. 'I've gone into this rather dry, church-type hall,' he says, 'with rows of not-very-comfortable chairs, and at the front of the room there's a photograph of a man with a bloody turban on, and a red beard. And I'm thinking: what am I doing here? And some bloke, one of the pupils, has walked up to this photograph, and there's a tape deck there, and his exact words were, "Unfortunately the Sheikh can't be with us this evening, but he's sent us a tape." And when his finger touched that button, my life changed.

'Up until that moment I'd been: "Oh no, this is some bloody religious thing, for sure." Everybody in those days knew about the Scientologists, they'd all been approached by born-again Christians, cults, and Bhagwash was big in those days. "Oh no, I've been suckered into coming to something religious. That's exactly what I don't wanna know about right now."

'And I don't know how long that talk went for, but the Sheikh spoke to me so directly—and he wasn't even in the room. All I was getting was a tape from God knows when, and he's talking to me in that tape, and I was just gone. It completely changed the way I think, and made me realise I'd actually met one of those blokes who really, genuinely knows more than me.'

You'd have had a choice, of course, if you'd walked into that church-type hall. According to the *Daily Mail* of 20 July 1972,[5] a jeweller in Birkenhead ran a promotion in which he handed out 3000 stones to people in the street. All looked like diamonds, but all except four were glass. Accompanying each of the 3000 was a leaflet explaining that some were real. Every recipient was invited to visit the shop and find out whether he or she had been lucky. Only one turned up; she had one of the four real diamonds.

The other three diamonds had been thrown away just like the fakes; and of the hundreds who came and listened to the Sheikh over the years, very few stayed. 'All the beautiful butterflies come and alight on my hand,' he said. 'They come, and they go.'

Ishaq was one who stayed, and Walid was another. He had read lots of books but could not make up his mind whether to attend one of the talks. 'I was boring my flatmate blabbering on about Sufism. So one day he threw

---

5 This story appears in Idries Shah's *A Perfumed Scorpion* and was quoted by Sheikh Abdullah in a lecture.

some money at me and said, "Go to that damn lecture! I don't want to hear about Sufism any more!"'

Walid went with a friend. 'We took our seats, and in walked this chap. Normally I could look at someone and size them up'—in fact the Sheikh himself later said Walid had natural discernment that enabled him to do just that—'but I couldn't suss him out, and it was like that all through the lecture. Just these vast . . . capacities. And I thought, this is it.

'I knew I'd never met anyone like that before, because with everyone else I could get a reading; I could sort of tag them a bit. So at the end I just walked up to him and said, "How do I pursue this?" It was a moment when our eyes met, and I went, "Oh my gosh." I knew that here was a person like I'd been reading about. They do exist.

'All the people you meet sort of pooh-pooh it. "It's just an analogy, it's just a myth—they don't really exist; you do realise that, don't you? They're just helping you to be better people, and can't actually do these amazing things." But the "Oh my God!" was "Oh my God, they do exist!" Thank God. And I knew it would be a lifelong connection as soon as I looked at him.'

Says *The Rubaiyat of Omar Khayyam*:

> I often wonder what the vintners buy
> One-half so precious as the goods they sell.

Sakina had never heard of Sufism and had come with her Muslim boyfriend. The lectures struck her as 'every word being absolutely and obviously nothing but the truth which is already there in front of you, but which you don't know you know, or you can't see or understand, until it's pointed out. They explained life as it is, and they made me feel as if I'd come home.'

It's hard to convey the seriousness, the precision, or the soaring and occasionally searing quality of what the Sheikh said. But even doing so would reveal little of the relationship into which his listeners had the opportunity to enter. He said to us, who kept coming, 'You were with me on the Day of Promises'—the day on which human souls have testified to the divine lordship.

Asiya says she was in 'this crisis of my life, a state of great grief over a really hurtful break-up and loss, and I kind of cracked, and in the crack a voice told me to go to the Sufis. And I looked in *Time Out*; and I remember that first time—when I walked in he looked at me, and he had this bolt of lightning in his look. He looked at me in the way he looked at the ones who he knew would become his students. And then during the lecture I got this sensation of tingling up my arm and across my chest; and that's when I thought: this guy's the real thing.'

Zainab, separated from her husband and their Christian Pentecostal church, had prayed, 'I don't know what I'm doing, my head feels like barbed wire, but please guide me.' She ended up in London with her two young children and was introduced at a lecture. 'As I shook his hand and looked into his eyes I thought: this is the answer to my prayers. It was as clear as—I thought: this is it.'

Farida just says, 'I fell in love with him the minute I found him.'

Hakim is French. Although his English was extremely patchy then, and he still often talks in broken sentences, he found to his amazement that he could understand almost every word the Sheikh said. But he adds: 'My attraction was on two levels: intellectual, because the talk was refreshing, and answering all my questions, and it was like, "What! Somebody who knows?" And the second level was the feelings.

'One day we were at the bottom of the stairs, and he stopped; and for some reason he looked at me. And he said, "*Salaam alaikum*,"[6] but in a very direct way. And from that moment—He went through me, and my heart went soft. And since then I always loved him.'

Attraction; magnetism; concentrated force. The Sheikh radiated it, and Sufis have a word for it: *jasbet*, or charisma. Like the lunch hostess at the tomb, people were drawn to him and to his circle; and as Khalida recalls, he would teach almost anyone. 'I used to admire him for having anybody in his group. He was that good that he could be prepared for anything coming at him.'

Nevertheless, the journey still lies ahead; and as he said, 'I will take you as far as you want to go—but you will all get off at your own station, and you will decide yourself which one it is.'

Ahmed once remarked how inviting was the famous verse of Mevlana ('Our Master') Jalaluddin Rumi of Konya (1207–75), the Sufi saint and poet best known in the West:

> Come, come, whoever you are,
> an unbeliever, a fire-worshipper, come.[7]

We knew it because the Sheikh sometimes quoted it, and he had it emblazoned on one of the banners displayed when we publicly conducted the *sema*,[8] or turning, the ceremony of the 'whirling' dervishes, the Mevlevis, named after their founder Mevlana himself. But he replied, 'I don't use it as much I used

---

6 This Arabic phrase ('Peace be upon you') is the greeting used by all Muslims whatever their native language.
7 The lines have also been attributed to Abu Said Abu'l-Khayr (967–1049).
8 Pronounced 'semah'.

to. I don't want people to think you can *go on* being a fire-worshipper.' He preferred another line from Rumi:

> First I was raw; then I was cooked; then I was burnt.

He took you into the kitchen despite yourself, as Khalida put it. 'If you couldn't handle the heat in the kitchen, then leave. We dug our heels in—"No, I don't wanna go in there!"—and he still dragged us in. Who else do you know who, against what you said, would still have tried to get round you and work on you in every possible way he could? He would try every method in the book. He never gave up on anybody. He never gave up on me, ever.'

Although his talks were open to all comers, regular attenders found themselves joining a body of perhaps thirty or more who were actually his pupils. Often he spoke about 'the group' as a focus of loyalty and warmth, but on the other hand, he would bitterly disparage its failings in an attempt to make its members realise that they had work to do; because the reason for the journey is to get from where you are to where you are not. You have your bad points and blind spots, just like everyone else you know, and you can't stay put.

So even if ineluctable attraction brought you, and you don't know why you're here, you are due to find out. The moth, unlike the butterfly, will be consumed by the flame; and for the novice, the flame is the sheikh himself.

The Sheikh told his Thursday audience, 'People believe they can fool others—and they do, for some of the time, or even most of the time if they are skilful. With all pupils, whether it takes a short time or long, I don't listen to their words: I watch their actions. And most of them come to me with personality patterns which they have groomed, false personality attitudes which they have learned from books or social contact.

'The Sheikh is gentle with those on the periphery of the group and flatters their egos, which is what they love, so they will be drawn further into the group. With those closest to him he is much harsher. A teacher may be stricter with students than he can ever be with strangers. Real seekers need intensive and energetic supervision; strangers may not be capable of working with a more intensive form of truth.'

He likened the process to teaching grammar, saying again: 'One is much stricter with the students who already know the basic language.' But by that time many of the butterflies have gone, because the classroom of the Sheikh's company is not the meadow they expected.

People, he explained, don't want others to see their real motives, so they are at 'devious pains' to cover up their real activities. At the same time, the average person's concentration is poor. So if you are watched carefully—for example by the Sheikh—it will be seen that your words or false surface activities will last for a short time (or, as he said, slightly longer if you're more alert): but eventually the truth comes out, and when you're caught unconscious of what you are doing, your real behaviour patterns emerge from a deeper level, and the falsity of your words begins to show itself.

As he pointed out, this often happens in an intimate relationship like a marriage. With familiarity, people let their hair down. 'Slowly but surely their behaviour deteriorates and their selfish, grasping nature and self-obsessed ways begin to show. When such petty behaviour is eventually exhibited, the scales fall from the eyes of those who believe the other to be good and true.'

Yet he included in the group's letterhead the Koranic sentence, 'The noblest of you in the sight of God is the best in conduct;' and the pathway to excellence was pithily summed up in his remark that 'the way you operate becomes the way you are'.

Like an apprentice in any trade, you must imitate and emulate until the right approach and the necessary skills come naturally. 'To achieve any permanence of good you have to repeat and repeat the desired actions so they become ingrained and instinctual, and still come out even under conditions of shock. If you only have gold coins in your purse, you can only give out gold coins. If you only have the most noble attributes and continue to perform, in your life and actions, their meaning, then you can "give gold from your purse" because you have no base metal.

'Humanity is attracted to gold as a beautiful, soft, rich metal which appeals to us at deep levels. When we have only gold in our purse we draw all life to us. This why we have to act on the essence of your being to engrave the most noble attributes [there]. The whole of Allah's[9] attributes are reflected in us, and they range from constructive to destructive.

'When we think entirely of self and are motivated towards personal gain and advancement, we contact certain ignoble attributes all the time, and that becomes engraved in our being [instead], and comes out under stress.

'Sufism in its ultimate aim is concerned with the redress of this inner imbalance, and tremendous efforts have to be made in order to be of constructive character and perpetuate constructive characteristics in our being.'

Such patterns are acquired at deep levels and make their way right to the surface so that you can reflect nothing else. This development of what used to be called 'moral character' really has nothing to do with morality or religion.

---

9   The words 'Allah' and 'God' have the same meaning.

Rather, it is a psychological journey of reorientation from imbalance to a state of balance, which can then be followed by the spiritual journey.

The Sheikh maintained that 90 per cent of Sufism was character. Because much of his work was the training of it, which he insisted had to precede any spiritual training, his pupils could be called to account at any moment, and in any available way, for any failure in the endeavour to maintain a high standard of behaviour. Although he would say that God judged you for your intention, no pupil could exploit that line as an excuse for thoughtlessness. He told Othman, 'I can be a nasty bastard sometimes. I only go by results.'

Besides, any excuse you give may well be made up, may it not? If you'd sat in one of the church-type halls with everyone else while he told us that we lied, and lied, and lied, to ourselves and to others, about our motives and our traits, and if you'd told yourself that of course it didn't apply to you—why, you would have been the living proof, too. 'Oh no, Sheikh Abdullah! You've got it wrong, Sheikh Abdullah!' went his chilling parody.

'Only when you can die to the process of self-obsession will you stop self-justification,' he warned. 'If you are too obtuse or stubborn to see yourself as you really are, it is the job of the sheikh to place your nose inexorably in the mess that is you. This is the process of real Sufi illumination—not reading tales of morality or making intellectual resolutions.'

Yet even thirty-five years later, the note of excuse can still be heard in some of his pupils' voices. 'And actually, in my defence, although I shouldn't say this. . . . I mean he wasn't always a hundred per cent.' In Koranic terms: 'The evil that they do is made fair-seeming unto them.' Or as Rashida says, 'We're still talking about the seven deadly sins sitting there.'

'Most people have a violin that they're playing all day long,' the Sheikh would say, drawing an invisible bow, 'and it only plays one tune: "Me-me-me-me-me-me." People don't grow up, they only get bigger.' He lamented that he had to correct the deficiencies of his pupils' upbringing, and in almost every respect he was, as he said, *in loco parentis*, in the role of a parent.

He was already alive to the characters of his pupils' parents, including those he'd never met, which was most of them. He would inform us accordingly: Naima, one of seven children, was the quickest learner because her father had used violence to enforce order; Ahmed got his naivety and some of his annoying traits from his mother; as for Sakina, he told her, 'Your mother made you the great nonentity that you are;' and she recalls, 'When I dressed up in something fetching, and once when I was given a very feminine gown as a birthday present, he said, "Your Daddy will fall in love with you all over again."'

His reformative character training could take the form of gentle advice, fierce rebuke, cajolery, silent example; even humiliation. With anything that people were overly attached to or obsessive about, he might resort to jibes and mockery until they could see the reality. The method is not the point. The point is to learn—and even the closest, those who eventually lived with him, sometimes found it a surprisingly easy point to forget. They were apt to become blasé. 'You appear to think I am bullshitting,' he remarked once.

Yet such complacency could never survive for long in his profoundly disturbing company, where one method encompassed all the others. He told us: 'My time is fully occupied as a mirror. It's like teaching a parrot to speak by hiding yourself behind a mirror in which the parrot sees a bird like itself, and thinks your voice from behind the mirror is that bird, so it responds. I just reflect to *murids*[10] (pupils) what they are. Some become so miserable they rush away. Some develop a spirit of resilience they think is progress. They look away from the mirror—unless they think my back is turned: then they make monkey grimaces in it.'

Grimaces apart, our companionship as pupils was always limited by the fact that our responsibility was to the Sheikh and the group, not narrowly to one another. He was very down on any attempt to cover up another pupil's blunder. 'You protect each other from the Sheikh, and from the teaching,' he said. 'Some *murids* mistakenly try to defend one who suffers the Sheikh's harsh tongue. This is a form of arrogance which they have to be cured of.'

Once or twice Masoud queried what he considered excessive pressure on other pupils—on Abdul-Malik, struggling with the electrics in the house we bought, and on Imran, whom the Sheikh set to fabricating a shower fitting for him that could not be bought in any shop—and the response came in a public lecture: 'The *murids* tell me I'm being too hard,' he said, or something similar. 'But I do what I do for reasons that they don't know about.'

The problem does not lie at his end. 'People who judge by outward appearances are lost in a world of dreams and illusions. They can see the surface of a thing but never attain to its reality. So very, very slowly, over a long period, we have to teach people how to observe themselves and the behaviour of others around them so that they can benefit from these revelations.

'In benefiting, they slowly strip themselves of all the regalia and paraphernalia they have been at pains to buy in the course of their life, and to cherish as something of worth. When they have been stripped entirely of these falsities, they can come to an understanding of the true nature of their purpose here—this short sojourn in the school of earthly life. You cannot understand anything

---

10 The plural in Arabic is *muridun*, often translated as 'seekers'.

outside yourself, and you cannot understand your lord, until you understand yourself.

'Human beings cannot see clearly what they are doing because they are doing it in a mirror-like sense. The senses reflect the world into our minds, and our attitudes and behaviour patterns condition this reflection in such a way that it becomes an illusion peculiar to our own particular thinking and development. These illusions are the veils which prevent us coming to the true understanding of our nature.'

So even the vastness of the task ahead is hidden from the newcomer—and that fact itself requires to be brought home to him or her. But how, exactly?

'We provide situations which catch them off guard. We emphasise setting you up in a situation. We know your armament, we put you into a set-piece battle, and we show you the whole process—what triggered it, how and why you reacted, the pattern of reactions in your life. We teach you how to observe them, and how to feel the force of the energy as well as the quality of the emotion or instinct which has swept you away.'

Let's spell out again that this kind of teaching, and learning, is not a matter of discussion, exposition or explanation. You have no 'input'. 'When you come into contact with the Sheikh and he is providing experience, you feel as if in a dream sequence. Your own will is subordinate to the situation in which he sets you up.'

A school hall once had to be hired temporarily for the weekly *dhikr*[11] (the exercise of 'remembrance', in this case a collective ceremony) because the usual hall was being renovated. By then we had bought a house in east London and turned it into a centre where some of us lived with the Sheikh. The traditional term he used for such an establishment was *zawiya*, with the accent on the first syllable.

On the first night of the new hall arrangement, with the Sheikh and four or five others about to set out from the *zawiya*, Naima ran upstairs to get something she'd forgotten. When she came down, everybody had disappeared.

'In hindsight, it had to be something funny going on,' says Khalida, 'because in normal life you probably would have found the group. It was only a very short time: she might have seen them going down the steps, they'd only have been at the car by the time she got downstairs. But in this situation, they'd gone.'

It was autumn: cold, wet, miserable and dark, and Naima didn't know where the hall was. By the time she'd walked the ten minutes or so to Dalston

---

11 Pronounced 'thicker' but with a hard 'th' as in 'the', and often spelt *zikr*.

Junction, she was enraged. It was a situation she hadn't been able to control. She hailed a cab and made the driver crisscross the whole area until they found the right school. She got out, went in, stalked up to the Sheikh with her anger on full display, and said, 'Don't ever do that to me again!'

Of course any such outburst from a pupil smashes the limits of propriety and mocks her or his ostensible reason for being with the Sheikh in the first place. But it demonstrates what you have already heard him say: *When you're caught unconscious of what you are doing, your real behaviour patterns emerge from a deeper level, and the falseness of your words begins to show itself.*[12]

The situation depends on the failing. One of Ahmed's failings was inquisitiveness. 'I was always trying to suss out what was going on and how it affected me,' he says. 'There always was plenty going on, and you could assume that you didn't know the half of it. If he sprang a shock on you, you never saw it coming. Nevertheless, I was an eavesdropper (which is how I heard the Sheikh tell someone to be careful because "Ahmed has very sharp ears"), and he would tell me to mind my own business. But then something else started to happen.

'At the time, I was living in the *zawiya*. When I came out of my room to go downstairs I would find Maymuna waiting on the landing. She'd follow me. Then she'd follow me back upstairs. When I went to the loo, she'd wait outside; then she'd follow me wherever I went next.

'This would drive me into an instant rage, and I'd swear at her, but it made no difference. I'm not sure she made any reply at all, and then she just went on doing it. I allowed myself the abuse because nobody, then or later, said what I secretly knew must be the case: the Sheikh had told her to do it. She was very conscientious about it. I think it was shock treatment for inquisitiveness—no doubt among other things.

'After days or weeks it stopped. In due course, too, I became clearly aware with some surprise that I had actually lost that particular trait; or at least it had lost its force. I can't say if the two events coincided, and it was at least five years later that he gave me a present of a keyhole saw (which was appropriate for the woodworker I had by then become) with the words, "Here you are, Ahmed, you're always looking through keyholes."

'But he did, at least once, explain what should have been obvious—that any treatment he administered was not handed out for the sake of it. It was intended to induce change; and once the disease was cured, the treatment ceased.'

That is why a spirit of resilience is not progress. His hope was that eventually *murid*s might stop (as he said) continually resisting, and instead become willing travellers who loved the journey.

---

12 The same italics will be used whenever the Sheikh's words are echoed from an earlier page.

'You know,' recalls Khalida, 'he actually told me, "You've got to imagine you're like an amoeba, crawling across a tank." You can imagine how slow that is, but the thing is that the amoeba will get there.' His fellow-master Sheikh Nazim Adil al-Qibrisi, who will appear again in this book, recalls of his own pupilship: 'I felt as though I were an ant with a broken leg, trying to crawl from Damascus to Mecca.'

You're going to need perseverance. But before that, resolution; and even before that, intention.

In Islam each group of formal prayers is preceded by a silent declaration of your intention to offer it, and the Sheikh once gave a whole lecture about following through on your intentions in life. Two newcomers hearing it were shaken by what sounded like a scalding broadside against the whole group, including bitter condemnation of an unnamed person who had promised him that he or she would fast during Ramadan and then failed to do so. This turned out to be Masoud, who had indeed made such a vow but had soon abandoned it on a camping holiday with his girlfriend.

Conversely, the fact that Aziza had returned from a visit to her family in Paris when she'd said she would was something the Sheikh mentioned even years later. Likewise he praised Malika for having uniquely stuck to her decision to eat only fruit one Ramadan, unlike the one or two other women who had said they'd do the same but abandoned their intention.

That firm intention is the least you will need if you are to learn from the experience that comes your way, however plainly the Sheikh has told you to expect it.

'He couldn't have spelt it out more clearly,' says Ahmed. 'It was at the beginning of our apprenticeship, so to speak. We'd all but finished renovating the basement, which he'd chosen for his quarters, and I was sitting there with him one winter's evening, basking in one of those moments of great calm and well-being in his company that were like honey—one never wanted them to end.

'He was looking at me from his green leather wing chair, as intently as he always did, when he said: "Whatever I do, whatever I appear to do, hang on by your fingers and toes."'

The coming challenge was faced by a female pupil in a dream. 'I was in a huge hall of some sort, and we all had a task to do that was incredibly difficult. And I just was determined that I was going to finish it. And when it came to the judgment and the judge came to me, he said, "Does not give up under any circumstances." I thought that was a negative thing.' Not at all, responded the Sheikh.

You must start with the determination you'll need all the way. He once described the kind of test awaiting a new arrival who sought acceptance by a sheikh of the old school, as no doubt he himself had done. 'A favourite trick is to throw you a pair of boots and say, "Clean these!"'

Sakina had attended only three of his lectures at most when she had to leave London for several months. On her return she knew she absolutely must find him again, and thought her only way of doing so was to make repeated visits to the hall in Hampstead where the lectures had been held, even though he no longer used it. She kept going back because it was the only place she knew, and eventually she stumbled upon the group, who were there for a *sema* practice.

The Sheikh himself had been adamant with his lady friend on her yacht before vanishing over the side. 'I'm going to join the Sufis,' he had told her. 'I must be with the Sufis!'

He loved an Etruscan wall painting from the Tomb of the Leopard that depicts a man playing the double pipes and striding, as D. H. Lawrence put it, 'with a strange, powerful alertness onwards'. It embodied for him the spirit in which he had left Southern Rhodesia for London in the late 1960s with nothing but two suitcases, free of all other encumbrances and looking only to the future.

'The true *murid* is one who fixes his desire on the court of Allah Almighty and who does not get attached to anything else on the way,' he said. The work of a seeker is to seek. If it's knowledge you seek, you will have to seek it even unto China, in the words of Muhammad.

On the other hand, the sinister ease with which a person can head off in the wrong direction was pointed out by Saadi of Shiraz: 'I fear you will never reach Mecca, O traveller, for you are on the road to Turkestan.'

The Sheikh would spare none of his blistering firepower in the effort to keep us on course. One midsummer the whole group was driving in convoy to Long Mynd in Shropshire. 'He was getting really angry,' recalls Zainab. Various rendezvous had been arranged, 'and each time we met, there'd be some group that hadn't got there. And finally when we did all meet again, there was still a group that had got lost. And—I always remember this because it was such a deep lesson, although it was sort of on the surface—when they caught up eventually, they said, "We had to help So-and-So because they had problems with the Saab."

'He was just shouting, "Bugger the Saab! When I say, 'Do something,' you do it!"'

'I always remember the feeling that the lesson was: if you're going to make it, you cannot pick up every stray as you go along. He wouldn't stop for do-gooders. He had a mission, and if you were with him you had to stick to it. And I can see why. He said, "People are going to get lost"—not on the road, but mentally. People are going to be lost if they keep stopping: if they cannot be concentrated and keep going.'

In the Sheikh's words, which AB had written on a piece of paper and pinned to his wall: 'Keep your eyes on the stars, not on the dungheap.'

Or you could ask Walid. He was there in Istanbul the day the tomb was opened, and even at breakfast he had known it was going to be special. 'We were due to cross the Bosphorus to a mosque, we were going to do a prayer, we were going to some dervishes' tombs; there was going to be great *barakat* ["blessing" or "grace"][13] there,' he recalls ruefully. 'So we were all into it. "Come on, everyone, all together, no one wander off, keep concentrated."

'As we came out of the mosque, Bashir said to me, "Why don't you buy a *tasbih* [a string of prayer beads] off that poor old guy there?"

'I said, "Look, we've got to stick together. We've been told. The Sheikh said, 'Be a flock of birds.'"

'The others had already gone down the steps, but Bashir said, "I'll go down and keep my eye on them while you buy the *tasbih*."

'"All right." I bought the *tasbih* and went down the stairs—and the idiot was running round in circles like a chicken with his head chopped off. He'd lost the whole damn group. They'd turned the corner and gone up the side street and he had missed it: and we missed the entire day.'

You must be one-pointed, insisted the Sheikh. 'When an ordinary person comes to the Sheikh they are shown that there is no single-mindedness of purpose in their activity and therefore no sincerity; but people resist this form of revelation of what they are really like.'

When a prospective follower told Jesus that he wanted to say goodbye to his family, the reply came that no man who put his hand to the plough and then looked back was fit for the kingdom of God, as Jesus called it. The Sheikh would allude to that reply, as he often alluded to what Jesus had previously told another man who had protested that he must bury his father: 'Let the dead bury the dead.'

He had a lot of time for Malika because she had left her son behind with the boy's father in England in order to join him in Australia. Hakim had likewise told his wife, 'I need to follow the guy. I can't stay here—my life's got

---

13 The Sheikh also translated this Arabic word as 'the knowledge of the energy behind the reality of the universe' (see below). It is a quality possessed and dispensed by Sufi masters, whether in this world or the next.

no meaning.' Hakim insisted that the couple sell their business, but his wife, French family and British in-laws were not happy. 'So the moving to Australia was very hard. But it was more than anything for me: I had to go.' His wife relented, as did his brother, who also became a pupil, and both accompanied him. 'When we arrived the Sheikh was waiting for us at the airport, and he didn't want me to carry the suitcase—he took it himself. He was starting to pick up, and I took it, and he said, "Give me the other one." I said no, and he insisted—"It's for balance!"'

Just as single-mindedness has its reward, the opposite can have a harsh penalty. On the Australian farm, Ahmed was heading off to a job the Sheikh wanted done: building a house for the geese. 'On the way the other blokes asked me for help in rounding up a young bull calf. Nobody had much idea of what they were doing. I wound his halter round my hand, he lunged, and I might as well have tried to hold on to a car. The rope tore off the tip of my right little finger. I was left with a small but permanent disfigurement. But the point of the incident only became clear later, when I wondered aloud what lesson I should draw from it. He told me I should have kept going to the goose job without pausing to help. "That's your lesson."'

Or did you believe that there isn't a lesson, and things happen for no reason?

His pupil Mike Hargraves was a karate enthusiast. The Sheikh believed strongly in the martial arts as a form of training that did not involve the intellect but instead sharpened alertness and instinct, and recommended or told many of his male pupils to learn karate. But when he issued a general invitation to the group to accompany him to a gathering in the north of England organised by the Pakistani Sufis who operated in the migrant community, Mike decided to attend a karate event instead.

A day or two later we were with the Sheikh. Without preamble, he said, 'For those who knew him, Mike Hargraves was killed in a road accident at the weekend.' We sat shocked as he added: 'Those who were with the Sheikh were all right.' Then he looked at one of those present. 'Death is always at your shoulder, Maymuna.'

Later he said more. Mike had died of the impact, and had not known that he was dead until he'd made a move to get out of the car, thinking he was still in a physical body. He had put his hand down to the handle, and his hand had gone through it. He had freaked out. 'The Sheikh said Mike would spend fifty years in this state of freaked-outness before he realised what was going on,' recalls Rafiq.

To be explicit: there are other worlds, and one day you will enter another life. Many people cannot conceive of that at all. Many more are like Shakespeare's dodgy pedlar and scam artist, Autolycus, who candidly declared, '[As] for the life to come, I sleep out the thought of it.' Either way, you will face a challenge as you read on; but the greater challenge will come when you die. The next life will be far more real than this one, and your journey will continue—but learning will be much harder there.

When you die, explained the Sheikh with awesome clarity, you awake. 'There is a threshold world in which the spirit is opened to its real nature. You will find out what you are really like: but it is no longer possible to act differently.'

He was continually having to dismiss the pleas of what he called hungry ghosts, who knew he could see and hear them. As he walked through London's streets they would accost him in a desperate bid for his help in warning others, often their relatives, of what lay in store. The same thing happened indoors. 'People are constantly visiting me at night, pleading, "Please tell them not to be like me!" Sometimes my pupils can even hear their footsteps.'

Although he taught of other worlds beyond that threshold, spiritual realms which are not just psychological states but can be traversed in the fabled 'summer caravan' of actual experience in this life or the next, there is no short cut. If you are to reach them, you cannot skirt this first trip in the winter caravan—the psychological journey to the centre of your own being, which Sufis and others say you must make while still in your physical body, or face the consequences afterwards.

He compelled our attention because we understood that he knew all these things at first hand. 'I have travelled the way. I know.'

And he warned: 'Many want to step into spiritual experiences and states while still blind and deaf to themselves. But in order to know your lord you must know yourself. The innermost nucleus of your own being is an immortal creature which has nothing to do with all the opinions, notions and psychic colouring of the experiences which you have undergone since birth.

'People don't understand this. They believe that the personality and ego they have developed is themselves, and believe that it has some meaning in a permanent sense.' It doesn't. 'Egoism is the fundamental illusion that we possess something that is our own or is our self. This is the greatest lie by which we cut ourselves off from our destiny.'[14] You don't have any ego. All you have are behaviour patterns and attitudes which are completely mechanical and formed

---

14 The Sheikh here adopts a remark of J. G. Bennett in *The Masters of Wisdom*.

by the environment—by the climate of your times and by society—which may stretch back hundreds or thousands of years.

'Our endeavours are concerned with giving you psychological patterns and templates which will enable you to find out what you are really doing: to take you from your own delusions, to show you your real motivations, and to show you your needs as you move away from the realms of your wants.'

And if you—the reader, the seeker, the pupil, or anyone at all—haven't done this, at death you will possess only the habit patterns that you have ingrained in yourself and the impressions that life has stamped on you. 'All your deepest impressions remain after your physical death'; and the result is inevitable. 'You go to your own place.' In other words, you will join others like you on one of countless different levels. That is why Jesus said, 'In my Father's house are many mansions.' The Sheikh would quote him, and often described how the Salvation Army, for example, were still to be seen and heard banging drums and singing hymns in the next world, as they do in this one.

Most people, if they believe in the next life at all, assume they will go to heaven. Not necessarily. 'You make your own heaven or hell,' said the Sheikh. 'Mankind has been given a freedom to deal with life in constructive or destructive ways. If you deal with it in accord with the divine will, you will benefit from the beneficent aspect of Allah Almighty in the worlds to come. If you do the reverse, you build up the processes which lead to your misery in the worlds to come.'

Many people say that you make your own luck, and everyone knows that what goes around comes around. 'Heaven and hell are within you,' the Sheikh asserted, and he quoted from the following paraphrase of the great Swedish seer Emanuel Swedenborg, who he said was one of only two people outside Sufism[15] to have recorded detailed experience of both: 'The attitude that causes a drift toward heaven is in the feeling that there is a higher power and an effort to relate to it. This same spirit of humility and respect for the greatness of creation goes with an effort to be with others and to be of some use. The one bound for hell serves himself first, last and foremost. By this he is cut off from the opening-out possibilities of heaven.'

The Sheikh reminded us that the ancient Egyptians had depicted a person's heart being weighed against the feather of truth after death. A monster crouches waiting to devour the false heart. 'Heaven is created by your lightheartedness in dealing with life,' he said. The reverse is true for a heart that tips the scales, its owner's real actions having failed to match the account he or she has

---

15 The other was Dante Alighieri, whom he considered to have been influenced by great Sufis like Suhrawardi (1097–1168). The quoted passage occurs in Wilson van Dusen's *The Presence of Other Worlds*.

given. 'Psychological states fit you for a particular place in one of the heavens or hells, where you will be with your own kind.'

He told Imran, whose diabolical laugh could often be heard above a circle of his companions, that if he ever realised where that laugh was coming from he would never laugh again.

'Mysticism is not mere psychological adjustment—it is a complete spiritual reorientation. Spiritual values have now been abandoned in our culture because they have been equated with formal religion and the failure of dogmatism, but experiencing heaven or hell within yourself before you become discarnate is very, very important.'

He would speak about the two angels who come to examine you in the grave, implacably reviewing with you everything you did or thought, which you cannot now go back on, and demanding: 'Who is your lord?' Then he would mimic the sinister, cajoling voice of Shaitan (Satan): 'Go on—tell them! I am your lord!'

He once previewed the angels' questioning of his pupil Sadiq, who had fathered three children but did not seem keen to provide for them: 'What about your children, Sadiq?'

As he explained, 'You have two films, the actuality and what you think is your life. At death these are run against each other and an analysis is made regarding your intentions, and a lot of questions are asked. The more self-deluded you are, the longer will be the questioning time. Eventually those questions will have to match up with the reality.' So he continually tried to pre-empt this process by calling us to account beforehand.

He had more opportunity to do so for those who lived with him, and he exercised it to the full. Ahmed relates: 'You can't live in a *zawiya* and believe, as I did, that the world revolves around you, even a little. The difficulty does not lie in your surroundings; on the contrary. He would point out that I was the difficult one. "We could give you so much chapter and verse your head would spin," he told me, and indeed he was working from close observation. "The way you grab things"—how I used to snatch things that were offered to me: one symptom of a crassness and abruptness of which I had had no inkling.

'In the end he threw me out because, as I seem to remember him telling everyone, I could not learn what the *zawiya* had to teach. I moved in with Masoud, but only a week or two later I was part of a group who accompanied the Sheikh to Turkey.

'Now the Sheikh often characterised people in terms of their star signs: half playfully and half not, he'd refer to the sting of a pupil born under Scorpio, for example. I was born under Aries, the ram.

'We were sitting at white Formica tables in an Izmir restaurant eating meatballs and rice and teasing Muktar, who had a quick wit himself. After copping one particular gibe, he hesitated for a second over his rejoinder, and I yelled over to him, "Come on, there's not much time!"'

'Instantly the Sheikh's voice knifed through the hubbub with shocking seriousness: "There's not much time, Ahmed."'

'Everyone fell silent as he continued: "Don't go home and put the horns into Masoud."'

Why would you take that kind of advice and instruction from someone? Because, unlike you, he knows what lies ahead.

In 1995 he wrote to one pupil about another: 'Caroline Donovan has just departed in order to return to England and her family after spending seven weeks here in the [Australian] *zawiya*. She has been happy here and fitted in well. Her original intention was to spend six months here, but I sent her away to continue to put in order certain things which, if they are done now in her life, will not be required for restitution at another time in this world or in the worlds to come.'

He expanded the point in a BBC radio interview.

'Suppose now you have enjoyed a certain experience and have forgotten it for a number of years, and suddenly you smell a certain perfume which brings it back vividly because a charge of energy has passed through your system, and you recall this in a very vivid manner. It's so clear that you could be re-living the event, [although] intellectually when you try to do this you have a vague, hazy conception.

'Now this is the real quality of repentance: you have to re-live every experience and compensate everybody and everything for all the wrongs you have done.

'I know one instance of one great Sufi teacher who had a pupil who was formerly a governor of a province, and he made him go personally to all the people whom he had wronged and put the matters right. Then, to cure his pride, he made him carry sheep's stomachs around across his shoulders and sell them as any seller of tripe would sell it in the marketplace.

'And it's the curing of deep impressions made at the instinctual level that matter[s]: so a mere surface repentance, of saying, "I repent," intellectually, has no real significance.'

When a mutual crush developed between Ahmed and an older woman at work who wanted to leave her husband, the Sheikh was not unsympathetic. But he reminded his pupil, 'This bloke's never done anything to you'—adding that it would have been different if, for example, the man had been violent to his wife—and warned Ahmed not on any account to sleep with her: 'If you did, I would feel sorry for you.' Ahmed had no doubt that he was talking about the penalty in the next world, and took his advice.

None of this is a matter of religious belief. It's a matter of knowledge arising from experience. Almost everyone who found the Sheikh was seeking knowledge and experience, whether they were ready for it or not. Most were Britons, and a few came from other Western countries (France, Canada, Australia, Germany, Spain, Switzerland); none had been seeking religion of any kind.

Yet in London he converted more than 100 people to Islam. That's a great many, especially when you consider the gravity of the simple thrice-repeated sentence that constitutes the profession of faith and makes you a Muslim: 'I bear witness that there is no god except God and that Muhammad is His slave and His messenger.' When the Sheikh's pupil Abdul-Aziz, by then a Mevlevi sheikh in his own right, was himself receiving people into Islam and giving each a Muslim name, he mentioned that he was apprehensive about the extent of the responsibility he might be assuming in doing so. Our Sheikh's comment was: 'It's the whole of your life.'

That did not deter Sheikh Abdullah from his successful endeavour to convince us, despite our backgrounds. But his aim was not religious conversion for its own sake, or the sake of numbers, and his task was not accomplished by means of argument. The fact is that the longer one spent with him, the more it became obvious that the Sufi way which he taught and exemplified was inseparable from Islam. He embodied both. Both are, as he said, integral parts of one unity, and he took pains to make that apparent. His essay 'The Inner Jewel' (pp.181–5) is one among many demonstrations of his eloquence on this point.

In fact his contagious faith was inseparable from his experience. The central statement of Islam is that fundamental declaration that God is One and Muhammad His messenger. The Christian churches state that Jesus combines the divine and human by being 'God's son'. The difference is obvious immediately, but the reality does not lie in the words. Part of it lies in the Sheikh's statement: 'I have seen Jesus weeping for the things that have been done in his name.'[16]

At that point theology crumbles, just as it did one evening in Australia when he was watching an episode of *The Bill* in which a devout Jehovah's

---

16 He also wrote, 'The picture that has been developed from the [Turin] Shroud is the nearest in looks that I have ever seen represented of Jesus.'

Witness was harassed by hospital staff when she refused a blood transfusion for her son. He was intensely focused on it, and indeed appeared consumed by his sympathy with the mother, as one believer concerned for the plight of another. At one point he exclaimed with fierce indignation, "Look what they're doing to this good woman!"

In Islam itself he had no time for what he called externalism. Although he pointed out that he had brought more Britons to Islam than any number of externalist preachers, fundamentalists will find a great deal to condemn in this book. He criticised 'Koran-punching' clerics and 'mechanical Muslims' as being 'religionists', representing the husk of Islam but not the germ.

'The Saudi Wahhabis now say that Sufis are not necessary in the modern world; the Koran is enough. The Sufis say the process is an individual experience which has to be encountered in all its freshness to be understood in a unified being,' he said. 'We teach the real Islam.'

Rashida and her brother Mansur responded to that. Almost the only pupils to have been born Muslims, they come from a family of Indian business people who lived in Eritrea, and were both studying in London. Rashida's parents had tried in vain to arrange her marriage to an Indian, but in her words, 'The Sheikh saw them and said, "Not the right guy. Rashida is not brought up Indian-slash-whatever: she's not going to make chapattis. You brought her up more open—the culture is different." So that engagement broke, and I was very happy, and so thrilled the Sheikh backed me up: "I can do my studies. That's it. I'm free. I want to learn."'

He also took care to inoculate the rest of us, whose Muslim identity was grafted on to our Western one, against the risk that we would contract the over-zealousness of the convert. In our first few weeks at the *zawiya* in London, before he moved in himself, the pupils there somehow got acquainted with two American converts: a little man much older than they were, his domineering black wife and their two hapless children, who were all frequenting the mosque where we went for Ramadan prayers, and who wanted somewhere to stay. The Sheikh said they could stay with us, but emphasised that in Islam we were only obliged to offer three days' hospitality.

Fellow-Muslims will often pick holes in your conduct, especially if you're a Westerner or they think you're a convert. The residents endured three eye-opening days of having the Koran quoted at them in order to criticise the meals they served, or the way they served them, or other things. Then the family vanished, along with their hypocrisy—but not before the wife had recounted her endeavours on behalf of the Prophet, who is often called Rasul Allah, the Messenger of God. "I go to the library," she had said in a sinister drone, "and I find all the books that tell lies about Ra*sool* Allah, and I take them out and I *burn* them."'

The great Persian Sufi Abu Said Abu'l-Khayr (967–1049) said, 'Not until every mosque beneath the sun lies ruined will our holy work be done. Never will a true Muslim appear until faith and infidelity are one.' The Sheikh explained, 'This simply means that when people are overcome by mere mechanical dogmas the spirit of the unity is lost. All the prophets came to mankind to show the way to the spirit of the unity. This spirit is part of an attitude and a way of life.'

Yet fundamentalists have been trying to make trouble for Sufis for more than 1000 years. Many accounts tell of visitors to Sufi gatherings, including those of Abu Said, asking stupid questions designed to catch the master out on a point of religious law or practice. Once a convert attended one of our Sheikh's lectures and began telling Ahmed afterwards how the Sheikh was out of line in this or that way.

'I disagreed, but hesitantly,' says Ahmed. 'When I reported the conversation to the Sheikh, he objected bitterly that most of his pupils would not retaliate against such critics. "If Amir had been there," he told me, naming one of the keener ones, "he would have known what to say! He would have put that bloke in his place!" It worked on me perfectly. When the guy turned up the following week and again started to pick holes, I gave him the biggest verbal barrage I could manage. He never returned.'

When we visited the Luton mosque, which at the time was a grotty little terraced house, the Sheikh had disappeared out the back to the toilet. One of the locals must have given him free advice on how to perform his ablutions before prayer, because suddenly we heard him roar, 'I've been in Islam for twenty-five years, so don't you try and bullshit me!'

He protected us from the age-old censure of the hardliners by making sure that all the converts learned all of Islam's essentials. We recited the profession of faith at the outset; he taught us, and had us taught, the prescribed prayers, and encouraged us to perform them; he laid great emphasis on the fast of Ramadan; he insisted that we made the obligatory contribution for charity at the end of it. He also formed an intention to lead his group on the pilgrimage to Mecca, although that was not realised.

He always said emphatically, 'You can't be a Muslim on your own,' and we all embraced those five pillars of Islam, as they're known, along with many other customs which form part of the *sunnah* or way of the Prophet—from which, rather than from the Koran, many aspects of Islam originate: hailing one another with the 'greeting of peace' ('*Salaam alaikum*'); leaving your shoes at the door; eating and passing things with your right hand; and so on.

But although this emulation is of great importance in persuading one's footsteps on to the beaten path, the Sheikh was fundamentally concerned with the spirit, not the minutiae. He was always practical, never picky.

In Islam some things are prescribed and others *haram* (forbidden): dishonesty, adultery, alcohol, murder, usury, pork.... It was probably one December that the Sheikh was enjoying some of the Harrods Christmas pudding he was especially fond of when Maymuna started reading the ingredients, which no doubt included brandy. She suddenly exclaimed, 'Oh! This pudding's *haram*!'

'I don't believe they'd put pork in a Christmas pudding,' replied the Sheikh.

'No, no, no –' she insisted.

'I don't believe they'd put pork in a Christmas pudding,' he repeated, still tucking in with relish.

'No, no –'

And he said firmly once again, 'They wouldn't put pork in a Christmas pudding!'

Muktar recalls that the Sheikh once sent him and Amir off to see a couple who lived in a broken-down cottage in Wales. Although he forgets the point of the mission, he remembers part of their briefing.

'It was a long drive and we had to stay overnight. Before we left, he said, "Now whatever you're offered to eat, or they ask you to do, I want you to do that. You're not holding to any external set of rules here," so to speak.

'I thought, "Yeah, whatever." Drive down, and we talk to them, and then evening comes, and we say, "What's for dinner?"

'And they say, "Pig's-trotter soup."

'And so there's this moment; and then both Amir and I say, "Fantastic! Can't wait!" Then we piled our way through this pig's-trotter soup, which even if I wasn't a Muslim would have been a big challenge for anybody.

'But you know what we learnt from that? Humility. We learnt someone's offering of hospitality when they had very little. They had very little material goods: they had little food, even, and the best they could give us was pig's-trotter soup.

'And it was like a Sufi story come alive, because you had to realise all of that—Who were they? What were they offering? What was the *love* that they gave you? And who cared if it was a pig's trotter?'

At a certain point we switched to using, among ourselves, the Muslim names we'd been given. Though done on the Sheikh's instructions, that never generated an odour of sanctity. In several cases he himself adopted shortened versions dreamt up by his pupils (which was how Abdul-Barr became AB); and when he had bestowed on one young woman the name Yasmin, denoting the jasmine flower, he commented, 'Now she can get up everyone's nose.' We called the *zawiya* the 'za', and Ramadan was sometimes 'Rammers', though not in front of him. In one all-male household the jug from which a Muslim pours water over his or her private parts after visiting the toilet was known as 'the willy water'.

The *barzakh*, sometimes translated as 'isthmus', is the threshold world referred to by the Sheikh: the soul's first port of call after death, and the realm in which your actions in this life catch up with you, for good or ill. So the phrase '*barzakh* points', on the analogy of Brownie points, came into use, again among the males. The Sheikh once used it himself, in the tone of one resigned to adopting whatever idiom he must use to make himself understood.

On the other hand, we observed a clear limit. He said that with Allah Almighty, 'There is a relationship, but there's no familiarity,' and we would never have made a crack about the Prophet, for instance, or made fun of the Sheikh himself.

It is true that he would sometimes contrast our attitudes with those of dervishes trained in the Islamic world, declaring, 'You're not *murids*' backsides!' He made it clear that our situation was not like theirs, either. 'I have made things easy for you,' he told us, and spoke of the shock we would receive if we were in a traditional *zawiya* as 'real *murids*': 'constantly under the eye of the sheikh, fed on scraps'.

Nevertheless, he gave a kind of imprimatur to our unique little culture when he said that the real master was the one whose teaching inspired strange jokes. Loyalty and sobriety do not entail continual solemnity. Once the people at the *zawiya* were invited to a Turkish wedding at a big hotel in Bloomsbury. Though we were seated with other guests who had been adjudged similarly religious, when the band launched into rocking Turkish pop or folk music the Sheikh got up to dance: so we joined him. He was wearing his usual tweed jacket, plus his crocheted prayer hat, and bopping with an expression of fierce concentration as if his life depended on it.

It was surreal, if only because obviously we had all stopped partying long before that.

'When I met him I was drinking far too much,' recalls Zainab, 'smoking, meeting in pubs, thinking, "It's really great, I can down whiskies and I can do all this"—and he went along with it. And suddenly it wasn't right—And he didn't say, "Don't do it," but somehow I knew that it wasn't right.'

For Khalida too, 'His teaching was not "I think you should be doing this". It was because it was the best way to live. He had to teach us very gradually how to come round to think what was really best for us as human beings.' One day he said to another of the women, in a gentle and serious way: 'Malika, know your heart's desire—and always, in every moment, strive to be the best of yourself. That is the way to live your life.'

Khalida has no doubt that such guidance was needed terribly. 'Things had gotten so bad that people like Paul Williams [my former partner] were around who could have children from multiple women, and us women foolishly went along with it too—and I deeply regret those days. I tell you, those were really bad times. I don't miss them at all. There were no rules, nothing. And you thought it was all OK, and you didn't realise how much damage you were doing to your own psyche. So of course the Sheikh saved us. You look back and you realise—What would have happened to you if you hadn't met him? You owed him a lot.'

Likewise her daughter Samira, who last saw the Sheikh when she was nine. 'Apart from my Mum, he had wildly the biggest impact on my life, easily. It was a BOUM!' she says, striking the table, 'that I never wanted to let go of; although I could thank my Mum a lot for that, because she held on to it.'

Samira became a Muslim at the age of five, and in her forties she is absolutely a Muslim still. 'I always had the Sheikh—*always*—at the back of my mind. [Even as a teenager] I had enough of an impact from the Sufi group to know when this New-Agey stuff was fluff, so even though I did read a lot about that sort of thing it was never, ever satisfying, or it didn't make any sense. So I always reserved judgment; I never got carried away.'

'I thought I was free when I met him,' remembers Zainab at sixty-two. 'I was enjoying doing all the things you're doing as a young person when you think you're free. But I've come to realise that you're only free when you're free within yourself. So the sense of freedom—I can only really be free if I'm free with God: if that makes sense. So that's the only freedom I can really identify with. If I felt cut off from that, I wouldn't want to live.'

By the time the Sheikh featured in Bill Nicholson's good BBC *Everyman* documentary 'The Dervish Way' in 1981 he had a group of pupils to bear witness to what he told the camera, in what is probably the only video footage of him speaking:

'Many people in the West believe that the externals of Islam are hard, perhaps harsh, and they are not accustomed to them. But there is in Islam a word called *ijtihad* which literally means "effort". Now this has been applied by the Muslim fundamentalists in the external sense, but we also apply it internally, in terms of our psychological training; and we use the discipline of Islam as a framework for rebuilding a new structure within those who come to us. And we find in almost all cases that people are grateful for this framework.'

He rejected the misconception that those who have undergone mystical development can proceed to ignore the dictates of religion. 'I used to have notions of this kind myself,' he told us. 'But I was sitting with my sheikh in his *zawiya* when he gave a talk that made me change my opinion.'

Although none of us knew who that sheikh had been, there was no doubt about Sheikh Abdullah's acceptance by the Muslim community in Britain, and especially among Sufis. He associated in particular with Sheikh Muhammad Aslam (1934–99), who came from Pakistan but lived in Blackburn, Lancashire, and Sheikh Nazim Adil al-Qibrisi (1922–2014), who was based in Cyprus but acted as spiritual leader to London's Turkish community. Each represented a different branch of the Naqshbandi Order, to which our Sheikh and his pupils belong.

Although the oral teaching and *barakat*—what the Sheikh defined as the knowledge of the energy behind the reality of the universe—had been passed down from master to pupil from the earliest times, it was only in the twelfth century (some 600 years after the time of Muhammad) that groups of disciples began to form themselves into orders to perpetuate the teaching and methods of particularly outstanding Sufis who had made an impression on the Sufi community. The biggest orders have been the Qadiris, Mevlevis and Shadhilis, as well as the Naqshbandis.

The orders are not sects of Islam but a variety of groupings providing for a variety of spiritual temperaments. Many people are drawn to the Mevlevis because they have music and *sema*, to the Chishtis because they have music and *ghazals* (a type of verse or song), and so on. All genuine orders are distinguished by adherence to the rites and tenets of Islam. From the orders mentioned, a whole range of new orders have sprung up because particular saints have deemed it necessary, or been ordered, to found them.

When one comes to Sufism one is traditionally bound by oath to the sheikh, who is a link in a chain of transmission which is regarded as a living thing, although historically all its previous members are dead.[17] This chain or spiritual pedigree, the *silsilah*, is exactly like a family tree, listing all the sheikhs in order and beginning with God and the Prophet himself.

---

17 This sentence and the preceding two paragraphs are based on a modified quotation from R. W. Austin's *Sufis of Andalusia* that formed part of one of Sheikh Abdullah's lectures.

The School of Celestial Fire

When our Sheikh used the word 'we' it usually denoted Sufi sheikhs as a group, or in particular the masters of his *silsilah*—irrespective of their era; and when, speaking of the experiences awaiting the developed pupil, he said, 'We introduce you to our friends,' that could only mean his fellow-masters of past times.

'We believe in an after-life, and can communicate with these men,' he explained. 'They can speak to us across the division of time and still give us counsel. This form of communication has a synchronistic quality of its own. When the things of this world cease to attract us, and our concentration relates to the area of reality within our own being, there is no further contamination of the intuitive factor, and the symbols and visions are true. Then you can relate to the *awliya* (literally the "friends" of God, or saints) in a form of direct communication, heart to heart.

'When you think of them, it's like telephoning somebody and seeing their picture. People can talk to each other. They are at the centre of their being and therefore at the centre of the universe, but they have died to themselves.'

The Sheikh occasionally indicated that he followed guidance, as we followed his. 'My superiors brook no disobedience from me,' he explained, and the identity of those superiors was implied on another occasion when he dismissed the question 'Why?' with the words, 'The *silsilah* never give you a reason.'

The names of Sheikh Muhammad Aslam and Sheikh Nazim were last on the list when our Sheikh read out his *silsilah*: that is, they were technically his immediate seniors. He showed great courtesy towards them in person and observed the precedence of the order—to the extent that, when Sheikh Muhammad Aslam once queried why our Sheikh did not wear a beard when it was *sunnah*, the Prophet's custom, to do so, he immediately grew one (although he later declared that 'Beards are filthy things') and kept it for the rest of his life.

From Sheikh Nazim—who was, our Sheikh commented, very much a royalist, having grown up under the British Crown and lined the road with other Union-Jack-waving schoolboys to cheer King George V during a royal visit to Cyprus in colonial days—he accepted an instruction to attend Lord Mountbatten's funeral in Westminster Abbey, despite holding Mountbatten responsible for the deaths of a great many Muslims during the partition of India in 1947.

The pupil, however, is not entitled to look to any higher authority than his or her own sheikh. Although many people thought these two sheikhs had chosen ours as their follower, he said it was not so. 'I chose them.' His relationship to them was emphatically not that of pupil to master, and on occasion he would criticise them and their pupils, sometimes vehemently, while the advice and instructions we received were given as his own.

'All sheikhs are the same in their degree of submission,' he said, 'but they differ in their degree of knowledge.' And again, 'Every one's like a diamond. Some have flaws in them. They try to reflect the diamond reality, but not all can reflect it properly. Or, they have different lights—some have stronger lights: you can put it that way.'

The world of another sheikh is more than likely to differ markedly from that of one's own. When the son of a Malaysian prince began attending the talks, the Sheikh took him aside and told him that in reality his teacher was Sheikh Nazim, whom he had never met. After our Sheikh had introduced him, the youth asked Sheikh Nazim whether he should continue attending our Sheikh's talks, which were appropriate to a London audience among whom were many non-Muslims who shared no common spiritual heritage. Sheikh Nazim told him that although our Sheikh had kindled the spark in the young man, the talks would be lost on him, and said, 'We have a different method.'

Other worlds of difference were obvious in our contacts with Mahmoud Hussein and his brother Marufa, who were deputies of Muhammad Aslam in the north and Midlands. The Sheikh was fond of them both, but our association with them entailed a wilderness safari, even on the phone. When he tried to reach Mahmoud Hussein at his Birmingham lodgings, he got a woman with a strong Brummy accent. 'It's Sheikh Abdullah here,' he began.

The reply came: 'F--- off, you silly black –'

'– And she used a word for a woman's sexual organs,' the Sheikh reported. He had come off the line chortling, for what choice did he have? He was a man of high education and perfect manners whose own occasionally vehement expletives and even apparent rudeness were carefully deployed for teaching purposes. Although he expected us to behave with perfect Muslim propriety on our trips to Birmingham, Manchester and Bradford, and never to embarrass him, and although if required he would deliver a fiercely traditionalist speech that drew applause from the audience, he was blunt about the cultural chasm we were crossing.

Sometimes the occasion for the speeches, the sermons and the subcontinental fervour was the *urs* (pronounced 'oorss') or death anniversary of a saint, in which case he would rarely fail to complain that it was a pain in the *urs*. One Saturday morning when our excursion coincided with an England-Scotland soccer match at Wembley, and we were setting out from a Euston Station already teeming with singing, drunken, flag-draped Scotsmen, he proclaimed, 'You are going from one kind of madness to another kind of madness!'

'We' were the men of the group, for the Pakistanis were typically phalanxes of black-bearded males in identical snow-white prayer caps and black Nehru jackets, with no woman in sight. Unlike most boys' outings, however, our day trips with the Sheikh to visit them by train or coach owed all their real pleasure to his presence.

For sure, the great Sheikh Suhrawardi was wholly correct when he wrote in the twelfth century that 'Companionship with the master is by obedience, so it is not really companionship, but service. Complete obedience and respect towards the master are required.' Yet such companionship can be fascinating, warm and uproariously funny, just as it can be lethally awkward, stressful or even frightening. And when Suhrawardi added that 'The master in the midst of his followers is like the Prophet in the midst of his community', the glow of a powerful comradeship shines out irresistibly.

Sohbet is a Turkish word[18] that Sheikh Abdullah always translated as 'association with the sheikh', although in practice it usually referred to the times when we sat with him, often over tea, and he would talk. He was emphatic that *sohbet* was central to Sufi teaching. It was certainly central to the life of our group—and for the men, lunch and *sohbet* at a Little Chef on the M1 were wonderful compensation for what could later be an afternoon spent in wretchedly uncomfortable squatting on the floor of the Manchester mosque, listening blankly to a ranting Urdu sermon.

That version of Islam, from which the women of our group were spared, was not ours. On the contrary, 'Writers who have seen Islam as a wild, male religion coming out of the hot desert are far from the truth,' said the Sheikh. 'The presence of the Prophet was cool and feminine, and there was a completeness of wisdom within him which was later lost as people were taken away from the true path by the influences of this world.'

Malika's son was born five or six months after she had begun attending the Sheikh's lectures. A week or so later, she had the urge to go out with her new baby in a sling. She usually headed for nearby Hampstead Heath, but that morning she walked into the village—where she bumped into the Sheikh, who blessed the baby and gave him his name then and there.

'A week or two later he called on me unexpectedly one afternoon. I tried to offer him hospitality, but he refused even a cup of tea, and told me to carry on as usual with my routine. He sat on one side of the fire and I on the other,

---

18 The 'h' is sounded. In everyday Turkish the word means simply 'conversation', 'chat' or 'talk', including in the sense of 'lecture' or 'sermon'.

and I breast-fed as usual. We were mostly in silence, and he stayed for two or three hours, emanating a lovely peace. Later, whenever I struggled with motherhood after having become a single parent, I would recall that afternoon and the feeling of pervading love and calm.'

Khalida was another single mother. Her break-up with Paul Williams had been nasty, and she feared what he might do. She was at the *zawiya* once when the alarm was raised: '"Paul Williams is coming up the road!" And they said, "Just come here, hide—don't let him see you," and the Sheikh offered me to go down into his flat. That taught me something: that these people were going to help me. Because I always had this tendency to feel alone all the time.'

She and her daughter both make the same point. 'He gave us a feeling of safety whenever he was around,' Samira says. 'And it doesn't happen very often, that sense of security. I don't know how else I'd describe it.'

Furthermore, in the words of Asiya, 'It was really nice to feel that he respected us, and that he was teaching the men to respect us, because I would say that Western men weren't particularly respectful of women.'

It was the sight of an old woman struggling across the street that prompted the Sheikh to beckon a male pupil who as usual had been eyeballing every woman on the way, and to tell him in front of his mates, 'She's feminine too, you know!'

Walid once made a flippant remark to one of the women at the *zawiya*: something about coming to look at them, or perhaps 'Phwoar!' or its equivalent. The following Tuesday the group met for *dhikr*, and as soon as Walid appeared and sat down, the Sheikh rose from his seat, advanced and stood over him. 'Now you don't come to the *zawiya* and talk about the women like that!' he thundered.

Walid shrank in his chair. 'He ripped into me,' he recalls. 'I was in tears in front of everyone.'

'Boy!' comments Khalida, who saw the incident, 'that was pretty scary.' As far as she could tell, he had personally been affronted by what Walid had said: 'and I didn't see that too often. It was very rare that he would make it personal—it was always teaching. He was telling your ego.' However, the Sheikh's own words cast a different light on what she saw.

'If you become angry, you needn't let it out,' he explained, 'but you can become angry and decide to let it out because that is what you feel like spontaneously. In this way you are not carried away by your anger. You are using it as a means to deal with a situation.

'Being angry is a totally different experience from giving way to an emotional rage. You have it under control [and] you can use it in a cool, detached way like a sharpened sword. This is the fighting spirit of the martial arts of the ancient East. You stop and time it to a minute; you have the complete measure over the emotion at the point you choose to let it out.

'This is the paradox of being consciously spontaneous. It's an active, conscious control: you are not the passive partner of your own rages. You have to develop spontaneity with a conscious feeling relationship: a feeling detachment which doesn't allow your heart to leap and be overwhelmed by the event and be carried off. You have to be cool within; it's like a retarded spontaneity.

'When Rumi said, "First I was raw; then I was cooked; then I was burnt," he was describing the process leading up to this linking of control with spontaneity. This is physiological as well as psychological. Fire has to be felt within one's being, and it has to burn, because eventually that fire becomes an inner cool—the fountain of camphor.'

A stocky, thick-set Englishman called Hatim felt the edge of the sword just like Walid, for he had inflicted physical violence on his wife and fellow-pupil Rawda. 'I reduced him to tears in the Birmingham mosque,' the Sheikh recounted. 'I was so angry about what he was doing to Rawda. He brutalised her.'

Ishaq, too, was brought to tears, but not by anger.

Any tourist in Istanbul can visit the tomb of a Sufi master named Sünbül Efendi (1451–1529)—painted, to this day, with hyacinths, because *sünbül* means 'hyacinth', and the saint always wore a hyacinth in his turban. Ishaq was in the party when the Sheikh took us there, very deliberately, in 1983. At the time the complex included a girls' school. It was evidently a boarding school, even though the girls were not yet in their teens, for each had her own simple room opening on to the courtyard. He encouraged us to note the charming, feminine eau-de-nil green and pink in which the rooms were painted; but that was only part of the lesson that unfolded.

The real Islam of which he continually spoke, and which he taught and demonstrated throughout his life, relies on steadfast faith, but already you have seen that it carries no prohibition on passion, laughter or pleasure. It allocates a time and place for anger, rightly employed; a time and place for sex. It has no room for arrogance, idleness, selfishness, greed or belligerence. Instead it guides towards kindness, sobriety, thankfulness, honesty, altruism, forbearance, restraint, modesty for both sexes, a clear focus, the channelling of one's energy into the effort to be of use.

'The Sheikh stood in one of those little girls' rooms, and we had to file in two by two,' Ishaq relates. 'He said, "Look at that. Have a look and a feel of this room."

'And there's a young girl, a tiny bed. These girls are wearing their little scarves. Their mums and their dads have sent them there. When they're not in the school they're going back to a home in which everybody's living a Muslim life, and they're building up a lifetime of experiences that have been shaped around the teachings of the Prophet, one way or the other.

'They're getting a proper Islamic education. Now who knows—how right was the school getting it? To me this looked like a really good version of Islam that was being done for the right reasons.'

At this point you should know that the Sheikh spoke a great deal about the 'impressions' of what a person encounters in life. In fact, he said, you live not in the real world, but in the world of your own impressions. 'The world [itself] *is* real, but what you see is only impressions: and these are fantasies coloured by your intellect, emotions and instincts. You have to recognise that your impressions are your own harvest. To harvest well you have to sow well.'

So Ishaq continues: 'These young girls were growing up in a world in which their impressions were being formed in a constructive way. It was the femininity, the sweetness, and the idea that these little virgin girls—one day they'll be married, and that marriage will be a good one, and they'll have a family, and they'll raise their children—that whole sense. That was the message.

'He's effectively saying to us: see how these people are living. And then he pointed at me and said, "Not like you, Ishaq! Yours is a lifetime of whoring."

'That's what he said to me. "A lifetime of whoring. That's what's you should be comparing it with." You know: "There's this—and there's your effing life."

'That might have been when I finally broke down. I was crying like a baby: I just was beside myself. It's the only time it's ever happened in my life. It was a sense of sorrow—and not just for me. I just could not help comparing them and their lives with me, at the age of twenty-seven or so, and all the impressions I'd caught to get to that point. And I just was sobbing, because there was nothing that could be done to undo the way that I'd lived.

'There's nothing that could be done to give me anything like that, and there's nothing that could be done to un-give me my experiences up to that stage in my life. That hit pretty hard, that one.'

The men who embarked on the journey of Sufism with Sheikh Abdullah had no excuse for failing to understand clearly how it is one thing to identify a woman as a sexual object and quite another to build a relationship with the feminine. Female pupils travelled a parallel route.

'I'd come from Western culture in the era of the feminists,' notes Asiya. 'We were supposed to do our own car mechanics, we were supposed to do this and that—and the Sheikh didn't go for that.' Indeed he once said that the ways of men and women were completely different in this world: 'We are very different, male and female, and need different environments to grow.'

'He taught men to treat women right,' Asiya continues, 'and for me that was amazing. It made me so much more able to relax as myself, as a woman, because I wasn't expected to have to be both a man and a woman. It was very good to be able to feel that you could be feminine, and bring out the feminine side.'

The Sheikh made no demands for the women to dress as traditional Muslims, except at the mosque and the *dhikr*, any more than the men. His concern was something else. 'One of the teachings that he impressed on us women was to honour and respect ourselves,' says Malika. 'And he would say to us, "Wear beautiful undergarments, because they make you feel good."'

Sakina recalls that those who lived at the *zawiya* had to learn to get their underwear into respectable order for display on the washing line. 'This was part of the same process of improving one's appearance that all the women went through. I realised my clothes were not up to scratch, and I started to buy for a totally different look—going from shapeless hippy mess to smart, feminine and conservative, but never dowdy. The women also had exotic Middle-Eastern, or floor-length and colourful Western, outfits for special occasions.

'The Sheikh would pay enormous attention to all sorts of small details, such as when a slip was needed under light clothes, and Aziza's struggles with static in her clothes so they stuck to her instead of hanging right. It would be fair to say that all of us felt much better about ourselves as a result of all this—more comfortable with our appearance, since we looked much more attractive and knew it.'

Malika did not live in the *zawiya* then, but a morning in Paris brought her the same quality of experience. 'We were in the dining area of a cheap and unpleasant hotel that had been booked for one night at the start of that trip,' she recalls, 'waiting for the Sheikh to come downstairs. We were noisy and excited, ready for our adventure.' For a pupil, however, it is never wise to be ready for A, B or C. The better plan is to be ready for anything, for the Sheikh may exercise his absolute power to disconcert or disrupt at any time.

'He entered in a thunderous state and delivered an enormous bollocking aimed especially at the pupils who had booked according to their convenience rather than for the good of him or the group. Then he turned on his heel and walked out with Naima, leaving great confusion about what to do next. Luckily I saw Aziza, who had lived with him for several years, grab her bag and run out of the door. I leapt up and ran after her. In the street she paused and said she knew where he would be'—the lingerie floor of the Galeries Lafayette. Once there, Aziza relaxed.

'Very soon we heard the Sheikh's voice nearby. I'd been looking at a particularly pretty set of underwear and was just asking the price. Next moment he was beside me in a most delightful mood, encouraging me to buy it and congratulating me on my choice. The three of us had a wonderful time shopping with him.'

The Sheikh made sure that the women were included when he taught and encouraged his pupils to learn the *sema* ceremony, and later to perform it in public. Sakina took part until she was fifty-nine. He expected criticism from hardliners for this policy, but pointed out that it was merely a return to original practice from the thirteenth century, which had subsequently been stifled.

For the *sema* itself he had what he always called 'a great love'. The 'turning' is no frenzied spinning, but rather part of a sober, complex, many-layered ceremony that possesses immense gravity and beauty even for spectators. He had practised it in earlier years to the extent that one ankle was permanently swollen. In London he supervised its development to a high pitch of perfection, and he saw to it that Abdul-Aziz, who was installed as a sheikh of the Mevlevi Order, transplanted the ceremony to Australia.

'Jalaluddin Rumi: he's a lovely man!' our Sheikh would declare gravely, as of a mutual friend, when he and Sheikh Nazim were sitting together presiding over the *dhikr* and other functions, as they did many times.

Sheikh Nazim customarily spent Ramadan in London. Being a lunar month, Ramadan arrives about ten days earlier each calendar year, and it was heading into high summer. So for twenty-nine or thirty days, until the sighting of the new moon, we new Muslims found ourselves going without food or drink from, say, 2.30am until 8.45pm. We broke the fast with the Sheikh, did the sunset prayer, had dinner in haste, and rushed off through the warm night to the Turkish mosque, at first a converted synagogue and later the former cinema, both near the *zawiya*. It could be getting on for 11pm before the prayers started.

Those prayers are long, but to Ahmed it felt almost like party time after the interminable day. 'There was the energy hit from dinner, the bustle, the communal atmosphere, and Sheikh Nazim's beautiful voice leading the prayers,' he recalls. Afterwards the Sheikh would often receive pupils for tea, and the usual chucking-out time of 11pm was much extended. The fast starts at dawn, not even sunrise, but one night everyone was still eating croissants around the mahogany table when he pointed out that they'd better stop—it was already past time for the dawn prayer. Once the company was even drinking tea after the sun had come up. 'The Sheikh always said he wasn't that fussed about the early start,' says Abdul-Malik.

If everyone had gone to bed, he would conform to the *sunnah* by allowing tea and biscuits or suchlike to be served when they rose just before dawn: but he wasn't really keen, commenting that 'the Prophet knew his people, and he knew how fond of their bellies they were'.

In the same spirit we relished the Eid al-Fitr festival at the month's end. 'How soon the miseries of Ramadan are forgotten!' remarked the Sheikh one year as he watched his pupils wolfing strawberries and cream on a celebratory boat trip up the Thames.

On the other hand, he could change a lifetime's habit in a few seconds.

'He put a very, very strong emphasis on Ramadan,' says Asiya. 'During my first Ramadan he gave a talk about fasting. He looked at everybody and said, "I know if you've been going around eating buns and things." Then he'd glare and ask, "Who is your lord? It's the bun!"

'When he talked he would pump it into your gut and your heart. So the message wasn't filtered through your head; it was going straight in. And when I went out, I started to take a cigarette and I thought, "Oh my God—who is your lord? This is ridiculous! I want to be a Sufi and I can't even do this."

'So each time I took a cigarette I'd say to myself, "Who is your lord?" and I would put the cigarette away. I carried that pack of cigarettes around for about two weeks doing that. I never smoked one; but I always had them there.

'I was still going through this when I had a meal with some of the other pupils. One of them was still smoking, and she asked for a cigarette. I said, "Here, you can have the whole pack." I gave it away and never smoked again.'

Hakim gave up immediately after a talk during which the Sheikh had directly castigated those of his pupils who smoked. 'I managed to give up for seven years,' he says. 'My wife gave up, my friend gave up; my brother gave up, and he's been free from tobacco since that talk.'

The fact that different masters have different ways is illustrated by the curious fact that Sheikh Muzaffer Ozak of the Halveti-Jerrahi order (1916–85) and his pupils were dedicated smokers. But that did not hinder his firm relationship with our Sheikh, which was established at least from the time the two met in Istanbul, where Sheikh Muzaffer was based. There is a photo of their initial embrace, which left a powerful impression on those who witnessed the attraction between them. We visited him again later.

In Istanbul with the Sheikh in 1983 we also met the noted Naqshbandi Sheikh Mahmut Efendi, born in 1931; and on the previous trip, contact had been made in the city with associates of another distinguished Naqshbandi, Sayyid Muhammad Rashid Erol (1930–93), who lived far to the south-east of Turkey. Thus began the crossing of another great divide.

'We were told that in order for the Sheikh and all of us to meet with them, there was some sort of test,' recalls Muktar, who was sent with Amir for a first meeting. The pair evidently survived the scrutiny, just as they had survived the pig's-trotter soup in Wales. Then Muhammad Rashid's people arrived at the hotel. 'And the Sheikh gets tested: they immediately say, "Lead the prayers," because they want to know he's got some Islam, he's got real grounding. So he did it, and they watched, and they participated, and at the end of it they said, "OK, you can now go down and see him."'

Abdul-Malik takes up the story: 'He sent an envoy to escort us: and this bloke was an absolute externalist—he was ridiculous. First of all he comes to the hotel and we're doing the prayers in the corridor, and he's complaining. He says, "You can't do the prayers here! This is a public place!" Then we're on the bus, and the bloke's saying, "This is prayer time! You should be stopping and doing the prayers!"'

'The Sheikh said, "Where are we going to do the prayers? There's no mosque here."'

'"You stop the bus, we'll do them by the side of the road!"'

'"You were complaining about us doing them in the corridor in the hotel; now you want us to do them by the side of the road!"' the Sheikh retorted. He really hammered him.'

It was a twelve-hour drive to Konya, another thirteen hours the following day, and a further two hours after dawn the next. Stops were few, even for the toilet. The trip ended at a dusty compound only 100km or so from the Syrian border. Here the men had to separate from the women, who were almost uniquely wearing full black chadors. 'We understood we were in a more fundamentalist situation,' says Muktar. 'But the women there were so loving,' adds Zafira. 'They were so welcoming, just because we'd arrived and we were their Muslim sisters.' The place vibrated with the attraction of Sayyid Muhammad Rashid himself. The women were singing songs about him and the men were clasping his hand. 'He was very loving and gentle and open,' says Zafira, 'and there was none of this feeling of heavy maleness. It was beyond protocol and ritual.'

In all this, Sheikh Abdullah was welcomed with great esteem, and his Turkish hosts remember the visit to this day.

At other times he spoke of his friend Sheikh el-Mehdi Bentounès, of the Alawi Order, who had been based in Algeria but also taught in Paris. El-Mehdi had died in 1975, and after his name our Sheikh would always add, 'May Allah be well pleased with him.' He had had Westerners among his pupils, including well-known figures such as Martin Lings, best known for his biography of Muhammad. Our Sheikh recounted how these people, bewildered by their own sheikh's words or behaviour, would come to him looking for explanations: 'What's he up to? Can you tell us what he's doing?'

El-Mehdi only gave his pupils one exercise: 'Visualise the name of Allah in letters of fire, and sob your heart out.' Sheikh Abdullah explained this as making the essential connection of mind (through the first part of the exercise) with energy (the second part). El-Mehdi never did tell his pupils what he was doing. As far as he was concerned, if he performed the teaching he had done his job.

'But the Western mind demands answers,' said the Sheikh. 'Although I had to respect el-Mehdi, I could give them answers. You can ask me a thousand questions, and I can give you a thousand answers. But you cannot penetrate mysticism by learning from books or talking. Instead, we say: "Come—taste the honey!"

'We give students exercises at many levels to start a whole range of processes operating. Most people can't understand this, and become unbalanced by only doing one or two things of what they are told. If they do exactly as they are bidden, the range of qualities will develop, and advanced knowledge about our own being will be the harvest.

'I take people out into the country at certain times, particularly the solstices and equinoxes, so that they can feel the changing of the seasons.' (That was why we had travelled to Long Mynd, among other places.) 'You also have to become sensitive to feel the energy of the Sheikh: it is the energy of life, the same energy that excites you in a tropical night, which he has held in himself. The pupils are like iron filings round a magnet, until they become magnets themselves.'

It's a matter of attraction. Even Samira as a little girl knew what she felt when visiting the *zawiya*: 'We would go and sit there—and it wasn't just sitting there.'

El-Mehdi would pretend to get lost in London and expect his pupils to find him by inward means: 'rather like radar that bats use', explained Sheikh Abdullah. 'There is a stimulation in ecstatic terms which is greater closer to the sheikh.' When we went to Turkey, the fast pace caught some out, as you have seen. One evening the Sheikh and the main body of the group ended up in a restaurant minus four of the men, who had been left stranded. They turned up some time later, having found him in Istanbul's teeming labyrinth with no information at all to guide them. He greeted them brusquely but was pleased with their success.

Abdul-Malik, too, got stranded, this time in Konya. He surprised himself by walking very directly and purposefully through a trackless jumble of streets and then suddenly stopping outside a shop, wondering, 'What am I doing here?' The Sheikh and the others were inside.

On the hunt in London once for a new job, he'd asked the Sheikh's advice, but received no immediate answer. A few days later he was at work in Victoria when he found himself delaying going to lunch. At exactly the same time, a pupil who was with the Sheikh a mile or two away in Chelsea was startled to hear the Sheikh exclaim abruptly, 'Come on, we've got to go!' When Abdul-Malik finally left the office and crossed the road, the two of them were standing there. 'And the Sheikh just gave me a hug, and continued the conversation that we'd had a few days prior, as if nothing had come in the way.'

By contrast, when another pupil was gripped one day in Melbourne by a strong urge to go to Brunetti's, the famous café, he told himself not be so self-indulgent—but if he had gone right then, he would have met the Sheikh enjoying an ice cream, as he did on random visits every few months. The pupil had ignored a fleeting intuition of the kind that, so the Sheikh taught, must be nurtured in order to grow.

The Sheikh himself deployed intuition on a much vaster and occasionally intimidating scale. As Zainab says, 'he always knew what everyone was doing, and he would often be cross with someone before they'd said what they were doing. He knew it.'

'He could read your thoughts,' affirms Walid. Another pupil recalls how, if you visited him with something on your mind, the conversation he led would work its way towards it. And as Abdul-Malik stood one night yearning for the old days when he and others had joined the Sheikh every Saturday for lengthy sessions, he had no sooner thought, 'Oh well, we have to let these things go,' than someone came up and said, 'The Sheikh says can you come at 3 o'clock? He wants to get back into those sessions again.'

Many would bear out Walid's statement: 'If you were in a room with him, it was not like being in a room with an ordinary person. If you thought it was, you were soon caught out. I was in an interview with him when I let my mind wander, thinking about something I shouldn't have been thinking about—something to do with ladies—and bang! He suddenly shouted, "Unngh!" [a jolting, visceral noise like the *katsu* yell of a Zen master]. So in other words, don't think you can sit there idly fantasising.'

'Fantasising' was the term the Sheikh almost always used for the endless stream of associative thoughts that run through everyone's mind, including yours. Many times, too, he quoted the words of a female Sufi, Nunah Fatimah bint Ibn al-Muthanna, who knew the renowned mystic Muhyiddin Ibn Arabi (1165–1240): 'Of those who come to see me, I admire none more than Ibn Arabi. The rest of you come to see me with part of yourselves, leaving the other part of you occupied with your other concerns, while Ibn Arabi is a consolation to me, for he comes to see me with all of himself. When he rises up it is with all of himself and when he sits down it is with his whole self, leaving nothing of himself elsewhere. That is how it should be on the Way.'

The pupil had better get used to the fact that the Sheikh himself knows or can actually see not only how much of you is with him, but also, by the same token, where the rest of you is. In Australia, for example, he was out on the veranda one evening when Ahmed walked up the drive. 'Yeah?' the Sheikh greeted him inquiringly, as he would sometimes do—checking on his first impression, often with a note of jollity or warning. Ahmed explained that he'd been to the doctor, who had started him on a new asthma medication for which he had high hopes. The Sheikh nodded. 'I saw you with a party hat on.'

We had plenty of opportunity to practise being both physically and mentally present in his inescapable presence, because he made himself constantly available. Although he often lamented that he needed pupils like a hole in the head, he dedicated himself to them. After dinner in London, five nights a week, they would visit for *sohbet*. Most came at least came occasionally, and some almost every day. The exceptions were Tuesdays and Thursdays, when he respectively conducted *dhikr* and gave his weekly talk, both in hired halls. The whole group went to both, give or take backsliders and a few who lived a long way off. But visitors were received on Sunday afternoons as well, and at one stage on Saturday afternoons. It was rare for them to leave without seeing him. So he was accessible, generally speaking, for more than two hours every night and something like eight every weekend. Not infrequently he would also receive individuals on weekdays.

During sessions of *sohbet* he sometimes gave personal advice, perhaps in answer to a question. At other times he spoke more generally, and the topic could be domestic as easily as it could be political, financial, religious, historical. Often it was his pupils and their antics. He was teaching on many fronts simultaneously, counselling on a series of personal problems and supervising any number of projects. 'The Sheikh has to keep all the balls in the air at once,' he would say. Sometimes he was genial, sometimes admonitory; sometimes animated, meditative or silent. He sometimes addressed everyone, but sometimes went deep into conversation with a particular pupil, the rest mutely listening.

Although most people understood how to behave even if they did not grasp the true nature of the encounter, one of his lectures included the following pointed remarks: 'Some people come to visit and they end up lecturing to the other *murid*s about their view of life and their philosophy. At such times the Sheikh reads a newspaper or goes out into his garden. After he has done so several times the offender generally stops visiting for a while.

'The offender has been following his impulses, wanting attention and praise from the Sheikh and expecting to be entertained. What he should have done is to control his impulses by sitting quietly repeating "Allah-Hu" to himself and thus trying to sense the Sheikh's presence.'

That is a reference to what the Sheikh called 'the most important exercise of all'. With occasional exceptions, it was the only one he recommended publicly, but he did so often. His own practice, his advice to all, and his instructions to his pupils were to repeat the words 'Allah-Hu' constantly, 'every minute of the day'—and he meant what he said: 'We die with "Allah-Hu" on our lips.'

Think about it. Would you do exactly as you were bidden?

This exercise, the repetition of what in Hinduism and Buddhism is called a mantra, is one form of *dhikr Allah*, the remembrance of God, which lies at the core of Sufi practice. Its exact nature varies from order to order and sheikh to sheikh. It is sometimes performed aloud, as it was in our collective session every week, and sometimes silently, as explained here.

The Sheikh was asked at a lecture why anyone needed to recite 'Arab words'. 'Because the Arab words do the job,' he replied. '*Dhikr* acts at first as a mental blockage, but eventually, through constant established use, it relates to the sensitive transformer stations ["plexuses" or "centres"] along the central nervous system which a teacher can gradually open, and in so doing response mechanisms are established. This causes a definite linkage between mind and energy.'

Illustrating this point, he quoted the Buddha: 'If you have not eaten sour plums, you cannot salivate in retrospect [when you think about them].' But if you have, your response may be established.

'Eventually mind awareness and energy become concentrated in such a way that we have a concentration of a kind that is constant,' he said. '*Dhikr* is not a means for introducing people to another mechanical system, but of bringing them in a more centred way to take cognisance of every moment.

And we have "Allah-Hu" in our hearts and we respond to it with each breath we take.

'The Sufis, who are the lovers of God, derive their spiritual strength and energy from *dhikr*, the remembrance of His names. To us, His remembrance is like breathing mountain air or drinking the crystal-clear water of mountain streams.'

He had owned a chain of record bars, or music stores, in Salisbury, Southern Rhodesia (now Harare, Zimbabwe), with his office above one of them. He recalled that, although the shop downstairs was belting out loud music all day long, the silent repetition of the *dhikr* was so strong in him that it blocked out the sound.

Another day as we sat at the table, perhaps talking about some of the born Muslims we had been meeting, he began to recite loudly and vigorously, as occasionally also in his lectures, 'Allah-Hu! Allah-Hu! Allah-Hu! Allah-Hu!'

Maymuna remarked, 'Something in me revolts when you do that.' Another pupil afterwards gave her marks for honesty. Not so the Sheikh, who rounded on her and told her that her attitude was the difference between someone like her—'all your drugs, all your lovers'—and a Syrian born in the faith.

But again this is not a matter of religious observance or belief. Very early on, a female pupil remarked that silently reciting a passage from the daily prayers could have a remarkable effect: for example, she said, if you did it while you were getting on the bus, the crowd would part and make way for you. The Sheikh was unimpressed. He told her severely that rather than deciding to 'pray' on a whim, she should be saying 'Allah-Hu' according to his instructions.

'If you apply the techniques I have given you,' he explained, 'you'll be so busy concentrating that the mind won't run on loosely, and you'll start to control the process instead of having it controlling you.

'It is possible for the Sheikh to know someone is entering his house, returning from their work, and to know that their mind is in a faraway place—and for his mind to have a conversation with theirs in that faraway place while *at the same time* the person comes physically into the room and the Sheikh greets them and converses about their day's work. This is all done by concentration.

'As a child I practised adding columns of figures at the same time as holding a conversation with somebody. My father was able to add up two diagonal rows of figures which crossed each other and give the answers to both additions simultaneously. This is the kind of concentration required.

'I used to say to pupils, in a typical Naqshbandi way, "Begin by saying to yourself every single action and thought, registering it as you do it." People found it hard to do and gave up. People don't like hard work and are inherently lazy. Nowadays I say, "Life is all a dream"—in the words of Rumi, "dreams within dreams within dreams".

'These statements appear diametrically opposed, but they are telling you to do exactly the same thing. When you relate to every single activity, you are relating in a positive way to your experience. Most experience is absorbed in an unconscious state while the mind is in fantasy elsewhere, so the aim was to make you conscious of your own presence and "I am". Nowadays I am saying you are all in a dream—day *and* night. When you are caught up in a night dream you're incapable of standing aside from it and saying, "This is all illusion." Most of you couldn't even pick up your fingers and look at your fingernails in a dream. You wouldn't have that much control.'

Yet the stakes are high—far higher than you know: far higher than anyone knows, except the Sheikh. Sitting again at the table one day, he told Maymuna with shocking seriousness: 'I am eternal life!' The very sentence transgresses the limits of common understanding, let alone religion. What could he have meant?

'Immortality is concerned with acquisition of conscious control over the mind's activity. That's all it is.' The method he prescribed for achieving that control is set out in great detail in the last of the nine discourses at the end of this book. 'We are not saying life is illusionary, or that registering every thought and activity is "it". We are saying that if you identify with these [prescribed] repetitive processes in the way you become identified with *dhikr* all day long, you will develop a sense of presence within yourself.

When he said, 'Make all your problems one problem,' he was referring to this continuous endeavour; and those words embody the profoundest of truths.

'We are not here to destroy your consciousness, but to expand it—but most people confuse ego with consciousness. This new presence is not identified, as the ego is. It is an awareness of being separate, and this separate identity begins to give you a freedom in your night dreams as in your day dreams. In night dreams you begin to understand you are dreaming. In day dreams you realise you have been fantasising and have to return to the *dhikr*. You realise that the automatic fantasising processes are dreams. They are death.

'Life, or immortality, lies in this process of consciously controlling your being. Consciousness is the road to immortality. Sleep and death are the same. They are the automatic identification with the things that have made you the pattern you are. We teach you how to observe your reactions, and how to feel the force of the energy as well as the quality of the emotion or instinct that has swept you away.

'That is the process of living in a *zawiya* with a teaching sheikh.'

There is nothing on earth like that process. Indeed it is next to indescribable. 'Intense' doesn't even come close. It was not for nothing that those who lived there would be asked, 'How's life in the old pressure cooker?'

The household was not a commune. It was run a bit like a British country house, but with the pupils in the mixed position of servants, family and guests—sometimes all at once. And life with a Sufi master is life in the raw. As Khalida said, there was a lot of heat in that kitchen. There was also a can of 'anti-bullshit spray' on the mantelpiece.

When the Sheikh said, 'Nobody can fight me,' it was a statement of fact, but that did not stop people from trying. Of the five pupils who lived there at the start, only Masoud refrained. Ahmed would argue and sulk. Maymuna and Aziza would sometimes shout. Naima, the Sheikh's wife as well as his pupil, once told him, 'I'm not one of your f---ing *murids*!' Aziza, more creatively, bent over, pulled her skirt up and bared her backside.

At least their anger was visible. Two Sufi generations ago, Sheikh Nazim's master Abdullah Daghestani (1891–1973) had lived with his own teacher, Sheikh Sharafuddin Daghestani (1875–1936). For reasons not recorded, their housekeeper bore them a grudge. As they began to sip their tea together one day, one remarked how peculiar it tasted; the other agreed. They investigated, or perhaps meditated on the problem, and the answer emerged. She had pissed in the samovar.

Although the Sheikh usually referred to his female pupils as 'ladies', he often said he did not put women on a pedestal, and once told those in his household, 'You can be a lot of tiresome bitches sometimes, and that's why you're called the ladies of the *zawiya*!'

Sakina recalls, 'The women of course all noticed the smallest details about each other, and sometimes about the men, and would talk to the Sheikh behind each other's backs. In reply he might tell his informant what that person was feeling behind the behaviour she had observed. You had to get over the knowledge that your own behaviour and appearance would undoubtedly get the same treatment when you weren't there.'

Malika too experienced what she calls 'the reality of women and our consuming jealousies when living in the *zawiya*. I had many difficult experiences. Once a large kitchen knife landed with point embedded in the floor where my feet had smartly left. Another time I had one foot in the car and the other still on the pavement as the car took off. But in spite of being mostly at the receiving end, when I similarly felt my insecurities activated I could behave in the same way. As women, we are capable of being endlessly tricky.'

We teach people how to observe themselves and the behaviour of others. By the same token the Sheikh rarely took sides, and would only accept one pupil's accusation against another if he found enough truth in it.

One day all of us were doing the midday or afternoon prayer in the prayer room, which was right next to the dining room and kitchen, all open-plan. The Sheikh was leading the collective part of it, as he always did. Once you've started each part of the prayer, you mustn't stop; but halfway through, a smell of burning arrived from the kitchen.

It grew stronger and stronger. Every time the Sheikh said, '*Allahu akbar* ['God is most great'],' to signify the next movement in the cycle, he said it louder and faster, until by the end we were praying at the double and he was nearly shouting. As the smell filled the room he finished the prayer, as prescribed, by turning his head, at top speed, to right and then left with the concluding sentences: '*As-salaamu alaikum wa rahmatullah* ['Peace be upon you, and God's compassion']. *As-salaamu alaikum wa rahmatullah*. WHO HAS LEFT THE PAN ON THE STOVE?'

Naima said, 'Maymuna did.'

He retorted: 'Well, if you can't bloody well cooperate –'

During that period he remarked that he wished the three women of the house got on as well as the two other men.

He had already said, 'I don't need a *zawiya*. You need it.' Nevertheless, he had put great pressure on everyone to find suitable accommodation, and after many false starts we had managed to buy the Victorian semi-detached house in Dalston with three storeys and a basement. Everybody had chipped in for the deposit.

It wasn't the worst area, but it had not yet moved upmarket. Four of us went with the Sheikh to inspect the house, which was sound enough but no treasure. He said little at first, but Aziza saw his dejection at the unattractiveness of the building and the neighbourhood. When we left, he confirmed it with the words, 'On this path you get what you need, not what you want.' There was no question of pulling out, and we moved in in early September 1979.

The Sheikh would often say that certain of his predecessors in the *silsilah* had been Pathans who had lived in sheep pens all their lives. 'One or two rooms is enough for any dervish,' he asserted. We did up the two basement rooms for him. Under his direction they were made lighter, more comfortable and a great deal more pleasant. Their chief feature was a Georgian-style glazed screen between the bedroom and ensuite, made by Jamal, on which Munira painted a copy of the beautiful Pompeiian fresco of the goddess Flora, her back turned and holding blossoms.

Not all the pupils came to lend a hand with the renovation; some stood chatting while the others worked. Imran would turn up in his cowboy-fringed black leather jacket, and one day accosted the Sheikh: "Ere, John—what about the sheep pens?' The Sheikh explained that it was not the things you possessed that counted, but whether or not you were, as he always put it, identified with them.

'When the Sufis refer to poverty they are not making a distinction between riches and non-riches,' he said later. 'Sufi poverty is a total state of detachment from all the distractions to which ordinary people subject themselves. This is physically felt within the central nervous system and is a state of withdrawal not known in intellectual terms.

'My humility is not an outer garment put on to impress you. It is there for its own reason. The person you feel yourself to be is a false person which has no reality. When humility is exercised, people begin to realise they do not exist at all, which is what we mean by poverty: to be not identified with anything, which is part of the *sunnah* of the Holy Prophet. One day he was content with hunger, tying a stone to his belly to assuage it; on another day he would feast. At one time he had fine garments, at another patched robes.

'Sufis don't identify with any situation. They can be wealthy one day and poor the next. The griefs and sorrows of life do not affect us in the desolating way they affect the identified person. We feel sadness, but the bitterness has gone from our sadness. We feel joys—the sweetness has gone from our joys. Yet our hearts are bubbling over with joy [itself]: we are filled with ardent, violent inner love.'

One day many years before, Sheikh Nazim had been walking through crowded streets when he caught sight of his Sheikh, Abdullah Daghestani, grasping the hind leg of a donkey and trying with all his strength to lift up its hoof. He rushed over to help, and between them they succeeded. On the ground underneath lay a crust of bread. That was their lunch, his sheikh told him, and they ate it accordingly.

The Sheikh spoke of being content with your *riziq*, or allotted portion in life. A pupil once complained of having been given sugar in their tea when they didn't want it. He replied that he had been at a function with Sheikh Nazim when someone had poured Coke into his tea. 'I just drank it.'

We had been with him to Patisserie Valerie in Soho, where Maymuna, savouring a pastry, remarked how good all the other pastries looked. 'Oh yes,' he said: 'torturing yourself with what you *could* have had. This is not being a Sufi.'

As another pupil recalls, he didn't like people dithering, either. 'Make a decision!' he would say—and as Zakiya points out, he insisted that when necessary you must be able to explain in basic language why you've come to that decision. 'He had no room for sentimentality. None. Very down-to-earth and rational. It's not about feelings.' As he explained himself: 'The sense of identity we all have with objects and situations is a relationship with the ego.'

Ishaq expands on the point: 'Maybe it turns out that another decision might have had a better or a different outcome? No. I'm not gonna dwell on that. If I make a good decision, basing it on everything I know at that moment, I've got no reason to doubt it, next day or in ten years' time. I should stick with it and not worry about it. Maybe it works out, maybe it doesn't: I'm entirely at liberty to separate myself from it. It's taken nearly twenty-eight years for that to sink in.'

Muhammad himself counselled: 'If something bad happens to you, do not say, "If only I had done such-and-such." Say, "God decreed that it take place, and whatever He wills, He does"—for "if only" begins Satan's work.'

Indeed the first experience Asiya had on becoming a pupil was one of huge gratitude. 'I hadn't felt gratitude for I don't know how long, because I was one of these people who complained—I wasn't happy with my life, it wasn't going where I wanted, I didn't get this, I didn't get that, bla bla bla.' We all have pre-conceived ideas, as Jamal says, and we project various dreams. 'We want them all to happen. No, I'm sorry. That's not reality!'

As the Sheikh often put it: 'People all want what *they* want.' *The sense of identity we all have with objects and situations is a relationship with the ego.* 'In reality you are only habit patterns and attitudes. The purpose of seeing through the false self is to see beyond, to what is really there, to which the real self can relate.

'Humility is concerned with the quest for absolute truth. It is not a virtue, but a necessity in order to learn. The real humility is the realisation that one amounts to nothing at all. But humility is prevented by pride—by being attached to a sense of oneself created by secondary things, such as believing one is learned.'

When it was mooted, for example, that Yaqub and Ahmed would go into business together making painted mirrors, it was an unequal partnership, because Yaqub had been to art school while Ahmed had not—and Ahmed was an intellectual rather than a businessman, as the Sheikh reminded him. But none of that prevented him from dismissing each of Yaqub's ideas in favour of his own.

Casting around for a clever name, the would-be partners finally settled on 'Journeymen', at which point the Sheikh remarked dryly, 'You haven't *got* very far.'

'I had grown up with asthma,' Ahmed recalls, 'and although it wasn't a big problem by then, it had left its mark in a certain way. The Sheikh told me succinctly, "An invalid child can be a vicious child." You always expect the time and attention your mother gave you.

'When I got engaged to a Turkish girl, one of Sheikh Nazim's people in London, who had a severe limp resulting from polio, Sheikh Abdullah remarked, "You will have to give her the care you have always demanded for yourself." I never had to face the challenge, because after returning home she started a career and got preoccupied, and in the end it was he who had to spell out to me that the whole thing was over. He knew my disappointment and said, "You may be lonely." But he added: "I have suffered years of loneliness."'

Before the *zawiya* he had lived in one rented room in a shabby house off the Kilburn High Road. 'Home is with your lord, not where you reside,' he said later. Aziza and Masoud lived there too, and Aziza cooked for him. He received pupils in that room, conducting intense one-on-one sessions in which he advised us and interpreted our dreams. Before that he had lived for a time with Amira and her husband and their cats, and even now she is embarrassed at the memory. 'I mean, what a dump,' she exclaims. 'It was so small: it was literally two up, two down, with a bathroom and a kitchen on the end. But he had nowhere else to go.'

To get from his room to the bathroom, with its toilet, he used to have to come through the main bedroom when the couple were just waking up. 'So we weren't actually *doing* anything—he would have known—but the number of times I apologised for the fact that he had to do it! I used to feel so awful. I just wanted him to have absolutely no problems, because he always sorted our problems out. He was so kind. And then to give him problems—oh dear.

'The feeling was basically very unusual, heightened affection that you didn't have for anybody else at all, and you never would have for anybody else. I've never had feeling like that for anybody, because it's so strong, and it's so right; whereas feelings for other people can go. There's just nobody on the planet like him.'

'Kind, supportive, loving' are Samira's words; and her mother: 'He's the only person I've ever trusted in my entire life, basically. That's it. Full stop.'

Later still, Rashida, the Eritrean, felt what she calls 'that beauty of fatherly love. But it was more than fatherly, it was a love that the Sheikh gave unconditionally to everyone. And—it's very hard to explain in words, but this connection—that I'd always known him, and that he would always be there in my life.'

Like Rashida, Abdul-Ghaffar was with him for only a couple of years. 'I was a young guy, didn't know anything, and here was this incredible, fearsome but hugely wise and insightful figure. He was just unfathomable, from my point of view; and hugely knowledgeable and powerful: and yet ultimately kind. And I loved him. I don't think there's any other way of describing it; and I knew that he loved me. But he loved the me that was the good me: that had the potential to become something better than I was.'

Rashida adds: 'I was a very shy girl, and I was very afraid of talking to the Sheikh, let alone giving him a hug. There was this respect, culturally, that you give to your master. When I came to the *zawiya* he would say, "Rashida, sit here next to me," and I'd wonder why I was trembling. It was only later I realised that there was something about him. It was loving fear—but it was an energy.'

Female or male, few would not echo what Zakiya says: 'For me, the Sheikh's physicality was quite important. The size of him; the feel of his beard when he hugged me; the smell of roses that he wore; his old tweed jacket. All these things, they're imprinted, and whenever I think of him they all come together and invoke his presence for me. He was very aware of that impression of physical things; in fact I heard him once say something to that effect—that he wanted to create a consistent image of himself. And because of that consistency, there's a timeless quality about the memories.'

Even though you may picture all this, you probably cannot smell it or feel the presence which was, as he himself said, like standing next to a big diesel locomotive. But you will already have felt the force of the current that energised all association with him: never predictable in its direction or its turns, yet inhumanly compelling, and above all constant.

'That relationship will never leave me,' says Zakiya. 'That knowledge of him will never leave me. And I'll think of him on my deathbed.'

The same message glows from Hakim's broken French-accented sentences. 'He used to come to Melbourne for the turning [*sema*], and a few times he caught me in the kitchen by myself. Again, he stopped and—sometimes you don't need words. You feel. Even if it's a brief moment, it's like, "Ohh –"'

In Sufism, complete absorption in the guide is to be sought and desired; and yet it is not an end in itself. It is ultimately succeeded by absorption in the divine. Amira had already written:

The School of Celestial Fire

The heavens that You have promised, I do not long for.
The fluttering birds, the sweet scented flowers that carpet the fields,
 the shimmering trees, the streams that sparkle with moons
 and stars,—these I do not seek
I drank deeply of the golden bowl of milk You gave me
 and since that time, I only long for You.

WHEN SOMEONE falls into the ocean, said Shams-i-Din Tabrizi, who was mentor to the great Rumi, 'if he moves his hands and feet, the ocean will break him . . . unless he makes himself dead.

'The custom of the ocean is that as long as someone is alive it swallows him down until he is immersed and dies. When he is immersed and dies, it picks him up and becomes his carrier.'

In the Sheikh's own words: 'The infinite ocean of energy absorbs what is now the cleansed energy of an individual, so that the drop represented by the individual can return to the ocean which is represented by that all-powerful attraction which holds the whole of the universe within unified activity.'

Once a person drowns, he or she is transmuted entirely. Like *The Tempest*'s king, who was presumed drowned fathoms deep,

> Those are pearls that were his eyes:
> Nothing of him that doth fade,
> But doth suffer a sea-change
> Into something rich and strange.

So very strange. A new visitor came to one of the Sheikh's talks, and when it was over he just stared at him and muttered to the person next to him: 'What a strange man!'

For his people he was both stage manager and shape-shifter. 'Every sheikh has his own Punch-and-Judy show,' he said. 'We're the consummate actors.' A colourful Austrian baroness who stayed a pupil for many years was in the habit of exclaiming, 'He ist ein Vizard!'

His given name and surname were the same as those assumed by T. E. Lawrence (of Arabia) on joining the RAF incognito, and although Lawrence had died in a motorcycle crash in 1935, at one time the Sheikh's pupils became absolutely convinced that he had survived and the two men were the same.

Other accounts tell of Sufis assuming the form of, for example, a lion. When our Sheikh was speaking once about Sekhmet, the ferocious lion-headed goddess of ancient Egypt, he warned, 'I am nobody's pet tiger!'—and straight away his companions saw him as a tiger before their eyes.

3

COOKED

We must walk a knife edge between the inner and outer worlds.

— Sheikh Abdullah Sirr-Dan al-Jamal

THE SHEIKH planted the featureless rectangular back garden in Dalston almost entirely with roses. He was still planting them until the day he left for Australia nearly six years later. There would often be blooms on the dining table. 'Even now', says Ahmed, 'I associate the scent of roses with the *zawiya*, and with the peace that even I could feel there, along with the sound and fury and jokes and inner upheaval.

'We sat there one afternoon—I think it was just him and me and Aziza. She was crying. He was trying to comfort her, though in vain, and the roses were right in front of them. He told her, "Smell this rose—Papa Meilland." It was one of his favourites.

'Picturing that moment, I recall his counsel to us all. "Use the mood as a path as you go deeper down within yourself, changing one word for another. The opposite of hate is love."

The opposite of grief is happiness. "Smell this rose," he said to Aziza again. "When I'm in my tomb, you won't be able to bring me even one rose."'

Aziza is buried not thirty yards from him, but no one has planted roses. The squawking of the cockatoos in the tall pine trees is louder than anything else, and on a still day you can hear the currawongs' wings thudding as they pass by.

Egoism is the fundamental illusion that we possess something that is our own or is our self.

'I had to face death in every moment,' says Rashida as she recalls her life before she encountered the Sheikh. 'It was about experiencing and learning, and you were not going to be there forever. I understood that from childhood, because we had just come from war in Eritrea. At seventeen I was seeing young people [in Britain] going to discos and having fun, when I'd been seeing dead bodies and blood in the streets.

'In London I had to make a decision: do I continue my life this way or worry about my parents back in Africa? I came out of the Sheikh's lecture, I saw the world in a certain way and I tasted what he was. I would leave everything.'

Still at business school, she visited the *zawiya* for the first time and sat down at the table. 'You know when you take a tape recorder and you forward, rewind, pause? A noise of when you delete something on a tape recorder: zzzzzzz—that's what I felt. Complete, utter—I was just stunned. Trying to drink this tea, and he would look at me and talk normally to all the ladies, and this brain was going zhzhzhzhzh-tak.

'My father used to sell cassettes and tape recorders, and since small we were fixing them. I was very good at rewind, forward—and I knew this sound is "delete": something from my memory, my brain, is being cancelled out; everything is cancelled. Gone. I couldn't believe it.

'I had half a cup of tea. He just continued that session, but it was instantaneous; it was this noise going on, and I was scared. I look at the Sheikh and the Sheikh is normal, and I'm thinking, "How come everybody's normal and I've got this brain that's going blank?"

'We hugged the Sheikh and left, and it was a new beginning. It was like a new person. I got in the car, and that's it. Perhaps never thought of the war again, never looked back to—whatever there was. I don't know what got cut. All I know is, that moment I left that room and that house, it was like starting from scratch.

'The best way to put it is, that's the very first time that I felt like I was just still, and there I was, and everything was perfectly all right. And there was no worries, no harm will happen: no this, no that. I was at peace. At that point I realised that that house was a holy—Experience Mecca, and this: this is reality.

'Then one day when I was there again, he took me out into the back garden. I don't know what happened.

'There was a different kind of light. In Mecca I had similar experiences where I'm away from the world in another world. I can't explain it in words. I'm looking at all these beautiful roses—the scent was incredible—and I'm in fear, and I wasn't sure what the Sheikh will say.

'And he said, "Do you know why the Prophet liked roses?" I said no. And he said, "Look: as the rose grows it opens up and then it dies, and after it's dead we make all sorts of things out of it: from the dried flowers you can get the scent, and even the oil smells nice. A rose always gives. You should be like that."

'And that was it. That moment of waking, this heart felt love beyond everything.'

They can come to an understanding of the true nature of their purpose here— this short sojourn in the school of earthly life.

'He said to me: "Do you ever go to flower shows?" I said no, and he said, "I want you to go to the Chelsea Flower Show."

'I said, "What? Me? Flowers? I don't—Really, I'm doing a business course, and, like—*flower shows*?" I was a bit of tomboy, having brothers.

'But he said, "I highly recommend you go. It's next week."

'Typical young people—when your parents tell you something, and it was the same with the Sheikh, the first thing that comes is, "No way I'm going to go to the flower show." But you sleep on it, and next morning I cut off the advert from the newspaper, and within two days I ended up in the show. The first flowers I see is from Ethiopia, so that made me feel oh! my home. It was paradise. It's totally, completely inundated with sense and nature, and it was something of myself that I had never experienced. I was really in a heavenly place. What happened in his garden happened again, ten times more.

'The Sheikh was very good at this. He just said, "Go here," and you did; and the energy and the power of all those flowers and trees just woke me up. In those days I never understood it. But having been married, and in a lot of experiences going back to Mecca and Medina, there is this deeper love within you that's there, and that was what he's trying to—what was waking up. It's like the Sufis say: taste the wine; but in droplets—slowly.

'Let's go back to the roses. He's saying that even a flower can be all these things—so be, at least, like that flower. The flower is totally surrendered. It does not judge; it does its purpose, drops the leaves, somebody can cut it; it leaves this world in peace. Rain, sunshine, whatever. And its purpose is to give that scent, and Allah created it so that all of these benefits will come out of it.

'But I'm a human being. We are instruments of nature, except we have this mind and senses and movements. Lucky the flower: she hasn't got free will. She is what she is. Human beings are the most highly prized creation, but I'm well below—forget animals! I haven't even reached flower level.

'I can still go back to that moment. It's like a photographic image. When I'm having trouble I can go to the same rose and use my reasoning, my intelligence, to fix things in life. But I still can't be like a drum or a rose and just perform.'

Our endeavours are concerned with giving you psychological patterns and templates which will enable you to find out what you are really doing—or failing to do. The gift may be concealed in the smallest incident; on the other hand, you have to be present to receive it.

For example, visiting the Sheikh when he still lived in Kilburn, Abdul-Ghaffar had walked from the station, knocked on the door and waited; but nothing happened. He knocked again, and still nothing happened. 'And I thought, have I got the wrong address? Have I got the wrong time? Does he not want to see me? I was there two or three minutes, and nothing happened, just complete silence. And I turned to walk away—and the door opened, straight away.

'I can't tell you how much of an icon that is in my life. It keeps coming back to me, that notion: "Be patient. Just wait. You'll get there in the end."

'I know he was behind the door, just waiting for the right moment to open it. And that little thing, of being just about to go and then it opened, resonated with me then, and it still does. It mirrors something that in recent years I've come to understand and start to manage as best I can. Being patient and being consistent is one of the things I'm here to learn.

'It's part of my personality that I've had a tendency to dip into things: go a hundred per cent and then move on. And the Sheikh was showing me that. Working in the basement, one of my jobs was sweeping, and I remember him showing me how to sprinkle water on the dust so that it didn't fly up. That was about being gentle, and consistent.'

And yet, Abdul-Ghaffar left the Sheikh a couple of years later. He knows it was an example of his failure to be consistent. He says so.

You will possess only the impressions that life has stamped on you and the habit patterns that you have ingrained in yourself.

Ishaq left too, in the end, despite how he started. 'I don't think I ever missed a talk,' he recalls. 'At twenty-five, that was the first thing in my life—apart from go to school, where frankly all I did was turn up—that I'd ever done consistently. That in itself introduced a pulse into my life which I started realising was very important. The idea of rhythm started to make sense.

'The first thing he ever told me to do directly was to start karate lessons. I found that quite stressful, but I kept doing it, and I kept doing it. And right there, just attending a talk, attending two karate lessons a week, eventually going to the *sema* and the turning practice, these things started to create an actual pulse in my life which was critical to my growth and my understanding of the Sheikh's teaching, which is also about your inner life.

'And as my day-to-day life became more disciplined, then my contemplative moments also started to develop a feeling and a pulse and a rhythm. That's a lot of teaching in a very short time. Within a year I suddenly understood why people that I knew who were more successful than me *were* successful. I'd been a notably unsuccessful person, and it was simply through complete lack of discipline, rhythm, pulse and regular habits and activities. He built me up. He made me a stronger person.

'Early in the piece I was quite unhappy. The changes that I was having to go through in order to accommodate having a relationship with a Sufi teacher were hurting me. There were things I was having to leave behind: I stopped drinking and taking drugs, for a start. I stopped chasing girls. You know, there was always something like that going on whenever possible. Little did I realise how unsuccessful those pursuits were in themselves, with regard to bringing me any real satisfaction.

'But that came much later, to understand the alternative. At this time I wasn't getting any blissful meditative experiences, and the turning [*sema*] in particular made me very, very uncomfortable indeed. I guess that's what it's designed to do—stimulate an energy within a system that wasn't very stable, and that largely resulted in long periods of quite intense depression. I was no longer living in a shared house with all my mates, "self-medicating", *et cetera*.'

Ishaq had long been seeking to end the pain of chronic depression—'and yet, hold on a minute, now I feel even worse! That was a valuable thing, because those regular patterns of behaviour started to become really important, and I started to see, OK, this isn't just about turning up, this is about having a life with actual regular things in it. A lot of other things weren't in it any more, and it was a *quid pro quo*: I was getting something back.'

The Sheikh would repeatedly quote from the pantomime *Aladdin* (in which Sufi references can be found at the heart of British popular culture): 'We give you new lamps for old.' The illumination conferred takes a hundred forms: some exalted, but many uncompromisingly practical.

'In those who have had a poor relationship with both parents, there are often many difficulties when it comes to the stage of going out to work. The

The School of Celestial Fire

sheikh's first task is to put them in a job and make them stick to it,' he noted. 'They have to learn to do every job with full dedication for its own sake.'

For Khalida, his teaching was founded on getting you started. 'We were like infants in the cradle; and step number one, get a job. You had to be able to be doing this before you could do that, otherwise there was no point. There was a definite method and sequence, just as a baby has to learn to crawl before it walks.'

Another pupil, Jamal, nails something that is oddly easy to overlook by readers or *murid*s who are set on exaltation and hidden wonders. 'In a way he wasn't a mystery, was he? He was pretty predictable as far as practical things were concerned: a very commonsense person, a good counsellor, good heart.' That was all true, and in an average week he did a great deal of just plain life coaching.

Latifa (incidentally the third French person among our fellow-travellers) says she didn't see much of the Sheikh at all, 'but what I liked most about him is when he was looking after the *murid*s. He was saying to you, "Go and get a job," and he was helping you in looking for one. He did that with me. Never talked about anything else—just, "I've got that for you: go and take it." 'Not only that—he wanted you to have somewhere to live. And he found it for me. It was superb.'

Walid says he was just bumming around. He worked as a gardener with a local council, but only picking up rubbish and mowing lawns. 'I casually walked up to the Sheikh after a lecture and said, "I'm leaving that job: I don't really like it."

'He poked me in the stomach and said, "Walid, I want you be a gardener!" That was like a butterfly being pinned, and it was my first real teaching. I didn't know anything about gardening, but because I'd read about Sufism I knew you don't not do what the sheikh tells you; because, even though it may not be what you want, it has a way of working out in your life. So I just bowed my head and went: Right, that's it. I'm going to be a gardener.'

Malika recalls the Sheikh saying, 'The greatest sins in this world are poverty and ignorance'—meaning, as she says, that they are something to strive against. Indeed Walid was later able to shake off his stepfather's taunts that he couldn't learn, because, as he expressed it, the Sheikh was putting things in his mind of a positive nature to combat that discouragement.

It was done in a particular way. 'I went to [horticultural] college up in Hertfordshire. But I just hated it, because I had to live away from the group, miss half the lectures and miss the Sheikh, and I left.' Soon afterwards the group went on a trip. 'We were in the hotel, and when I came in for breakfast in the morning every single chair was taken except one at the table where the Sheikh was. I was looking around desperately, and the Sheikh was glaring at me like an owl, going, "Sit down, Walid!"

'When I did, it was: "By God, I could have kicked your backside for leaving that course!" He was hammering me right through as I ate my breakfast, telling me I had to learn to finish a thing I started.' And when Walid enrolled in another course, he stuck it out, although he hated that too. When you set your hand to the plough you must plough the furrow.

As Hakim puts it, 'when you do anything, do it to the best of your ability. You can't do more than your best, even if it's not good. If you have been *there*'—that's to say, present in yourself and concentrating—'when you do the stuff, you can't do better than that. Be the moment.'

In Malika's words, 'One of the very first lessons he taught us was to perform every task, however simple, without daydreaming. I remember him saying to me, "Peel every potato with your whole being." Particularly when I prepare vegetables, I am still mindful of that simple and useful instruction.'

The Sheikh told us, 'The blackbird singing is being the best blackbird it can,' and frequently: 'A tiger has to be a good tiger!' He insisted that being good at each task must never be shirked. He also spoke a lot about the importance of letting go at the last minute to let a thing take its course—but only once you had striven as hard as you could.

'You need to make an effort towards constructive actions to ascend to a higher level. The Sheikh is a guide, but you have to make the effort. If you do not yet know what you should be doing because your intuition is not developed, you have to have the courage to do the best you can and be ready to change course at any moment if you do develop an intuition.'

Doing a printing job, Abdul-Malik was getting nowhere and had told himself he couldn't do it. But the Sheikh sent word that he must try again: 'He *can* do it.' Abdul-Malik did try, and he was able to rig the printer. Recalling the episode, he echoes his friend Abdul-Ghaffar, who realised he needed the patience to wait for the door to open: 'It's one of those things where the Sheikh planted the seed and it's come up in many different forms. I'm trying something and I think, "No: I've got to try this again in a different way, because it is possible."'

When an ordinary person comes to the Sheikh they are shown that there is no single-mindedness of purpose in their activity and therefore no sincerity. People have to learn to do every job with full dedication for its own sake. That's your first assignment.

'The second task of the sheikh is to make people stand back and become aware of their own patterns, and of the unpleasant aspects that they have incorporated into their personality,' he said. 'They may find this very painful. It is done through practising exercises and through the relationship with the sheikh.'

He likened that relationship to a mutually trusting marriage. "When we do trust, then the wounds of childhood and adolescence can be exposed, because we no longer fear the risk of their exposure; and by this means they can be looked upon in the light of love, and can therefore be healed. The feeling function has to be put to the test in this way, together with love; and no other function can substitute.

'This is the relationship which has to develop between the sheikh and the pupils: in that when certain things are revealed which have been jealously covered up and guarded [i.e. from public view] from childhood, even if the sheikh appears to be cruel in the way that these things are revealed, it has to be understood that the revelation itself—the facing up to the problem—is one which the pupil has to undertake. This facing up to the reality of the situation is very important: facing up to all the inferior reactions, to all the inferior feelings, as well as the highs which are sought, for example, in a love relationship.'

Even trust itself is not essential: what is imperative is not to run away. 'Pupils may trust the sheikh, or they may mistrust or even hate him; but so long as the relationship goes on this can be worked out.'

Wait a minute. Hate him? Sure: because you must remember that he will always do what he knows he has to do; and as a pupil, *you get what you need, not what you want.*

'If you are lazy,' he said, 'count yourself lucky if somebody points this out. Laziness is your fault—a sign that a human has persevered in uselessness for too long. It's the one thing people like doing in perpetuity: it's so pleasant, and you all colour it with this soul quality.' That's only one example, because he'll tell you if you're greedy, too. Or selfish; pushy; forgetful; sleazy. And he'll be correct. If you decide not to believe him, you may as well leave now. But when he's told you, will you like him? Indeed you may hate him. It's not hard.

The Sheikh's devastating rebuke was a distinct experience familiar to all, if not suffered by all, and we referred to it as he did. 'I gave So-and-So a hammering,' he would say. At full force, it was burning, withering fire. It was not random or casual, ever, even if you pretended to yourself it was. His words always hit their target. *Fire has to be felt within one's being, and it has to burn.*

'I don't remember the details,' says Abdul-Malik, 'but I do remember the intensity of that feeling in the stomach. It's like your guts are being ripped out.

I was aware at the time that it obviously isn't just because the Sheikh's talking to you. There's something physical going on. It's extremely uncomfortable, to say the least.'

On the group's second trip to Turkey the Sheikh had allowed Muktar to record the *sema* in Konya, its birthplace. Back in London, Muktar went and played the tape to his mother. But meanwhile the Sheikh had not yet listened to it, and he started asking where it was. Muktar returned to the *zawiya*, where he and his wife were staying: 'I walked in, and he was sitting at the table with the others. I was standing to his left, and he looked around, and when he started I felt like someone had taken a stick and hit me in the back of the knees. That caused me to hit the floor: I fell to my knees, and then my neck was forced down, and I was in the position of one being beheaded. This was not some mental impression. I had no control over my body at all.

'I explained what had happened. But this time he decided he would go at me in public—it was the only time.'

He said, 'Big boy Muktar! You just want to be a big boy in front of your mum and stepfather and show them how important you are! Big boy Muktar in front of his mother!' And there was something along the lines of 'You just want to impress your social set. I *shit* your social set!' he roared. 'And then he hammered me, hammered me, hammered me like that, and it stopped.'

Please don't under-estimate the fearsome impact of an incident like this. It gains much of its charge from the fact that you are not a helpless conscript suffering the capricious rage of an ill-tempered or vindictive sergeant. You have chosen to receive it, along with everything else that the Sheikh may throw at you or bestow upon you, by seeking and gaining acceptance as a pupil in the first place. So you have—or should have—no means of explaining it away, no chance to rationalise it, and certainly nowhere to run.

'There was a second wave of it, on something else,' says Muktar, 'where he got me down to his apartment and had another go at me. So then I was sick. I couldn't get out of bed for three days because I ran a massive temperature. I was really ill. When I got back he just disappeared for a few days. That whole week I was so distraught; and then it was the Saturday morning. We were all sitting there, and he suddenly came in. He just looked at me, and he had a most amazing smile. And we never talked about it again.'

So long as the relationship goes on. . . .

'I suspect he just needed to have you under his control for a certain amount of time to change you,' said Jamal. 'If he can't hang on to you, he can't do anything. You have to think to yourself seriously whether you want to actually *leave* or not, or should I just plod on a bit longer? I'll just see this through.'

For his part, the Sheikh was insistent that he would never chase after people who had left him. 'My hand has always been open, and anybody may alight on it or jump off elsewhere at any time,' he said. 'I don't need pupils.'

Yet by the same token he sometimes made it poignantly plain that the relationship need not end. Dain, practical and inventive, had helped to install the remarkable plumbing system at the *zawiya*. Having joined the group with gusto he duly migrated to Australia to be with the Sheikh, but fell into dispute with him. When Dain was arguing down the phone, about to sever all contact, the Sheikh asked him, 'But who's going to do my plumbing for me?' The question had little to do with pipework or boilers. It was a hand extended to a man who was about to dive into an abyss of his own making.

Even so, the invitation is not issued for sentimental reasons, but because there is unfinished work to be done. When another colourful character, Amir, had finally left, the Sheikh remarked, 'What a shame. Just when I was going to show him his dark side.'

And that showing, asserts Walid, is the teaching in a nutshell. 'You have to use logic. You say, "If I was all right, I'd already be a saint, wouldn't I? And I obviously am not like him." So you've got to take the medicine, otherwise you're going to get nowhere. You're going to have to eradicate something to become like the Sheikh. You're not going to become like him by hiding your problems.

'There's not many people you can meet where you're genuinely challenged like that. You know where you're really at, rather than where you might think you're at. So you didn't take a meeting with the Sheikh one-to-one lightly. Part of you was slightly frightened of him. You didn't want to encounter him in a frivolous way, and you went there because it was going to help you spiritually.'

There is a relationship, but there's no familiarity.

'Plus', says Khalida, 'you knew that he could just look at you and he knew everything about you.' We would all have agreed that he could see through people. 'And I soon realised', says Ahmed, 'that he knew me far better than I knew myself; better than I know myself now. It was hard to accept, but it was inescapable.'

Your dark side is in fact what Sufis everywhere call the *nafs*: the lower self—a tenacious, domineering, far-reaching alliance of intellectual notions, emotional urges and instinctual drives. If not constantly in the sights of the pupil (as it should be), it is certainly in the sights of the Sheikh, who would strive continually to bring it to our attention. He said you had to befriend your bad habits, and he told Malika, 'Live with the totality of yourself.'

She describes how she experienced what she calls 'the skilful undoing of my moody personality'.

'Mealtimes were a great opportunity for him. I recall a considerable period when for myself every meal, particularly breakfast, was abject agony. As he often said, he taught by repetition, and by stick and carrot. He would make a point of focusing on me: "Malika, how are you today? Did you not sleep well last night?" And to the others: "What is the matter with Malika today? Malika is Moody this Morning!" He put particular emphasis on the Ms.

'Slowly, so very slowly, I went through a process of becoming aware of my inner states, followed by underlying and uncomfortable emotions. The needling would continue in many subtle and not-so-subtle ways, always when I was trapped at table. My internal states would flare up into a range of diabolical emotions—indeed moody; miserable; angry; inconsolable; and (it felt) endless—all while passing the salt and drinking tea from our beautiful china. These were treacherous waters to visit, and the Sheikh always picked the most explosive, suffocating or despairing internal moment to ask me for the sauce.

'Eventually the day came when I found his comments (so many Ms) almost funny, or at least I could smile. Finally I laughed, at which point he laughed with me. I cannot do justice to the skill with which he operated, or even remember much of what he said, but I have the visual imprint and flavour of the meals we ate, marked with the experience.'

Psychological states fit you for a particular place in one of the heavens or hells. Malika comments that her gloomy temperament improved a great deal, and the Sheikh was explicit: 'One must understand oneself before one can gain any spiritual insights.'

Our three trips to Turkey were not, as he made brilliantly clear, tourist excursions. He was teaching continually, by reference to our surroundings, our encounters and ourselves. His own exaltation and vigour were even more palpable than usual. He was joyous, as Latifa recalled, and there was a strange excitement; but the intensity was too great to leave any room for comfort.

Abdul-Malik had found that second trip almost like Purgatory. 'I felt under a lot of pressure. A lot of pressure. When we came back, the Sheikh asked me, "How did you find it?" and I said I'd found it very difficult. '"Yes," he said. "You're not as wonderful as you thought you were." Ooohh: I got immediately uptight. But of course it's absolutely true. And straight away he said, "You've got to die before you die"'—the exhortation of the Prophet.

As Walid recalls, 'You'd be devastated from things he said, because he meant so much to you. He might say, "You've got no willpower." Trouble was, it was always true! So then you're struggling with a problem you've got.'

In all this your self-esteem is not merely roadkill but actually targeted for destruction, because to esteem yourself is to esteem those regalia and paraphernalia that cost you so dear. Instead you need to get the measure of your problem, whatever it is: to get an idea or a sight of it before you can target it. *Live with the totality of yourself.* When a rat ran past him as he left the house with Jamal one day, he said, 'There—there's your *nafs*!'

In Zakiya's words, 'There was no hiding place when you were with him. We all perform, don't we, in everyday life? But there was no point.' He adapted Robert Burns: 'Would that God the gift would give us[19] / To see ourselves as others see us.' He once remarked to Ahmed around the table, 'Your problem is you don't realise what a turd you are.' It was exactly the same thing.

As he said: 'The whole teaching in Sufism is to show people to themselves as they really are and as they behave. Those who inhabit the *zawiya* are merely pawns for the Sheikh to place on the chessboard, and each *murid* in turn is asked to look at the progress of the game. They see certain standard human patterns of behaviour and begin to connect motives with patterns—but when looking at one's own individual patterns there is always a failure, because there is no detachment.'

His account sounds chillingly clinical: yet there is more than one way to acquire that clinical detachment. Once the visitors had left each night, the house became the scene of what he called 'a sort of family life'. There was often more tea, there was usually joking, and he would discuss the characters and carryings-on of other pupils in a way that he did not always do more publicly. Nevertheless, by day or by night, the humiliation or criticism of one pupil served equally as a lesson for others, if they had the sense not to get distracted by relief that the target wasn't them.

As the Sheikh said, his spotlight would swing from one to another, and the rest would enjoy the 'pathetic gyrations' of the person whose weak points were on display: until it was their turn. Fatima wryly quoted John Donne: 'Never send to know for whom the bell tolls; it tolls for thee.'

The group process, he said, shows you all the frailty of human nature as you observe the others. 'Eventually you begin to realise that you suffer from the same frailties that you hate most, and you take action to overcome them by means of coming awake—and the only wakefulness is the complete and utter alertness of a bird trembling on a bough.

---

19 Burns wrote in Scottish: 'Wad some Pow'r the giftie gie us', or in other words 'If only some Power would give us the gift.'

'Death is always at our elbow. We are not in fear of him,[20] but ready to go at any time. So it is our purpose to use different teaching techniques related to reforming you.' Not sermons and books, but techniques that 'kick you awake every second of the day. That's what *sohbet* with the Sheikh is. It's a harsh road, but at the end you will gain inner peace and come to know an inner love. This is why we give emphasis to the spiritual aspect, not just psychological reorientation.'

He would say that if he wanted to explain a point of human nature he need not tell his pupils to read, for example, Dostoyevsky, because he could simply illustrate it with reference to one of them, or indeed all of them.

On moving into Dalston he had camped in the prayer room with his bed and all his things, in full view of everyone coming and going, while we spent a ham-fisted three months renovating the basement. The job involved almost everybody. He himself called it an exercise, and as he pushed ever harder for us to get it done, he persistently drew our attention to the ways of his workforce—from Paul Williams the plasterer ('an old soldier and a chancer', the latter word also used by Paul to describe himself), who had the instinctual coordination to achieve beautiful flatness but at the cost of spattering plaster all over the room, to Murad, a genuinely skilled carpenter who would do half a day's excellent work and then vanish for a fortnight.

The Sheikh's continual refrain was 'Don't listen to what people say: watch what they do'. *People who judge by outward appearances are lost in a world of dreams.* You can't necessarily see the traits of others clearly unless you let someone show you—or far better, show you how.

Even before buying the *zawiya* we had met one Sunday afternoon a month to manage the running of the group. The sessions were far from businesslike. The Sheikh would often come; but once when he didn't, he sent someone with a big cartoon cut from the newspaper. In farcical detail it depicted a gang of people building a sailing ship in utmost chaos, accidentally clouting one another with planks, falling into the sea, and so on. Underneath it, echoing Rumi in the Sheikh's forceful writing, was the caption: 'Find your dream within the Sunday dream.'

Hassan was trying to paint the basement ceiling, not only with gloss paint, which was a big mistake in the first place, but slapping it on, and it was running down his arm. He was weeping because the job was going so wrong. It turned out he was trying to paint with the turps that the brushes were soaking in. At the same time the Sheikh was fighting mediocrity at every turn, railing against 'shamateurism' and making his dismay fiercely obvious when one pupil

---

20 The angel of death, perhaps.

trashed another's work, for example by accidentally tearing the lining paper they'd put on the wall, or indeed by getting plaster on their fresh paintwork.

He declared, 'You must do a perfect job,' and in the *zawiya* he supervised every detail. Having someone do that would itself have been a novelty for many, let alone working to his standards. He admired professionalism and encouraged it in every activity.

For Ahmed, 'The keynote of his teaching, as we experienced it from day to day, was the imperative to get everything right, whether it be achieving a neat finish on the paintwork or helping when help was needed. "Everything is as important as every other thing, and that's the way the universe works," he admonished me once when I forgot to deliver a message.'

In the basement we were all amateurs or nearly so, and the pressure was intense. But he said, 'We teach people to do unaccustomed things in a skilful and controlled way so that the accidental effect is taken out of their lives and gives way to a skilful control.' Similarly: 'Where you are at your weakest you have to learn to be at your strongest,' and that goes beyond carpentry and plastering.

Paul Williams, a poor communicator, was causing some difficulty or other, and it fell to the mild-mannered Jamal to pull him up. 'I said to him, "Look,"—I became quite forceful—"you have to explain yourself and do things properly." That was not in my nature to do. And the Sheikh came up to me and put his arms round me, gave me a big hug, because it's something that I don't normally do. For me to have done that—He wanted to congratulate me on making an effort to be a bit more forceful.

'That's all I needed. I got the point. It's not how many times you get told something, it's what is told and when.'

Doing those unaccustomed things in a skilful and controlled way means aiming for better than you think you can do. 'That was imprinted in my head,' remembers Walid—one of several pupils, both male and female, who forged paths in unforeseen careers at the Sheikh's urging. The extremely bookish Ahmed discovered a fascination in woodworking, and the Sheikh's mentorship took many forms. When a length of skirting board was needed, someone drove the two of them to the Cohen family's hardware shop in Stoke Newington High Street, but they had to walk home almost a mile with Ahmed carrying one end and the Sheikh the other. 'Then when I did an unremarkable little job he praised it enormously and called others over to admire it,' Ahmed recalls. 'When I organised new flooring for Aziza's room, he told me, "You're turning into a practical lad."

'But of course, you transfer your accustomed pattern of behaviour to the unaccustomed task. Once after I'd spent quite a while fitting mouldings to a doorway and gone on to the next job, he caught me returning to fiddle with the doorway again, and said, "You seem to be drawn back over there!" That was a stone thrown into the pond, so to speak—because not being able to stop, to draw the line and move on, in any activity whatsoever including thinking, is ingrained into me very deeply indeed.'

Instead the Sheikh would always say, 'If you must do intellectual work, treat it like case-file work.' And he would explain: that means concentrating fully on one matter till you've finished working on it, and then closing the file so your mind is clear for the next.

Towards the end of the basement project Ahmed exclaimed what a pain it was to have to keep getting down off a ladder to change drill bits. 'I would have you doing this kind of thing for a number of years,' responded the Sheikh—and added, not long afterwards, 'You should go in for fine cabinetmaking.'

So Ahmed went to trade college. 'I entered a new world in which I saw that things were made, not born fully formed, and made in ways I knew almost nothing about. Now I'm thoroughly at home in it. That's been an expansion of my consciousness, and the challenge should last me the rest of my life. Some fourteen years later, when I showed signs of flagging, he told me sharply: "You must make furniture. That is your task."

'I made many pieces for him. Time was usually no object: the goal was perfection, and his approval. His encouragement was backed by his criticism, which, though usually direct, was sometimes oblique. The first big job I did for him was a display cabinet. The main material was to be blockboard, which has a core of solid wood; but in an attempt to save work I outsourced the veneering, which meant settling for fibreboard instead. When I mentioned this unilateral change of plan, his manner became distant. "Yes," he said. "If it's made of some kind of compressed paper board instead of solid wood, of course it will no longer be a personal thing for me."

'I went home, got a sledgehammer and smashed the half-finished cabinet to pieces. Then I re-made it in blockboard. When it was done, he said he was delighted. I mentioned that I hadn't finished the back to the same standard as the front. "Oh yes—a typical cabinetmaker's trick," was his cheering reply.'

And if you're wondering why all this was being done for the Sheikh, for no material reward, you are seriously not getting the point. *They have to learn to do every job with full dedication for its own sake.* It was the same with gardening, building, plumbing and all other work performed. Quite apart from the fact that the pupil is in the service of the sheikh and the other pupils, especially when master and pupils share the same establishment, there is skill and perseverance and much else to be learnt, and the learning is in the work.

'For example,' says Ahmed, 'french polishing can *only* be learnt by feeling, and it's taken me more than twenty years. In addition, almost every job was harder than the last, and often seemingly near-impossible. But I would make a drawing and bring it to him. He would pore over it, make comments and occasionally sketch something himself. His cherished period was the late Georgian and the Regency, with its links to classical antiquity, and my love of the same tradition was kindled then.

'Often he would call for something that I knew meant hours of extra work or would take me out of my depth—but to resist, whether on aesthetic or practical grounds, would have been putting respectively my judgment or convenience ahead of his. So I gained an understanding of 3D design; a craftsman's long apprenticeship, without his visiting my workshop; and an education in taste.'

Yaqub, who had trained as a sculptor, underwent a similar process when the Sheikh supervised him in creating garden ornaments, urns and planters of artificial stone in a refined classical manner. So did Aziza when she made the robes he wore at the weekly *dhikr* and latterly his lectures.

Zafira recalls, 'The teachings were conveyed most strongly in his commitment to perfection, which he demonstrated through his own commitment. His rose garden in east London was ablaze with glorious perfumed blooms. Through the tasks he gave us we were expected to do our absolute best—and what's more, he had confidence that we would. I was tasked to make him a set of net curtains and a pair of cushions: every stitch was done with intense concentration to ensure a pleasing outcome.'

Sakina had been doing small sewing jobs for the *zawiya*, and Farida started making hand-sewn presents. 'The Sheikh decided we would make a wedding dress to enter in the local Gown of the Year competition, to be modelled by Farida,' says Sakina. 'It was designed by the Sheikh, and there were further and further modifications as we went along. It had a boned bodice, which was technique I hadn't done before, but it fitted her exactly. Farida did a lot of work on the veil, an extraordinary creation with a spray of white fabric flowers glimpsed within a double layer of net fabric. It was a bit like the bubble-skirt fashion, but fifteen or more years early.

'By the night before the competition it still wasn't finished: yet more alterations required. We sat up most of the night sewing at our separate work tables—and time stopped for me. I looked at my clock, knowing I had a lot more work to do. When I'd finished, a good two hours later, the clock hadn't moved. It hadn't stopped, either. After that it went on showing the correct time.

'We made the deadline, but we didn't win anything. The other entries turned out to be finished inside to a professional standard which put my sewing to shame.'

Sakina's hard-won experience echoes that of Ahmed. 'Trying to make fine furniture for him, and then for others, has taught me that craftsmanship is another word for getting everything right at every stage. If you err in planning or execution, the result will be there to see. No verbal trick or sleight of mind can repair torn wood grain or fix a loose-fitting drawer. The final product is your judge, and there is no evading its verdict.'

'Check, check, check!' the Sheikh would say. He often drew attention to standard procedure in the RAF during the Battle of Britain, in which he had flown a Spitfire while still a teenager. If a pilot returned from a sortie and reported any problem with his aircraft, the aircraft mechanic—the 'erk'—who had serviced it was put on a charge straight away as a matter of course. It was automatically his fault. The responsibility was total, the accountability immediate.

A token of this law can still be found in AB's shed in Melbourne. Each night during Ramadan a folding chair had accompanied the Sheikh to the mosque in London, and Ashraf had been in charge of it. When he moved out of the *zawiya* in Dalston he approached AB, who was staying, and gave him a package—a spare wing nut, all wrapped up and taped. 'The Sheikh says you must always have it with you when you take the chair, in case the other one falls off and you lose it.'

'I've still got it,' AB says. 'Never touched.'

In Australia the Sheikh at one stage scrapped his practice of getting pupils to do building work at the *zawiya*, saying they were useless. Abdul-Malik recalls, 'One of the triggers was that I made an absolute cock-up of something. I was putting in some filler in the lattice work, and Zaid (an architect) had very carefully explained to me what I should use. I used something else, and as soon as it rained the red dye in the filler came out. When I turned up the Sheikh said, "Have a look at that." 'And my heart just dropped. It just looked crap. You could see. You're thinking: it's there. What can you even say? What can you do? I'd done completely the wrong thing. I was thinking I knew best.'

And yet—you can't panic if something goes wrong. In the workshop or the kitchen, panic is meaningless. It's meaningless anywhere. As the Sheikh would say, 'If you slip on a banana skin, all you can do is walk on.' Like many of his sayings, it sounds absurdly commonplace but embodies profound wisdom. Khalida is right when she says, 'These things are actually tools. If something happens in your life, you've lost your job or something, you can use that to get you through.'

Aziza was making an elaborate blackcurrant *bavarois* with multiple layers for the dessert for the Sheikh's birthday—itself the centrepiece of the year—and it didn't set properly. It was the big presentation dish and it was nothing but a terrible mess. All seemed hopeless, but she rolled up her sleeves, focused intensely and re-did it until she got it right. The Sheikh commented that he had taught her that, and she agreed that she'd learnt it when he had put her under pressure while sewing robes for him in London.

The women were always very busy in any case. The Sheikh was clear that they had to have their own realm while the men did all the building, maintenance and decoration; and the women looked after everything to do with food. In general it was of the highest standard, with top-quality ingredients. Sufi *zawiyas* of old were often noted for their cooking, and the Sheikh knew a great deal himself. He had learnt a lot from watching the cook in his grandmother's house as a boy, and some of the *zawiya* recipes were his own.

The women who were doing the cooking in any particular week had to get the quantities right because nothing was allowed to be thrown away or wasted. If they made too much they had to sit and eat all that was left, which they did not want to have to do; so they would encourage everybody to have seconds, and the Sheikh would make critical comments if they pushed too hard. However, his tone might leave doubt as to whether he was criticising them for pushing, or the others for not eating up, or both. He would taunt Naima that she didn't like his belly, but said it resulted from being surrounded by loving kindness.

Every Saturday morning in London two of the women would go to Soho to do the week's shopping. On their return they would often recount their dealings with Brian the butcher at Randall & Aubin. For a long time their shopping companion was Zafira, a striking, rosy-cheeked young blonde to whom they suspected Brian was giving the better cuts of meat for better prices. One Saturday they canvassed this view at great length with the Sheikh, who heard them out and then recited with ominous deliberation: 'Mirror, mirror, on the wall, who is the fairest of them all?' He paused before answering the question himself in a tone heavy with meaning: 'Zafira!'

I just reflect to murids what they are. After all, he said that he too was a mirror.

'I remember a very nice example of that,' says Abdul-Ghaffar. 'My relationship with Hamida was very volatile at times. She was wonderful in many ways but quite hard work for a soft guy like me, and on two occasions I managed to ask the Sheikh directly for help. He was always busy and there were people around, *et cetera*, so they were both snapshot conversations in the hallway in Dalston as I'm leaving.

'On the first occasion, I was feeling very fond of her and I was scared that she was going to go. I said something along those lines to the Sheikh, and he said, "Well, you must be very affectionate with her. Give her what she wants. You must look after her and love her."

'Some time after that I had an almost repeat conversation, except it came from a very different place. We were in the hallway, and my feeling then was I was quite annoyed with her. She'd been, I thought, messing me around a little bit, and I was quite fed up. And again I expressed that in some way or other to the Sheikh; and he said, "Give her enough rope to hang herself by."

'All he was doing was simply reflecting back to me my own mood, or my own thoughts. At the time I didn't realise that—but later I realised that's how he teaches. Knowing that, and then reflecting back on all the interactions you've had with him, was itself quite a profound thing.

'At first I took what he said literally, and that's what I acted upon. I just thought, "He's telling the truth." Which of course he is, in the same way that when he's doing a lecture he's telling the truth—a more profound truth than anyone else I'd ever met. But he was also showing me the truth of who I was in that particular moment.

'And the underlying message was: "Sort it out yourself. I'm not going to tell you what to do." About your life, your relationships: you have to work that through yourself. And it's true in the whole of your life. You can't actually have someone to tell you what to do.

'I'm talking about stuff that happened thirty-four years ago, but I'm still learning from it, even now—those little conversations. And that's because of the nature of who he was: who he is.'

That same length of rope, with which his pupils too could hang themselves, was an essential part of his equipment. He made it freely available, and we made good use of it. We would loop it round our own necks in acting as our various characters dictated—but our own wills were, as he said, subordinate to the situations in which he set us up, and it was he who would spring the deadly trapdoor when the moment of unpalatable truth arrived: as it unfailingly did. Via this route we were manoeuvred into exhibiting our own defects, and thus forming a closer acquaintance with them than any homily could have induced.

AB went to see him once, thinking he would do the right thing after starting an affair with a fellow-pupil. 'You know I'm seeing Muna?'

'Yes,' said the Sheikh, 'I did know.'

'I just wanted to let you know about it, and I'm wondering whether I should tell [her estranged husband] Sadiq what's going on.'

'Why tell him?' came the reply. 'He's just an idiot anyway! Don't tell him!'

'What, you mean don't say anything?'

'No! Don't say anything!'

If you were a pupil, and having read this far, would you follow that advice? Either way, you would be gripped by the tension and puzzlement that are a way of life for every aspirant.

One night as everyone was leaving, the Sheikh leant and whispered in Imran's ear, 'You'll never make a womaniser if you can't hold your tongue! You have to learn to keep your mouth shut!'

Another ladies' man, Yaqub, had devoted much time and talent to the chase. Even after several years with the Sheikh, when he was given the job of farm manager in Australia he contrived to keep up with a string of girlfriends in the surrounding hills.

In London he had got acquainted with an attractive redhead, an American artist whom he introduced to the Sheikh and his teaching. Being a committed pupil, although he didn't live in the *zawiya*, he asked permission to go out with her; perhaps it was for a meal. Certainly, said the Sheikh. So he did. Then he made a further request, perhaps to head out of town with her for a day. That was fine, said the Sheikh; so he did. After that, he asked if he could accept her invitation to stay the night at her cottage in the country.

No problem at all, said the Sheikh.

Two fellow-pupils were coming up the steps of the *zawiya* a day or two later when they met Yaqub leaving. He told them he'd just been the target of the Sheikh's rage: and when they asked why, he said ruefully, 'My donkey bolted.'

The donkey is the emblem of the *nafs*. 'Keep your donkey on short rations,' the Sheikh would say, and he had two rather charming framed pictures of donkeys on the wall of the *zawiya*, both in London and Australia: one was a photo, and the other was the Arthur Rackham illustration of Bottom with his ass's head in *A Midsummer Night's Dream*.

Darkness having fallen on the cottage, Yaqub had settled down on the floor while his friend got into her own bed. Perhaps it was she who then suggested he might be warmer if he chastely shared the bed with her. He got in. The further suggestion was made that they have a cuddle; and nature took its course.

The Sheikh once declared plainly, 'We let you down with a bang again and again,' and that was what he had just done to Yaqub after hearing his sheepish report.

At such times it not only pays to remind yourself that a crippling rebuke is not dealt for laughs, or 'for its own sake', but rather crowns a demonstration in which you or your fellow-pupil have been the star, and whose lesson cannot be wished away. You must also never forget that its aim is to haul you one more stage along the path towards emulating the extraordinary condition of the man handing it out—who once put Yaqub's ruling passion into perspective by saying, 'I can call up like this' (snapping his fingers) 'nymphs who are into things you can't even imagine.'

You can only teach by the method applicable to each pupil. So he dealt with Yaqub in that way. For Ishaq at the Turkish girls' school, there were tears. On Ahmed and Masoud (for example) he used other techniques. Each of them had had relationships, of different intensities, with women who lived in the *zawiya*. After the two men had moved out, one of the two women would sometimes ring up on the Sheikh's behalf to deliver a terse reprimand about something. Neither had any trouble finding the words to do so—and it was always the former girlfriend of whichever guy it was. After a few such scaldings, Ahmed remarked to Masoud: 'Have you noticed how when the Sheikh wants to hammer you he gets Naima to phone you, and when he wants to hammer me he gets Maymuna to do it?'

Masoud gave his deadpan look. 'Remarkably effective, isn't it?'

It was the Sheikh himself who said men were like little boys. 'We are always in awe of the mother.' He ended AB's affair with Muna by telling him his parents would be very disappointed. 'He knew how to hit me hard,' said AB. And it was the same only different when he told Sakina, who had failed to collect someone from the airport, 'If it had been your father you wouldn't have forgotten!'

His technique was that of the hunter whose quarry's unvarying paths compel it to its death, because they allow him after careful observation to set the trap exactly where the beast will pass. 'The only difference between a rut and a grave is the depth,' he said.

'The more often you do a thing, the more likely you are to do it again, whether constructive or destructive. Any conscious action or communication relates to deeper layers of the mind and is coloured there with a certain numinism individual to yourself, so the things which attracted you or compelled you to do something are given a personal note of invitation which comes from a deep level within, and you are likely to repeat the experience or activity. It has this attractiveness—a soul quality—about it that you find hard to resist.

'We reflect your behaviour patterns in order to chase away your misfortunes. People who fear something concentrate on it, so the very thing they fear most comes upon them.

'In general people do not understand that before they can work on themselves they have to put certain things in order which militate against the process, and which are being carried forward within their souls in a destructive way to prevent them from gaining progress under the guidance of a teacher—which they really desire, but for which they are not properly prepared because in their mental luggage they carry portions around which prevent their proper understanding, in an objective way, of the behaviour patterns which have gone to form their characters.

'Similarly, many people think that a teacher can help them to receive *barakat*. They do not understand that a teacher spends a great deal of time motivated by love and patience in order to prepare pupils to receive *barakat* in certain circumstances in which they find themselves when living their everyday lives.

'When the lessons of life resulting from experience are not fully understood, and are consequently ignored again and again, this brings about further trials and disadvantages—and with them ever-increasing intensity and trauma—in additional experiences flowing from their lack of comprehension of a similar prior experience.

'Many people do things out of fear or hate or anger. All these qualities are contained in an individual, and they give colour to the incident or encounter or experience. This is the colouring of the qualities of their own soul, the *nafs*. This quality re-emerges in order to attract you to do the thing again, until it becomes a well established pattern which shackles you.'

The Sheikh not only diagnosed, but prescribed. 'Pupils are given concentration exercises in order to bring their normal wild, uncontrolled thought patterns under control. This is the hardest of the areas, since mind relates not merely to intellectual content but to instinctual, emotional and intuitive processes—the last of which are contaminated by the first two. This revealing of oneself to oneself enables a pupil to see just how chaotic his or her past habit patterns have been. In many cases such patterns of thought and behaviour produce destructive consequences, and people have to be shown, through understanding of cause and effect, the poor quality of their mental control in relation to their daily lives.'

He told Khalida it would be about four years before she would learn to live with fear. She says, 'It was one of those statements that brought you down to earth. You were way off in some world that you'd created for yourself, and I remember hearing that and thinking, "That sounds so realistic—just to learn to live with something, rather than have it disappear." And that's how it turned out: I learned how to just watch that feeling.'

After making people aware of their own patterns, he said, 'the next stage is a long and slow one of consolidating the work on the pupil's patterns and ingraining new ways of behaving.' He had travelled that way himself, though it was a rare snapshot he shared when he once said, 'I used to be very arrogant as a young man—so, you know, I had a hard row to hoe.'

Equally, the road he mapped out was clear for those with the determination to follow it. 'Just as people have become mechanical through adherence to things they like or that give them pleasure, we build up within them new patterns and say to them, "Concentrate on these patterns, devote your energy to them, and thus starve the old patterns of the energy you used to feed them."

'Intellectual pursuits are absolutely worthless. I have pointed out continually that real understanding has to be grafted on to our instincts so we gain wisdom through instinctual processes, not intellectual pursuits.'

Ishaq testifies: 'The core of his teaching was we should be aware and awake, and he taught that to us through *dhikr*: repetition of God's name all the time. Hard to do.

'The very doing of it doesn't make you better, but it educates you. One of the reasons it wasn't hard for me to stop drinking and whoring and smoking marijuana was because when I tried to sit and do the Sheikh's exercises, sit quietly for an hour—look at a spot on the wall, for instance, and just repeat a simple phrase, I found that quite hard. I'd say, "I've got between 7 o'clock and 8 o'clock. I don't have anything I need to do now. I don't need to think about this thing or that thing. I need to remain focused on this little phrase." But I can't.

'So I started thinking why I was finding it hard—and guess what I found? The way that I lived had an impact on me.

'As we live our life we're building up certain impressions. If we get angry about something, we burn it in pretty hard; very passionately in favour of something, we burn an impression in quite hard. When we sit and try, at the end of a day, to meditate for an hour, the things that come back to us are the things that have been burned in hard. And a lot of the things I'd been doing up till then, which the Sheikh would have recommended against, were burning into my impressions all the time.

'I was constantly burning something new in, and referring to something I'd burned in yesterday or last week or last year: and when I thought about it I burned it in again—I went back to it like a dog to its vomit, as the Sheikh said.

'So I started to see that you could only be successful in the progress you were trying to make if you lived in a different way and didn't have those impressions revisiting you when you didn't need them. It wasn't so much what the Sheikh said to me that helped me to understand that; it was what I learned myself from trying to follow his practices as they were set out. I realised: "I did those things and thought they were good for me—but now when I try and do this, which I *know* is good for me, I can't do it because I did those things!" So it just resolved itself.

'I found that what he would call "constructive impressions" are the easier ones to set aside, and that gave me some clarity about what a constructive thing actually is. It's something whose impression is not difficult for me to set aside for an hour if I want to meditate. Now there's an insight right there.'

Understanding has to be grafted on to our instincts so we gain wisdom through instinctual processes, not intellectual pursuits.

'I cycle three or four times a week,' Ishaq continues. 'You're very vulnerable on a bike, and it's worse than in a car, because you're more likely to be physically injured. Even if all you do is tumble off, something quite unpleasant's gonna happen to your body—and it's very often that problems come along. Somebody pulls out in front of me or cuts across me. I've learnt I can get angry about those things; and when I get angry about them, I can shout and scream and holler at the person who did the thing. I can get to work and tell all my mates about the bad thing that's happened to me. I can burn and chew on that all day if I want.

'Or not. Or not. I judge that that's a thing I should be able to set aside. It's a practice that I can choose not to do.

'If I do it, I'm gonna remember it forever. If I don't do it, I'm not gonna be any less alert when it comes to getting out of people's way on the road, but I'll actually have a nicer day, even though there are idiots on the road apparently trying to kill me. It's a habit, it's a behaviour, and miraculously I find I can set it aside. Not because I heard the Sheikh say some words in a talk, but because he directed me down a certain road, and I went down that road with a sturdy intention.'

Explaining the need to aim for a stage at which you would no longer react unthinkingly to insult or annoyance by others, the Sheikh said you would feel no more anger than if a child had tweaked your nose. He meant that entirely literally, and you may pause a moment to think how easy you would find it.

Yasin recalls, 'I was very prone to lose my temper at work if I made some mistake or there was some mishap that set me back in schedule. On a bad day, a residual bad mood that had built up could attract such mishaps or cause further mistakes, making the whole thing a vicious circle.

'I had a girlfriend who came along to the talks for a while. In those early days the Sheikh tolerated such things in the context of a serious or ideally a loving relationship, and generally his pupils were taken as normal Westerners for practical purposes.' Yasin says that in evoking that six-month affair he is reminded of the Sheikh's oft-repeated assertion, 'We give people what they want.'

'I moved in with her, wilfully and without seeking his permission. We started to have fights, culminating in a bust-up, and I moved out again.

'Shortly afterwards I was with the group on one of our regular summer solstice trips into the countryside, where it was hoped we might feel the energies in nature. Although I was still gripped with the kind of melancholy one might expect, after a couple of days the mood lifted somewhat and I became philosophical, feeling a healing and a preparedness to move on, despite knowing this girl was already entertaining a newcomer.

'Just as I was having such thoughts, the Sheikh's wife came over, asked how I was and started commiserating, saying how fond the Sheikh was of Liz. This stirred me up, as if I were now duty-bound to go and win her back.

'In two days' time we were due to fly to Istanbul as a group, and the night before the morning flight I felt compelled, in the fit of jealousy that had now been instigated, to burst in through the bedroom window, catching the two lovers *in flagrante*. Of course things became very unpleasant, and this guy was a nasty Gypsy type. Next morning, after a sleepless night, I arrived at Heathrow with a black eye and my nerves frazzled and fried. The Sheikh made a wry comment.

'On arrival we were met by the press, and the following day we were on the Turkish front pages, with me sporting the shining token of a lost love and unable to recover from my experience. On account of my melancholy the Sheikh declared, "You're useless to us on this trip," and sent me home after a week of the three-week visit.'

It was the hard-copy version of something he told Malika—and he was never shy of using a stock phrase or proverb if it nailed the problem: 'When you laugh, the whole world laughs with you; when you cry, you cry alone.'

Yasin says he recovered, finding after what seemed only a few weeks that he was so buoyed up by the lectures and collective *dhikr* that anger and depression, when the usual prompts occurred, began to feel superfluous, foolish and anachronistic by contrast.

'On the other hand, perhaps the real breakthrough came in my workaday life, when I was able to apply the silent *dhikr* all day and use the mental reason factor to apply a watchful, alert vigil over the internal world. I can remember how wonderful it felt, on making a mistake or having a setback, to find that the being who had formerly reacted in an automatic, habitual way had disappeared.'

The Sheikh explained further: 'We have to learn to become rational about our feelings and to pause before we allow ourselves to be carried away. At that stage a repetitive process is established in the mind—of pausing as a surge of energy races through our being. The stimulus can be internal (e.g. thinking of something which has caused us fear in the past) or external. In most cases people behave wildly and indiscriminately. When they are centred by developing this repetitive process of pausing, the intuition can operate, and a strange knowledge, which is rational just as intellect is rational, advises us. It says, "Throw yourself down to the right," or, "to the left," or, "Leap on to that passing bus."

'This method of counselling has far more wisdom in it than mere intellect. Intellect is the calculating quality of the mind, which discriminates in relation to certain known data and then selects a course of action; but it can be wrong, because selection is made from the bank of our ego experience. The other form of selection is made from the vast area we all possess when we come here as infants: the soul of humanity.

'It is the memory bank of all the experiences of an archetypal kind which humanity and animal, vegetable and mineral life has experienced—a bank of knowing, to which we can relate; but normally intellectual processes stand in our way, because we are creatures of pattern and habit. Once we know a certain way, we follow it as habit to the exclusion of any other, so intellectual processes have to be forgotten at the time when new processes are being introduced.'

He described having seen a pride of lions passing through a group of antelope who did not scatter at the lions' presence. 'They know through archetypal experience whether the pride is hunting or not, and they feel it. They use right discrimination through feeling, and they go on browsing while the lions pass by.' In this way, he explained, the conscious experience limited to one lifetime is linked effectively at the instinctual level to the whole of life's experiences when it comes to dealing with a particular situation.

Such archetypal structures, he said, are deep within us all, and we have to get to know them. 'These are simply the collective experience of humanity as a whole relating to the world of experience, which lies outside time and space. We are born with this treasure, which enables us to feel fatherhood, motherhood, love for the opposite sex, a whole range of human feelings, in the same way we instinctively feel for our mother's breast. We don't work out that there is milk there; we just seek it, because we have this knowledge built into us from birth.'

From its gradations 'we draw the ability to correctly make our actions spontaneous, because we relate the conscious part of our mind to these archetypal structures, and they guide us'—just as they guide the antelope. '[They] cannot be visualised. We can only relate to them by inference, analogy, imagination, at a spontaneous level, without thinking intellectually.'

'We are so concerned in Sufism with the evolutionary process in pupils that we are constantly weaning them from their whims and identifications with life. When we do this the motives are often misunderstood, and the Sheikh is questioned or found to be wrong in the eyes of the pupil. We are only trying to wean the attention of the human psyche from the egocentric patterns set up by every individual, from all the natural desires of their ego, so they may relate spontaneously in their consciousness to the deeper, more lasting experiences stamped in their minds before they were born.

'Hence Sufism can't be related to a set of rules or written-down methods. It's a capacity at the feeling level. And at deep levels instincts and emotions are affected, and a common bond operates.' As the antelope understands the lion, a human can communicate with other humans, with animals or even with plants.

You have to develop spontaneity with a conscious feeling relationship: a feeling detachment which doesn't allow your heart to leap and be overwhelmed by the event and be carried off. You have to be cool within. The Sheikh spoke of a great calm and a strange, awesome stillness at such moments. In relation to the pleasures, sorrows and events of life generally, he advised, 'You must be like the distant stars.'

After the *dhikr* ceremony he would ask everyone what they had felt or seen during the exercise, and one day Zainab told him she had been seeing elephants and climbing over something. 'I thought, "That's obviously going to be quite impressive," so I related it to him. He shouted at me, "Where were you? Why weren't you in your body? You shouldn't have been anywhere else!" He was so intense about that. Whatever's going on around you, stay within yourself!'

In fact he said, in so many words, that you should be so detached that you could have one hand in a bucket of shit and be eating honey with the other.

'When people come to us we make them aware of themselves by the process of splitting them into observer and that which is observed, in themselves and outside themselves. This is extremely difficult to do because habitual habit patterns carry the mind back into old tracks. We carry this struggle to all areas of the human mind and body.'

A struggle it is. Asiya was among the women who worked on the costumes for the *sema*, and even after thirty years she recalls: 'Najiba was my nightmare, and he put her in charge of the sewing, which I was never good at anyway. That was a big *nafs* experience. Every time I had to go and be under her, she was revolting. I really could not stand that woman, and I'm sure she didn't think much of me either. We're completely different kinds of people, and oh, it was insufferable. But I had to keep it under control, and I used to dread those things.

'And also the turning itself, because Abdul-Aziz used to pick on me. Something was always wrong [with how I did it]—my arm was dragging, or whatever—and it used to infuriate me, because what's her name, the one he married? She never did it right, she never learned to move her feet properly, ever, but he never picked on her. He would always find fault with me. The Sheikh knew I was having a hard time, but he said, "You have to learn to deal with people that you don't like." He was very clear that I'd have to learn to accept Abdul-Aziz and follow his direction.

'The other thing he did was to put me in a tent in France with the woman who was with the guy I'd been with before, and that was really hard too. I know he did it intentionally, because he knew all the details of the story. So I had to deal with my feelings all through the trip. He was doing that kind of stuff all the time.'

Indeed the Koran says, 'We try some of them by means of others'—and the Sheikh, as Sakina says, was a living Koran. He embodied the Koran just as the Prophet did: its poetry, its grandeur, its subtlety, its strangeness, its clarity, its ferocity, its consistency, its unexpectedness, its implacability, its insistence. If you see seeming contradiction in those qualities, you will see the same in the Koran. 'Through him', she says, 'we could understand in turn that the Koran illustrated the way of Allah Almighty—the way of all creation. Like Khidr with Moses in the Koranic story to which he so often referred, he would often not explain himself. Our task as pupils was just to wait for the outcome, and it was a task in which we all failed repeatedly.'

It was Khwaja Ubaidullah al-Ahrar of Tashkent (1404–90), one of his spiritual forebears, the great Central Asian Naqshbandi masters of the eleventh to fifteenth centuries known as the Khwajagan,[21] who said, 'For those being

---

[21] Persian for 'Masters' and pronounced roughly 'Hojjagan'.

cooked on this path, a long time passes before they are informed that they have been cooked. It is like the cooking of a watermelon beneath the sun, where none but the gardener understands its condition.'

What is more, and to quote Javad Nurbakhsh again, 'By the master's accepting and rejecting of the disciple, by testing him in a multitude of ways, the disciple is both shown to himself, and known by the master. In such circumstances, many a heart has cried out, "I will either die on his threshold or reach the goal!"' In the Sheikh's own words, 'You have to endure till the end.' *You have to make a ruin in order to find a treasure.*

Sheikh Nazim would say that if your sheikh threw you out of the front door you should try the back door, and if that was barred you should make an entry hole in the roof. 'If the master expels the disciple, he should not go far away,' Nurbakhsh counsels; 'he should persist in remaining nearby, realising that grace is received by attending to and serving the master.'

Proximity ebbs and flows, and pupils must remain aware of where they stand. As Sakina said, 'You could find yourself more distant from him through your failures: not because of personal repugnance on his part, but as a reflection of how much you yourself drew towards him or didn't.' In this way as in all others, he was relentless in acting as a mirror—and as she testifies, he continued unflagging in the role after moving to Australia in the middle of 1985.

A few of us had preceded him and eventually many made their homes there. Some settled in Melbourne while he at first occupied a big house on the edge of town. But even before he bought the farm the following year, life had changed a great deal. Money was tight, and the emphasis was on making do. He again sat with us at dinner, facing the kitchen, but the room was smaller, his canvas chair replaced the Regency style, and a folding picnic table replaced the mahogany one. We ate off a sheet of orange building plastic on the floor.

Some time later he moved right into the country, creating at his new (and last) *zawiya* a large garden in which the women worked every weekend while the men were at the farm. 'Life at that house ended up hard for me,' Sakina says. 'Maymuna was in charge of the garden, with me and Farida doing her bidding, relayed from the Sheikh, and we saw less of him.

'It was fascinating and instructive to see him make the garden from scratch, very conservatively based around what was already there. He bought from nurseries all year round, building up an enormous diversity of plants which gave interest in every season—mainly flowering plants, and of those, beautifully scented ones. Each was set in a round hole cut in the turf, and for years we cut the narrow lines of grass between the plants with hedging shears.

'But unlike several others I was no longer invited to meals. That started because I was working late three nights a week, but I came to see it as an illustration of how everybody's fate is their own, and the Sheikh, or Allah Almighty, could visit different things even on two people living together. I would arrive later to give my housemate Farida and sometimes others a lift home, and every night I'd knock on the door of the drawing room and say at most a few words to him before leaving.

'I got very unhappy under this regimen, which made me feel constantly rejected and unwanted. We spent every weekend outdoors, with two cups of tea a day on the veranda, and a biscuit if Maymuna felt like providing it, and a trip back to my own place for an hour's lunch break and for the night once it got dark. If it rained we worked until we got soaked, but if the rain stopped we still went back.

'I felt angry and lonely and trapped, until eventually it dawned on me that coping with all this might be doing me more good than anything. I remember reasoning that I was getting an easy time in a good job at work, where by that time I was in charge of a hundred people, but getting the experience of being a servant at the *zawiya*, whereas someone else might be in charge at the *zawiya* but not at work. Besides, others were also getting a hard time and possibly fewer perks than me.

'I also learned that I wouldn't dissolve in a bit of rain. And, as the Sheikh said, the plants became my friends. That too has stayed with me ever since.'

He had assured us that if he appeared in a pupil's dream it was deliberate, and soon after arriving in Australia, Sakina had dreamt of him screaming at her so loudly that she woke up: 'You think you're here to have a nice life! Well, you're NOT!'

In fact you are here—not just in another country, but in 'the school of earthly life'—to acquire understanding. And *the real way to learn is a repetitive method; more often than not the thing has to be experienced before any hope of understanding can come about.*

The Sheikh's frequent impatience with the obtuseness of his pupils masked a lifelong patience when it came to the task of supplying the experiences they required; and he did not conceal, any more than any other Sufi, the truth that it was a long haul. 'We take the long view,' he declared.

It is also true that understanding, once attained, puts the seeming hardships of the journey back in their proper and inconspicuous places. He often recounted how as a young civil servant he had visited the office of the department's deputy secretary, a very senior official by whom he was over-awed. The man had gestured at the ranks of bulging case files crowding the enormous desk across which he faced his subordinate, and told him serenely, 'Time heals all these problems.'

Yet time, and often lots of it, is needed to impart or to acquire understanding. While Ahmed was engaged, or thought he was engaged (with the Sheikh's permission) to the Turkish girl, he came home to the *zawiya* one evening. The Sheikh, who was in the hallway, paused and greeted him with his inquiring 'Yeah?'

He took the cue and said, '*Salaam alaikum*, Sheikh Abdullah—I was wondering whether you really wanted me to get married.'

'Well, Ahmed,' the Sheikh began, and repeated something we had often heard him say: 'the Khwajagan never allowed their pupils to marry until they were fifty years old.' Then he added with even greater emphasis: 'And I'll tell you why!'

At that instant one of the women called from the next room, 'John!' and he broke off.

'Could Ahmed get us some milk please?' she asked.

'Ahmed, go out and get some milk,' he ordered.

So Ahmed had to go straight back out of the door and down to the corner shop. When he returned the Sheikh was occupied with something else. The conversation was left unfinished, and it was about fifteen years later and 12,000 miles away in Australia that the same topic came up between them one evening. Without any prompting, the Sheikh said, 'You know, Ahmed, the Khwajagan never allowed their pupils to marry until they were fifty years old. And I'll tell you why!'

Ahmed remembers: 'A thrill ran through me as the answer came at last. "Because they could see life clearly."'

Years earlier the Sheikh had told an interviewer that it was only after reaching that stage that male pupils were 'capable of dealing with femininity and not messing women about', and he expanded the point in a lecture: 'Beyond our drives, inner psychic reality serves to manifest a reality. It often chooses a powerful image of the cosmic man for its expression. A Sufi was asked why he had no wife, and referred to this stage. "A wife is when you have arrived at man's estate. I have not yet arrived there: I'm still travelling towards it."

'If you take a wife when you're not sorted out within yourself and not realising your own human potential, you are only entering into an area of conflict between two underdeveloped human beings. Humans are areas of chaos lusting after the next whim, [and pairing up will lead to being] at war outside as well as inside yourself.'

Ahmed married Sakina when he was forty-nine.

The Sheikh arranged Rashida's marriage to Dain and later gave her three pieces of private advice about her husband, family and business. By her own admission she ignored all three, and the couple left him not long afterwards. Three decades later she is in the middle of a divorce and declares, 'Ninety-nine per cent of this hardship I'm going through is because these three messages were not adhered to. Whatever happened in these twenty-nine years, it's what I knew in 1985 and I didn't listen.' Yet she adds: 'Spiritually, it's been the right marriage for me, because when I look back and what I'm going through now, I'm learning: every moment of this is my fault.'

The Sheikh continually reminded us, 'I teach like life.' As for life, it not only teaches as he did: it is also, as he warned, a harder taskmaster—as Masoud found out.

Masoud was a lovely bloke, and he and Ahmed were a bit like brothers during their couple of years in Dalston. When Masoud's foibles were discussed one day, Ahmed blurted out, 'But I do love him!' only for the Sheikh to reply, 'Oh, I love him too! But it doesn't affect my judgment *that* much,' and snap his fingers.

Masoud was hard to pin down. If you thought you'd agreed on something with him, you might find him doing the opposite. When the Sheikh was sending pupils round to help him do up his house after he'd left to get married to Munira, some of them returned to the *zawiya* one night with the news that Masoud was planning to remove a structural beam. The Sheikh said he must not do it on any account, and they relayed the order. But when they arrived again next evening the beam had gone, and they had to install emergency props to stop the place collapsing.

On Masoud's marriage the Sheikh had observed grimly, 'She'll teach him.' Ahmed found out why when the Sheikh threw him out of the *zawiya* and told him to join the couple in the house that he had helped to renovate.

'The reason for that was that I never really got the point while I lived with the Sheikh,' Ahmed says. 'He told me he had received many kicks from me. I think I was guilty of all kinds of betrayals and wrongheadedness. He spelt out some of it, but that wasn't enough to bring about a change in me, even though he said, "I have treated you in many ways as if you were my own son." It was absolutely true. But I couldn't fit in.

'And although it was cosy at Masoud's, we had barely made a start on the house. Sleeping and eating on a building site is always a trial. On top of that, Munira's shy charm turned out to mask a pattern of occasional but terrifying rages from which nothing was spared—her husband, the walls or their lodger.

When I returned to Dalston for a visit, the Sheikh announced, "Ahmed's found that the *zawiya* isn't such a bad place after all."'

I teach like life. But the course is accelerated, so that the pupil has a chance of gaining the experience in this world instead of the next. 'First we bat you one way, and then we'll bat you the opposite way.'

When Dante in his *Inferno* visited hell, he came to a place where 'a storm of warring winds, the hurricane of hell, never resting, seizes and drives the spirits before it; smiting and whirling them about, it torments them. . . . And I learned that here there suffer those who have sinned in carnal things, their reason mastered by desire.'

There he saw and talked with Francesca da Rimini, whose husband had murdered her and his brother, who was her lover, in about 1285; and if you had been at the table in Dalston you would never have forgotten the relentless force with which the Sheikh impressed upon Aziza the need for loyalty and constancy in her affections: 'Remember Francesca da Rimini,' he more than once told her: 'blown about by the winds of hell!'

We had adopted from him the word 'whirling' to describe not the *sema* but its very opposite: inner confusion, including that occurring under pressure from him. 'You must stay centred and stop whirling,' he said, 'otherwise you will be like a polo ball, whacked about on a polo field, out of control and at the whim or mercy of other people.' He retold an anecdote by Idries Shah in which the selfsame point is made in almost the same words. 'A visitor asked the question of Rais-i-Kabir, "Why do you behave in an exaggerated manner which makes people uneasy about you? Your conduct is too mixed." The Rais said, "The purpose of mixed behaviour is for people to notice how easily they are affected by it. A person is like a polo ball struck in any direction by a blow. Exaggerated behaviour says nothing about me and everything about the uneasy witness."

Instead, the Sheikh would say, 'You must be *here!*'—striking his chest, as we had all seen him do, to indicate where that was. It was with the same gesture that he said of AB, 'He is an example of a man who is *here.*'

The Sheikh's own demeanour was in many respects the centre around which our world turned and by which our own steadiness was challenged. It could change in a moment from clownish to awe-inspiring, or from tragic to sweetly gentle. The atmosphere changed with it: from miserable to joyful, humdrum to indescribably weird, in moments, let alone overnight. The process was testing, and like the Rais's visitor we were often 'uneasy witnesses': but it was mesmerising. *Every sheikh has his own Punch-and-Judy show. We're the consummate actors.*

Every day he would act the pupil, so to speak; and moreover, at least once he did it for real.

When we visited Istanbul for the first time in 1981 a strange man arrived at our hotel while the Sheikh was out, so he was asked to come back. Before he did so, the Sheikh said he wanted to test the man. 'Nobody's to say I'm the Sheikh. When he comes, you're just to pretend I'm a *murid*.' He dressed Ali (others say Othman) in his robe and turban, and said, 'You pretend you're me.'

Everyone was facing what they thought was the only door. There came in from behind them a small, neat, slightly tubby, slightly bald, very Turkish-looking but otherwise nondescript man in a brown suit, with a little moustache, who looked like a bank manager. Since that moment he has always been known as the man in the brown suit. 'He was in his mid-nothingness,' said Zafira; 'he could have been thirty or sixty. He was not demonstrative in any way. He was under the radar.'

He asked for the Sheikh, and Walid said, 'I don't know where he is. He's, er—he went for a walk.'

Just then the Sheikh entered. He was in his usual brown corduroy, and he'd stuck his hands in his pockets like a typical dozy pupil. 'Anyone seen the Sheikh?' he asked. 'Oh—oh –' He sounded bewildered. 'Where do we go?'

Someone had pointed Ali out to the visitor and said, 'There's our Sheikh.' But the man smiled, said, 'No, it's not!' and walked straight up to Sheikh Abdullah and hugged him, as much as to say, 'You can't fool me!' before they sat down together. He knew what the joke was.

When someone asked, through a translator, 'So how did you find us? How did you know the Sheikh?' he said, 'We've known each other by heart for many years. I know him well.'

Then he explained that he didn't have a sheikh himself; he had been taught by Khidr, the ageless and timelessly knowing being who appears anonymously in the Koran as a guide too bewildering for the incomplete insight of the lawgiver Moses. Khidr has visited and advised Sufis through the centuries, of whom Ibn Arabi is merely the most famous. His appearance is linked with a certain advanced stage of development where the ability is gained to deal with the apparently irrational—with the knight's move, that L-shaped move in chess that is neither straight nor oblique.

Khidr's surprising, Mercurial nature requires the flexibility of a green plant that can bend with the changing wind. That is not, of course, the same as being blown hither and thither. To be flexible you have to be centred, in the way that

AB demonstrated one day after coming home to the *zawiya* to be greeted by the Sheikh: 'Come here, Abdul-Barr. I want to tell you what's happened.'

AB recalls: 'At the top of the stairs the women used to keep a big cardboard box, and in it they had this huge plastic drum of cooking oil. He said, "This container's been punctured and all the oil's seeped through the floorboards and through my ceiling down below—and Maymuna said you did it."

'I said, "How would I have done that?"

'"Maymuna said that you keep the mousetraps in it."

'I said, "That's right, I chuck 'em in that box every morning."

'"Maymuna's suggesting you put a mousetrap in and jabbed it through the container."

'And because I'd been in the house a while, I thought, "Oh, it's one of *them*."

'So I said, "Yes, that's quite likely. It's possible. I'm sorry. If it was me, I'm very sorry—and what can I do?"

Put yourself in AB's place for a moment while you consider what your own reply would have been. Ahmed, for example, would have reacted quite differently, far less impassively, and the consequences would have been different accordingly.

As it was, AB continues, 'The Sheikh's going, "Hang on a minute, let's go and investigate." So we investigated the empty carton, and he goes, "Can you see a puncture hole anywhere, Abdul-Barr?"

'I said, "No, I can't see one."

'"No," he goes. "What I can see, though, is an indent. It looks to me as if someone's kicked it with their foot."

'The long and the short of it was that Maymuna had done it, and she sort of remembered that she might have kicked the box and punctured the oil.'

In Sufism the way of *malamat* is the way of blame[22]—of not minding when people think ill of you, or even encouraging them to do so in order to show them how foolish it is to criticise. The aim, said the Sheikh, was for the seeker to come to an understanding of how to die to his or her self: 'a slow process because it is concerned with all emotional identifications with objects, events and people'. He remarked in passing that people were always blaming him for something.

When Ahmed complained that on joining the group it had become awkward to explain to friends uninterested in mysticism why one's habits had changed and one was suddenly unavailable several times a week while in fact

---

22 There was a group or order of Sufis called the *Malamatis*, but the term has broader application. The topic is discussed at length on pp. 261–5.

attending Sufi activities, his unexpected reply was, 'Just tell them you're having an affair with a married woman.'

'If someone slanders or attacks you,' he advised, 'do not be concerned with yourself, but with what your lord has commanded. As long as you do not defend yourself He will defend you. He incites [your adversary] against you in order to test you.'

Or the Sheikh might administer a similar test himself. There was the matter of the cooking oil; and again, one day he wanted AB to drive him to the Royal Horticultural Society garden in west London, the area where AB had grown up and which he knew well. '"Don't forget, Abdul-Barr, tomorrow you're taking me to Syon House."

'I said, "Yeah, I remember."

'He goes, "Yes, Syon House in, umm—Oh, where is it?"

'"It's in Isleworth."

'"No, no. . . ."

'"Brentford, then."

'"No, it's not Brentford."

'"Well, it's, umm, Hounslow."

'The Sheikh said, "No, no, no."

'"Ealing?"

'"No, it's not Ealing!"

'"Well, Kew then. It could be Kew."

'"No!"

'It went on and on, and it's getting silly. I'm going, "Putney?"

'"No!" he retorted. "Putney's nowhere near it! Oh, God—I'll go and find out!" He stormed downstairs and came back with a map. He'd obviously looked at it downstairs, because as soon as he opened the door he said, "Isleworth!"

'I said, "I said Isleworth first."

'He goes, "No, you didn't!"

'I was just about to say something when the women said, "No, you didn't!"

'I thought: here's one waiting for a hammering. And I said, "Oh, no, no—Sorry. I thought I had."'

The moral? 'It doesn't matter if you're right,' says AB. 'It don't matter. Not just with the Sheikh. When you see other people doing it, it's easy to spot, isn't it? It's their own self-importance. But you can't see it in yourself. You'd be put down for it eventually—but I've seen the same thing happen to others.'

Indeed Abdul-Malik relates:

'The Sheikh said, "Amir gave me a lift from the talk." I was thinking that it had been Yaqub; but I didn't say anything, obviously.

'Ali said, "No, it was Yaqub."
'And the Sheikh said, "No, it was Amir."
'"No, no, it was Yaqub."
'"No, it was Amir."
'Ali said again, "No, it was Yaqub"—and the Sheikh absolutely hammered him: "If I say it was Yaqub, it was Yaqub!"
'I learned from that one, because he didn't get it, and I still don't think he got it by the end.'

The disciple must cling to his sheikh as a blind man on the edge of a river clings to his leader. The advantage he gains from the error of his sheikh, if he should err, is greater than the advantage he gains from his own rightness, if he should be right.

Conversing about some technical issue or other, the Sheikh once said something that prompted Abdul-Malik, who had a technical background, to exclaim silently to himself, 'You can't get energy out of nothing!' As a result he found himself starting to argue a bit. The Sheikh made a polite rejoinder, and then added—"You know, you can't get energy out of nothing."

'He just took the wind right out of everything I was going to say,' Abdul-Malik recalls. 'You want to just tear your hair out or something. The Sheikh always said he wasn't an intellectual, and basically he'd just taken the argument and banged it against the wall. You're just sitting there thinking, "Well, what can I say? There's nothing left to say now." The Sheikh wasn't going to argue about it.'

The key lies in his own words: 'The spirit of a thing is something irrational, not understood by the rational intellect; so you have to die to the intellect to come to a new way of knowledge—the knowledge of immediacy.'

A top-floor room was up for decoration, and AB was supervising. 'Loads of people were coming round painting, and my orders were to make sure that I knew where everyone was all the time. Then a directive came from Maymuna: "The Sheikh said that if anyone wants to go to the toilet" (which was on the floor below) "you're to go with them, because you've got to supervise people at all times."

'I said, "If I go downstairs with someone who wants to go to the toilet, and I wait outside the door, then I've got twelve men upstairs being unsupervised, haven't I?"

'She said, "Oh. Hang on."' She went off and saw the Sheikh, and came back. "The Sheikh said that if anyone wants to go to the toilet you're all to go down, all stand outside the door waiting, and then all go back up again."

'And I said, "You're having a laugh, ain't ya?"

'She goes, "No, that's what the Sheikh said."

'"I think he's having a laugh with you."

'"That's what the Sheikh said."

'I said, "I can't do that!" So I didn't do it. And I never heard any comeback from it.'

No intellectual knowledge from your background can help you understand the processes of Sufism. Only now has he just begun to wonder if he should have taken the twelve downstairs each time as instructed.

By this stage you will have realised why the Sufis (and indeed the Koran) talk so much about the inevitability of being tested. The fact that the pupil may be clinging to his or her Sheikh like the blind man, as instructed, confers no immunity at all: for he warned us, 'You can't trust me! All you can trust is "Allah-Hu, Allah-Hu".'

Whatever I do, whatever I appear to do, hang on by your fingers and toes.

One day during the basement project he came downstairs and delivered a hell of a hammering to the blokes working there. No one remembers what it was about, but it left us stunned. It was dreadfully powerful, and as on all such occasions there had been nowhere to hide. Ahmed said something to him afterwards about the impact. 'Yes,' he said. 'No refuge but "Allah-Hu" and Allah Almighty.'

AB recalls another occasion. 'He'd just finished hammering someone, and as he was storming out of the room he said, "Come with me, Abdul-Barr, I want you to finish that lock off." So I went downstairs, and all I had to do was put in two screws. I had the lock ready, I had the screwdriver ready. But he was standing behind me, still either raging or pretending to rage—fuming: and my hands were shaking.

'I'm saying, OK, just concentrate, concentrate: you've got two screws—two screws. I got the screwdriver in, and my hands were going like that, and I stopped. I remember now the conversation with myself. "Right: I'll give it another minute and then I'll just say, 'I'm sorry, Sheikh Abdullah, I'm unable to do this.' 'No, no, you just do it!' the Sheikh will tell you." It took me forever; and he never said, "What the hell are you doing with two screws?" He waited while I did it. It seemed to be an hour; it could have been twenty minutes. But it was forever.'

'Most people', said the Sheikh, 'haven't the staying power in themselves to go on constantly applying themselves to a particular task until it is completed with a mind entirely devoted to the task, [so that the task is] done to the exclusion of every other thought or any other attraction. This form of concentration has to be developed. [It] is very necessary in order to understand the real nature of will, which is a divine quality. This will is not what we think it is in ordinary intellectual terms. In fact we cannot find it by intellectual practices.'

At one stage Malika lived in the *zawiya* and worked in the kitchen. 'I would sometimes, in a state of nervousness, become clumsy and drop cutlery or bang the pans,' she recalls. 'Sitting watching from the dining area, the Sheikh would shout at me with full force, "Malika, get a grip!" The energy he projected would make a bodily impact on me and jolt me into full awareness, leaving nervousness—which is basically a state of mind—out of the picture: a tangible experience of what he meant by "being awake and being present".'

He said that your first task was to become constantly aware of your mental processes. 'The average person is entirely unaware: the product of their own rambling fantasies. The exercise of *dhikr* is damming this torrent. It teaches people to relate to blanks, and in these blanks there are no emotional or instinctual surges, no intellectual ramblings. These states are of heightened, alert awareness in which the physical senses act in the way that you act under great stress from fear, and you can hear a pin drop in the next room, or intensity in the atmosphere. This produces eventually a feeling of cool wellbeing, [as when you're breathing] in pine-forest air and mountain streams are gurgling away.'

You have heard such references before and will hear them again, because they convey a definite stage of experience. 'The air is filled with positive ionisation. If you are sensitive enough it produces Olympian detachment from everyday affairs.' The technique for achieving all this is *dhikr*, he said. 'Because it is a repetitive exercise it gradually brings about longer and more meaningful blanks. Eventually the torrent dries up, and you walk around in the state of preparedness of the Japanese samurai—highly alert.'

He often recounted how the great master Shibli had been to visit one of his peers, Sufyan al-Thauri, and found him sitting absolutely motionless. 'Where did you learn such concentration?' Shibli asked. 'From a cat watching a mousehole,' came the reply.

One evening the Sheikh said to Muktar, 'Get Hisham on the phone.'

Out in the hallway was a phone jack, which you could remove in order to take the phone into the main room. Abdul-Malik recalls, 'I could hear Muktar in the hallway: he gets Hisham on the phone and says, "I've got the Sheikh for you"—and unplugs the phone. Now I knew that when you unplugged a phone in those days, the line went. Muktar didn't know that. So he plugs the phone in at this end, gives it to the Sheikh, and it's a dead line.

'The Sheikh just put the phone down. And I'm thinking, "But of course it's dead!—and of course the Sheikh and Muktar are ignorant about these esoteric things of electronics, so they're making this rather stupid mistake."

'But the Sheikh looked at me and said, "Hisham's on the other end of that phone waiting for me. This is a heightened expectancy. He's concentrating more intensely than he's ever concentrated in his life." And I realised that of course my stupid arrogance was irrelevant. The Sheikh knew exactly what he was doing.'

It is our purpose to use different teaching techniques related to reforming you.

The Sheikh warned that whereas at night you have dreams, 'during the day you have fantasies, which are the same thing and perpetually fill your head. You are shrouded in the mist, like the dazed feeling after staring at a film for three hours when you come out of the cinema. You can't see your surroundings clearly.

'You need to be awakened from this state. When you reach that state of being awake, your mind will be empty of the endless fantasies and colourings. There will only be real perceptions. Like the neurotic person who feels their dreams are cracking up and obviously unreal, and who then becomes frightened, the mystic too lives with a certain tension at the absence of fantasies. He or she has to learn to cope with this.

'The state of being caught in your own inner processes stops when you find wild alertness. If you have awareness and constant alertness in the way that the wild solitudes teach you, as a wild animal is alert, you are no longer caught in anything. You are fully alert to forces around you. You have to be, to survive. There is a tremendous steadiness in the innermost core of your being. This is the reality, the philosopher's stone. The steady inner aloofness is very necessary in order to survive.

'You go on living spontaneously, but a part of you is detached all the time. You are not surprised. You are directed towards the source of inner peace. If you are as detached as that, you have reached to immortality, which is not altered by death. Death becomes a chance event which cannot shatter this essential nucleus.'

Immortality lies in the process of consciously controlling your being. The fact is that in Sufi training one's conduct must indeed be considered a matter of life or death. That is the case both in the *zawiya* and around the Sheikh more generally, and no less true for being a figure of speech. This is very hard to grasp if it has been not experienced, but it has left its brand on all those by whom it has.

In Khalida's words, 'He could come down hard on people where in the outside world we might think it wasn't that big a deal.' *One is much stricter with the students who already know the basic language.* Do you remember Muktar and the tape recording? When Farida gave Sakina the prototype of a tissue-box cover she was making as a present for another pupil at the Sheikh's request, he laid into her vigorously and told her she was currying favour with Sakina by means of something that wasn't hers to give.

The noblest of you in the sight of God is the best in conduct. 'He could nip things in the bud,' Khalida adds. 'That was always a general rule around the Sheikh: you just didn't say anything that came into your head.' *Now, you don't come to the* zawiya *and talk about the women like that!* 'He would make a big deal of it, and you sure didn't do it again.'

The need to abandon thoughtlessness coloured the very air around him. He told us to be at all times like the quivering sparrow on a branch: 'It doesn't want to be a hawk's dinner, or a cat's!'—and he would imitate its darting glances. 'You must be like a wild creature! This is how to live your life: always awake, with total presence. You must live every moment of your life as if it is the last. We lay great emphasis on being conscious all the time: so attentive and concentrated as to [possess] a wild creature's alertness—the wildness of survival, in which the whole of one's being is attentive to what is going on around, and no detail is lost.'

Our alertness was tested every hour. For a time Ahmed was the one who took the entrance money at the lectures. Once at Golders Green he got up from the table and moved a few feet away. When he got back, the money had gone. No one had come in except the Sheikh. In dismay Ahmed looked and asked around. The talk hadn't started yet, so finally and reluctantly he approached the Sheikh, who brought out the wad of cash from his inside pocket, saying: 'You know, if I see money lying around I pick it up.'

We lay great emphasis on being conscious all the time. 'But at the same time', he said, 'we insist there should be no emotional identifications or attachments. You must encounter scenes as an observer, with no reaction and no conclusion drawn.'

For meals at the *zawiya* a fine white tablecloth was laid, and impeccable behaviour was expected. Each resident had his or her own place, with the Sheikh at the head. Zaid and AB sat on one side with an empty chair between them, a radiator on the wall behind them, and Zaid next to the Sheikh. But when Zaid moved out, the places stayed the same. 'When the Sheikh needed water—and I had to see that, not be told—I had to serve him,' says AB, 'because Zaid would have done it, being next to him. So I had to get up from my chair, move into the next chair, move up to the end chair, pour him the water, and then go back—all without the chairs touching the radiator. And every time I did it the three women were watching, waiting for me to knock that radiator. It went on for ages.'

Do you say that AB should have moved along and sat in Zaid's chair, or at least in the middle chair? It's not a trivial matter. 'The paradoxes, inconsistencies, injustices and irrationalities can only be seen from the human standpoint,' the Sheikh insisted. 'The average person cannot understand the unity within the universe.'

He wrote Amira a characteristically pithy reply to her account of a dream in which she had been shown a heart that was a scorched fruit, and had told herself that it must have been a flower first—perhaps one 'like a lotus with many long delicate stamens'. First he told her she must understand that the heart was the fruit of marrying the instincts to the elementary rational aspect of her being 'to produce true emotional feeling in yourself so that you can relate to the world of flesh around you'. But then he wrote:

'The fact that in your dream you start analysing instead of observing the vision of the heart tells me that you have carried your intellectual approach into the world of the unconscious, where a fragmented aspect of your being is not asking the questions and waiting for the answers, but is in fact rushing ahead like a naughty precocious child in the way most people do in everyday life, tripping over themselves with anxiety to arrive at the WRONG conclusions.

'Why should the heart be the fruit of the lotus? You are taking three beans, and by waving your intellectual wand you turn them into three million. You will never make progress this way—you will only become stupidly neurotic.'

In Sufism, by contrast, he explained that the pupil undergoes a 'controlled neurosis' in which he or she enters into uncertainties, mysteries and the irrational without reaching for facts or reasons. *You have to die to the intellect to come to a new way of knowledge—the knowledge of immediacy.*

Very security-conscious, he had a burglar alarm installed. It consisted of a deafening siren on the top landing, next to three of the bedrooms, and a colossal bell on the outside wall. When they went off, both at once, it was terrifying. Talk about the knowledge of immediacy. Abdul-Malik wired them to sensors on the external doors that triggered after a short delay if anyone opened the doors without having switched the system off. It was left on overnight and occasionally went off in the small hours without warning. 'I used to dread that phone ringing,' Abdul-Malik recalls. He would arrive wretchedly, toolbox in hand, to find everyone in their night clothes waiting in the hall, glowering at him as he entered.

Early one Saturday the Sheikh came up from his rooms and cried out that he had just had a cold shower. The hot-water cylinder was in the rear basement and reached via the back steps. Masoud ran downstairs, out through the back door and down the steps. Just as he reached the cylinder, the alarm triggered. Desperately he ran back up in, raced to the front door and switched it off. In relief, he leaned back on to the hall radiator—which fell off the wall.

When you come into contact with the Sheikh and he is providing experience, you feel as if in a dream sequence. Your own will is subordinate to the situation in which he sets you up. Once the magician Prospero had conjured up the tempest of Shakespeare's title and thereby cast the royal party and their drunken retainers on to his island, where he would then restore harmony and right order, they found themselves in thrall to his powers: quite literally spellbound, and ripe for the errors of their ways to be corrected.

Sometime in that period a small fire started next to that hot-water cylinder. It was discovered before it did much damage, and the Sheikh led the household in a prayer of thanks, but it had happened on Ahmed's and Masoud's watch. He told each to write down and pin to the other's door a message he had dictated. Ahmed has forgotten which trait of Masoud's it was that, in the Sheikh's words, blinded him to the consequences of his own neglect. But he still has, on the front of an envelope with the drawing-pin hole in it, the message that Masoud was told to write for him: 'MY SMUG SELF-SATISFACTION WITH MY INTELLECT'S WHIMS ASSURES ME THAT I NEVER NEGLECT A SINGLE THING.'

Despite or more likely because of the men's best efforts, the plumbing was plagued by airlocks. Dain and another pupil decided to try to use the mains pressure to blow them out of the system. Lending a hand, Ahmed had no real idea how the plan was supposed to work, but he knew it was risky. After they had re-jigged various connections, the moment came for the two to test their work. They stayed on the top floor to turn the valve on and sent Ahmed down to the basement to watch the cylinder, with strict orders to yell if anything funny happened.

It did. There was a racket and a hissing in the pipes, and within seconds the hot-water-filled cylinder took on a lean, yanking the connection on top. As water streamed down the outside, Ahmed shouted and ran upstairs. They closed the valve. They had put so much pressure into the cylinder that its concave bottom had blown out and become convex, so that it couldn't stay upright.

They had to buy a new one and plumb it in. The Sheikh indicated that the three men should share the cost of some £200, nowadays worth at least £600. The two others decided that Ahmed was the innocent party and they would split the charge between them. When the Sheikh found out that he'd accepted this offer, he criticised him severely, saying that whenever Ahmed found a loophole he would exploit it.

The plumbing system got so complicated that a manual had to be compiled. To obviate low pressure the Sheikh insisted that everyone's room be on the mains, which was against the regulations. He explained that the pupils needed a degree of comfort; otherwise, he said, if the accommodation were too miserable, 'I'll be hammering you for something, and you'll think to yourself, "Oh, Christ...."' It was an unexpected glimpse of the carefully judged path he had to tread. He would say, 'Allah Almighty never gives you any more than you can bear,' and at any moment he was fully aware of the reactions he himself was provoking.

Although he immediately qualified his remark about comfort by saying that when one had the inner television (as he sometimes called it) such things didn't matter, he added that most of his pupils were a long way off that stage. Even a decade later he was still pointing out that we ought to be able to stay in touch with him in a direct or inward fashion, using what he also called the communication of the heart—'But at the stage you're at, you have to speak.'

On the other hand, not everyone was, as he put, it dead. Zakiya, for example, remembers the powerful effects he had on her: 'Non-verbal, just directly, at an emotional level. Just sitting there looking at him, without words being spoken, he was able to evoke powerful emotions in me. One time in particular it was as if I had literally a lump in my throat. It was the emotion trying to get out. That wasn't me, that was him.'

At his lectures, recalls Asiya, 'He always illustrated what he was talking about with the energies in the room. Once when he talked about women having to wait for men—I think it was Penelope waiting for Ulysses—and the sadness and the yearning, the whole room was struck with sadness and yearning. It was in your body; it wasn't like you were imagining it or empathising. And then he would talk about energy; he would sometimes pump up the energy so that you could hardly sit still. You were burning inside, you were so uncomfortable in your own body that you'd squirm; and you'd look around, and everyone else was doing the same, and you'd think, "Oh God, he can't go on much longer." And then other times, he would send out the *barakat*, and you could stay in those hard chairs at the Holborn library forever just basking in it, it was so nice.'

'Tibetan adepts melted snow,' said the Sheikh, 'and my people will tell you I can burn them like the sun.' Muktar remembers getting suntanned while sitting with him inside the *zawiya*. 'I'd go red. I'd come out, and someone would say, "You got sunburnt!" And I'd go to the office, and someone said, "You're sunburnt!" So I remember the absolute heat and sunshine that he radiated when he was in that particular state. He said, "I have very positive states and quite negative states." He would emanate the expansion or the contraction in *sohbet*.'

He was clear that if his pupils could feel the energies outside in the world they would become more sensitive to the energies within themselves. By the Seine near Nôtre Dame he made everyone run up and down the steps to find where the energy line ran.[23] 'He was very sharp with people who thought they felt things but were just imagining them,' says Asiya. 'When he was asking and someone said they felt this and that, he might say, "No you don't! You've got to learn the difference between imagining and feeling."'

You also have to become sensitive to feel the energy of the Sheikh: it is the energy of life, which he has held in himself. The pupils are like iron filings round a magnet.

Sakina had a very strong experience of feeling his energy at a *sema* which was given in front of him. She had spent the afternoon with him and says she was probably more sensitive than usual as a result. 'In the *sema* I could feel peace emanating from him, and it got stronger and stronger as I turned towards his side of the room, and weaker as I moved away. When I told him afterwards what I'd felt, he said he'd known.'

How can such things come about?

'By orderly and disciplined stimulation', he said, 'the sheikh arouses in every pupil certain spasmodic feelings in the central nervous system. These are of a sporadic kind. They come and go—little quivers now and then. By constant stimulation and by the correct guidance, and by the force of the resonation, these feelings begin automatically to respond to the stimulation. When this takes place the responses become more orderly and gradually develop a life of their own. It is an inner life of feeling, which takes over from the feelings which are normally concerned with your ego and your wants.'[24]

The Sheikh said the Koran was meant for recitation. '[The word] really means "Recitation"—and this recitation, when it is done properly, has a resonating effect on the human body and produces physiological changes leading to psychological effects. For those who have been, say, in tropical countries [where they] have experienced the impact of a blue flash when they've touched certain man-made fibres on their clothes, or combed their hair and produced blue sparks, this is the same effect as resonating. Those who have held battery terminals on a low-powered battery get a zizzing effect within their body. The

23 See also p. 274.
24 See also p. 194.

resonating produces this because the volume of the sound disturbs the molecules in the body and in the air around, and the mind [starts] to work in a different way from intellectual consciousness—what has been described as the opening of the spiritual eyes and the opening of the spiritual ears.'

Again: 'The divine revelation [has the quality of being] strung together in certain harmonics which the human voice is capable of repeating so that the frequencies and the resonating effects can be felt again and again as they were intended.'[25]

He once exclaimed, 'I don't know why you people don't make more effort! There are a lot of states [of consciousness] which are very beautiful.' And he said: 'The vivid qualities of the inner world outshine the qualities of our physical capabilities. They enhance and expand our physical capabilities so that we see the objective universe with new eyes, and see things in it that ordinary people cannot see.

'When you realise intuitive experience is a wonderful, startling form of experience, and you are no longer awestruck by it, you realise that if you change your attitudes by conscious effort every day you start to change your [night] dreams. You sink deeper in yourself to new levels of experience.'

As so often, his emphasis in those words was on the expansion of consciousness rather than the altered state itself; but the state is real enough.

Walid had a job in a cemetery. 'I'd got in late and I was tired, and I was sleeping a bit in the hut. The other two guys had gone to walk round the cemetery for a bit and past the boss's window so he'd think they were working. As I was dozing I saw this bowl of eggs in front of me. I thought, "There's a bowl of eggs! I must be asleep. I'd better get up, because I'm meant to be at work. I'll straighten myself up."

'As I straightened myself up, the energy just came up and went into these centres, and I'm telling you it was like an express train. This little voice which is talking to you now just shrunk. I was going, "Help, help!" and getting hot; in fact I could feel my flesh starting to burn. I thought that I was going to catch fire. It was so powerful, and these centres were going like pistons in a train, and I was vibrating, and I was losing consciousness.

'It was actually quite frightening. It was a little taste of the sort of power that's there—and it's not your ego in control of it, so the ego would be frightened, wouldn't it? Because it's been brushed aside like a little leaf. The lesson was that this little person which we think of as "Good old whoever" is just a tiny little aspect of the power which is within us but we never experience.

---

25 See also p. 190.

'I told the Sheikh about it, and he said, "You should have just carried on and done the 'Allah-Hu' and trusted that you'd be all right."'

He admonished Abdul-Malik in much the same way after something that had happened at a lecture one Thursday. Sitting in the front row, Abdul-Malik received an intense stare from the Sheikh. What he calls 'a weird feeling' overwhelmed him: he passed out and could be seen slumped over and hyperventilating. The Sheikh stopped his talk and called for help. Khalil, a trained nurse, hurried over and lifted Abdul-Malik out of his seat with a view to setting him down on the sidelines and reviving him. He was disconcerted to find that his fellow-pupil, a man in his twenties of average build, had become astonishingly light in weight. 'I could have picked him up with one hand,' Khalil said.

Then there is the testimony of Muktar, mentioned above. He was in the Sheikh's sitting room, sitting opposite him and next to the old chimney breast, on which two pupils had highlighted the intricate detail of the embossed wallpaper by hand-painting it in different blues and gold. 'It was picked out in those incredible colours, so it had this eidetic effect,' says Muktar. 'He and I were talking about a dream or something. Sometimes I just would ask crazy, real questions, and he would answer them; and for some reason I looked at him and said, "Well, who are you, then?"

'I'm looking at his eyes. And at that moment something emerged—and then that wall lit up in multi-dimensions, and the whole of the room started to disappear. He was smiling, and I said, "Oh dear, I think that's too much. Better stop here." And it stopped. He just laughed and said, "OK."'

Very often when he was telling someone something, one or more of the others present would realise there was a message for them as well. 'Sometimes just an eye glance, or just a sort of feeling,' recalls Zainab. 'He'd suddenly make your stomach go all funny. He had that lovely belly laugh, and he'd sort of look at you, and you'd suddenly feel your whole stomach twisting, and he'd done something, energy, to one of your centres. Little things like that, I would know, and I would get the message.

'He sometimes was very angry. When Rasha had that sort of breakdown, and I had to leave her and go back to Devon, because I was only there for the week and I had to get back to my children and things, he rang me in Devon—and he absolutely bollocked me. "How dare you just disappear off to Devon? Why didn't you look after her children? Why didn't you do this? Why didn't you do that?" I was trembling with fear and guilt that I'd upset him and done something wrong.

'He would do things like that, and it would bring out a fear that I'd had as a child for my mother and for other things. I was in trouble, I was expelled from school, and he brought out that rebellious side in me.'

Farida recalls, 'If you were female he'd hurt you in a different way. He'd make you feel awkward, or embarrassed. So I didn't get screamed at. I couldn't have taken it. I would have been in tears—No, I did! It was different once we were in the garden in Australia. I remember being severely told off about something I did wrong around his roses; and I was so offended. I felt so hurt to be yelled at! "Why didn't he tell me nicely?" So now I know what it feels like. I really felt hurt for ages. Weird.'

We teach you how to observe your reactions, and how to feel the force of the energy as well as the quality of the emotion or instinct that has swept you away.

It will soon become obvious, if it's not obvious already, that you can miss the message, and miss it more than once. But not for ever: because the Sheikh was untiring in his work of delivering it, time after time if necessary, and in a seemingly effortless variety of ways, until the payload found its target and the impact could not be evaded.

Although our visits to Turkey were an exercise in sticking together, moving quickly, and being alert for the changing situation, Masoud was as elusive as ever. On the second trip the Sheikh was constantly calling for him. 'Where's Masoud? Go and fetch him. I want him next to me!' Masoud would always be dodging off to one side or lagging on a quest of his own.

Finally the group arrived at Istanbul airport for the flight home. The Sheikh called for Masoud. He was in a far corner of the terminal, buying one of those tasty bread shapes covered in sesame seeds—a Turkish pretzel. When he returned, the Sheikh laid into him vehemently in front of the group, excoriating him in full detail at last for his waywardness and lack of focus: 'Whenever I want you for something, you're off eating a pretzel!'

Back in London everyone still talked about this tirade, and no doubt Masoud himself was still smarting.

By the time the group returned to Turkey some time later, Ahmed was living with Masoud. He went on the trip while Masoud stayed at home. One day on Istanbul's eastern shore we passed a pastry shop in whose window were little pretzels, this time sweet ones. 'Go in and get one of those, Ahmed,' said the Sheikh, 'and when you get home, give it to Masoud.'

Ahmed bought one and carried it with him for the rest of the trip. Back home he exchanged greetings with Masoud and Munira, got the crumbling pretzel out of his luggage and handed it to Masoud: 'The Sheikh asked me to give you this.'

Masoud opened it and looked at it with his characteristic slightly blank expression—but he got the message. Giant swathes of his life and character were baked into that little pastry. He said later, 'I felt hammered all over again.'

From the conduct of several of his pupils the Sheikh selected a scene, unique to each one, that he would replay again and again to them and others, thereby flooding a blind spot with horrifying light (*Look: there's your nafs!*).

He would remind Aziza of the time he had arrived at her workplace to meet her and heard her say, or knew that she'd said, to her boss, 'Oh, he's here again! I wish the old man wouldn't keep pestering me and turning up like this.' He had only to mention the boss's name, Sandor, to call forth bitter denials; but in reply he would often invoke Francesca da Rimini.

You can only teach by the method applicable to each pupil.

In 1980 or so the Sheikh said he wanted to raise his public profile and attract more pupils. Ahmed began seeking coverage in the national media with what he calls blind eagerness driven by excessive faith in his own ability.

'In fact I had little clue what I was doing, and my smattering of knowledge about the media was underpinned only by a vast naivety,' he says. 'Often you get two warnings. First I gave a pathetic interview on BBC radio. Then I invited Stephen Pile from *The Sunday Times*, after I had talked up his writing prowess to the Sheikh, and he did a nasty sarcastic little piece. "How do you think I feel, being guyed like this?" the Sheikh asked me.

'While I was doing a phone interview with the Scottish *Sunday Record*, the Sheikh frowned at me as he went past in the hallway, and I should have taken the hint. I had no idea of how carefully you should maintain your guard against a reporter like that. Someone came to take a picture, in which the Sheikh wore his robes and posed with some of the women. During the week or so in which we were waiting for the story to appear, I mentioned the interview to the Sheikh, probably looking for reassurance. His only response was to quote from the *Rubaiyat*:

> The moving finger writes; and, having writ,
> Moves on: nor all thy piety nor wit
> Shall lure it back to cancel half a line.

'On Sunday morning I went down to Shoreditch, the nearest place you could get that particular paper, and returned feeling sick. He hadn't come up for breakfast yet, but I could see as well as the others what a disaster I had created. The headline made reference to 'JOHN'S SEXY SECT' and the story was a parody of the truth, in which the Sheikh fleeced his pupils and surrounded himself with a harem of dancing girls. It was horrible.

'When I showed it to him his first words were, "This is you!" He held me entirely responsible and made it clear that the story was a reflection of myself. I could feel the scorn of the others, too. The same day he sacked me as secretary of the group, and I was excluded from various meetings. It was searing and humiliating.' Eight or nine years later the Sheikh was still referring to it.

As he explained, people who have been with Sufis for some time quickly grasp certain psychological points they could never have grasped when they first arrived. But he said it was necessary to touch on a point in order to arouse the emotional effect. In the first instance, 'we require to immerse a person in a total situation.' At a later stage allusions were usually quite sufficient to set them meditating on that point—although, as he put it, some people had to be thrown in the bath again and again.

Ahmed had the dancing girls. Aziza had her boss Sandor. Masoud had the pretzel. Each stood for a certain character trait. To this day Sakina has a cartoon that the Sheikh cut out from *Punch* magazine and gave her in London.

'It shows the creatures of the Zodiac, both human and animal,' she says, 'including a very pregnant and slightly defiant Virgo standing facing all the others, who stare at her in angry judgment while the Aquarian water-carrier voices what all are thinking: "So much for Virgo!"

'The Sheikh (an Aquarian) made no comment at the time, but Virgo is my star sign. He had spoken of the virginal quality as a kind of psychological untouchability, not literal virginity. However, the visible evidence of Virgo's unapproved activity was prophetic, although I never literally went that far. It was not long afterwards that I disobeyed the Sheikh's explicit instruction not to travel together with a male pupil who was going to Australia at the same time. I was nervous of the long journey alone and I could see no harm in having company. In San Francisco, where we changed planes, he hired a car and we left the airport for a joyride.

'On our return things started to go wrong. The next airline rejected my overweight luggage and I had to go through an embarrassing and expensive re-packing exercise in the terminal. When we got to Australia the Sheikh initially said little, but my travel companion left the group completely soon afterwards, and it took the Sheikh to point out to me that my behaviour had first led him to assume I was offering him a relationship, and had then left him severely disappointed.'

Othman's case was different again, for his passion was 'alternative' medicine and he has devoted much of his life to it. After the Sheikh's passing he opened his own practice and said he was abandoning Sufism and Islam. Even before that, his hard and conscientious work as manager of the farm had been tainted with the belief that he knew better.

In Istanbul we were participating in *dhikr* with Turkish Sufis when someone complained of an ailment, maybe a headache. Othman produced some little white homeopathic pills which the seated dervishes furtively passed from hand to hand towards the sufferer. Either they were passed to the Sheikh himself, or he saw what was happening. He was highly displeased and later pointed out how much trouble could have ensued, Turkey being then under a military government and notoriously tough on illegal drugs.

Othman's keenness to promote his obsession could have jeopardised everyone's safety. Yet although the Sheikh would often pointedly recount the incident when Othman was mentioned, all Othman himself said when it was brought up was, 'I don't know what all that was about!'

The incident that triggered Ahmed's expulsion from the *zawiya* sounds banal indeed, but its consequence makes perfect sense. The Sheikh asked him to hang an ornamental plate on the wall. He used a modern screw instead of the old style the Sheikh much preferred, and it was visible. In vain did Ahmed protest that he'd chosen it because it would hold better. 'I knew he hated them, and a pupil with any flexibility or good sense would have done the opposite.'

Everything is as important as every other thing, and that's the way the universe works.

'It was a question of feeling. If I couldn't choose the right screw, how could I get any further?'

A question of feeling, indeed. 'If there were rules, the Prophet or Abu Bakr [Muhammad's immediate successor, the first *khalifa* or deputy] would have laid them down centuries ago,' the Sheikh declared.

Another test was set and failed when Aziza returned home from a visit to her family in Paris one evening before the visiting pupils had left the *zawiya*. Her trip had been emotionally stormy, but nobody thought to excuse themselves as she described its turbulence to the Sheikh. At last he lost patience and dismissed everyone, railing afterwards at 'cloth-eared donkeys' who had sat there dumbly, without feeling the delicacy of the situation or acting accordingly. Instead they had been complacent in the knowledge that he hadn't yet signalled it was time for them to go.

For sure, most people never wanted to leave. Abdul-Malik, who had dragged his feet on installing the burglar alarm, was visiting in the early evening when it got to 7 o'clock, the usual exit time. 'I got up to leave—thinking to myself that

I didn't want to keep him waiting—but he still sat there, and he looked at me and said, "You kept me waiting for the burglar alarm; you can wait now." And I thought, "If this is the only comeback I ever get, I'm quite happy with it!"'

Thus the carrot sometimes complements the stick, or the bitter sometimes complements the sweet to create another taste, as it did one day when the Sheikh was reading a book that Dain had given him, while Dain himself was pestering him with conversation. Finally the Sheikh rounded on him angrily and said, 'I'm trying to read this really interesting book, and you keep trying to interrupt me.'

Abdul-Malik missed the warning bell another time, even though the alarm itself was his business. The Sheikh told him it was going off unexpectedly, but he didn't offer to fix it. 'After I'd got home he rang me and said, "You were too stupid to get the hint earlier, so now I have to ring you up and tell you to come round."'

Subtlety equally failed on both men late one evening as they heartily accepted the lukewarm offer of a final cup of tea which they had failed to recognise as the departure signal. Accordingly they received a further signal which they could not mistake. The incident echoed the Koran's admonition to those invited to eat at Muhammad's house: 'Linger not for conversation [afterwards]. That, behold, might cause annoyance to the Prophet, and yet he might be shy of asking you to leave; but God is not shy of teaching you what is right.'

A living Koran, as Sakina said: spelling out, among many other things, the law of consequences and the price of heedlessness. On the Sheikh's instructions, Abdul-Malik went to lodge with Khalida. 'Samira was a toddler, and they were in a council flat—very depressing. She was cooking and everything, and I just took advantage in the way kids do. I was unappreciative. After I'd left, the Sheikh got me and Ashraf to do a load of re-decorating for her. "You return the favour! She looked after you and you didn't do the right thing by her."'

In Sakina's words again, 'He could be seemingly very harsh, particularly in leaving people to experience the consequences of their own actions. He would set situations up deliberately which put people to the test. If you failed, it was for real, and although he could be mollified (as he put it) if you succeeded at something else, the failure remained unless you truly understood it and repented of it.'

His word 'mollified' should not be taken to imply the human weakness of irascibility. He used it in an objective way to describe how he operated, as if he were talking about someone else; and it serves to convey in human terms an aspect of the relationship into which the pupil enters.

When Sakina got to Australia the Sheikh put some of the men on to finding her a car. They bought an old Ford Falcon in a local dealer's yard, built like a tank and cheap, and took it back to the *zawiya*. 'When I came to pick the car up I was invited to stay the night. I was lodged in Maymuna's room on the floor, on a lilo with a sheepskin over it and quite comfortable bedding.

'But as the Sheikh told me later, it was a test of what I'd do with the money they'd saved for me on the price. The answer was that I gave none of it to the group, having already spent most of it on replacing household goods I'd left behind in London. Furthermore, I thanked the men for their efforts by giving maybe two of them a jar of honey each.

'When I was invited a second time and put up in the same way, it was noticeable that there was no sheepskin on the bed. In due course the Sheikh told me that I'd shown little appreciation of the first invitation, and had told someone I was just there to pick up the car. I wasn't even aware of my attitude, but he was.

'When Yaqub, living on the farm, at some point earned the Sheikh's anger, the food rations sent to him each week were cut down to the basics—no more jam. That struck me as very like the removal of the sheepskin.'

Even the Sheikh's greeting on one's arrival was not to be taken for granted; instead you would take it to heart. It was a sign of proximity or distance. If it was cold, the problem was at your end; if warm, you were reassured. As Ishaq says, 'It wasn't about him. I could gauge on a scale of one to ten, based on the way he treated me, how well I'd been living in the couple of days or the week since I'd last seen him. If I hadn't been doing my exercises, hadn't been living as well as I should have done, I would get nothing. And I knew that was gonna be a tough night.'

'Yes,' said Abdul-Ghafur Lari, who died in 1506, 'this is not the path of those addicted to comfort. It is the path of the ardent lovers, who play with their lives. . . . For one who suffers no pain, there is no medicine in this hospital.'

In the Sheikh's words again: 'The dark fire of the *nafs* . . . carries you off through your impulses and wants. It has you imprisoned in its grip. The work of the Sheikh is to oppose these unconscious impulsive processes, the forces of the dragon. Your feelings may be anger, surprise, fear, *et cetera*. You are hot with emotion which burns in you. The Sheikh has to apply fire to fire—to burn up these emotions until you have a cold fire. This may not always appear cold to other people. Eventually you become able to sense things in a feeling way: you develop intuition.'

Perhaps a ton of pressure may be required to extract one drop of intuition. Abdul-Malik, for example, was in charge of the sound system for the *sema*.

Once a month the Sheikh himself would attend, and the entire turning ceremony would be performed in costume. The first time this event took place at one particular hall in Kentish Town, the recorded music suddenly went silent halfway through, and the ceremony was ruined.

Even after testing everything, Abdul-Malik could find no apparent reason for the problem, and next month it recurred. Still he could find no cause. A month later, when the music stopped without warning for a third time, the Sheikh said, 'If this happens again, I'm walking out.'

The pressure on Abdul-Malik was intense. No one was responsible but him. He checked everything he could think of. The fourth time came, and the Sheikh himself was turning when the majestic sound of the orchestra once again cut out. In the ensuing silence, 'He didn't literally walk out, but you just felt the energy stop,' recalls Abdul-Malik. 'It was palpable. Bang. It was like he'd turned off the tap.'

Then a very interesting thing happened. Abdul-Malik suddenly knew exactly what the problem was. 'It was so clear. There was no doubt in my mind. It wasn't like I'd worked it out—there was this element of absolute certainty. I realised the building had a volume cut-out, so that if the audio level went above a certain point it automatically cut out the mains. That's why we'd never tested it: it was built into the hall.' He is equally clear that it was only the extreme pressure on him that had resulted in the revelation required.

We are not here to destroy your consciousness, but to expand it. In the alchemist's retort, said the Sheikh, 'there was the liquid which had to be submitted to certain treatment of heat and pressure which brought about change.' *You have to die to the intellect to come to a new way of knowledge—the knowledge of immediacy.*

It was Abdul-Malik again who volunteered when some electrical thing needed repairing in Australia. 'The Sheikh was talking about going to visit the strawberry farm. And it was one of those things where part of me said no, I ought to not go to the strawberry farm, I should stay behind and do this work; but I didn't want to miss out on the trip. So I didn't start on it. And then, just as we were about to go, something happened—and the Sheikh just blew up and said, "No! That's that! I'm not going to the strawberry farm."

'I thought, "If I'd said, 'I don't want to go to the strawberry farm,' and stayed behind, this would all have looked different." D'you know what I'm saying?'

Do you know what he's saying?

'One of the things about being with the Sheikh which you don't come across in the ordinary world,' he adds, ' is the relationship between your own thoughts and what's going on outside you. When you're with him he's a reflection of your own thoughts. That's why these things are of no significance to anybody else, but it's like a knife right into your heart.'

Or in Khalida's words: 'Seemingly ordinary happenings all of a sudden had a deeper meaning to you on a psychological or a psychic level. He could do these double things so skilfully. He once said that a sheikh had to have the skill of a surgeon's knife.'

The message will find its target. After a lifetime during which Malik ibn Dinar of Basra had abstained from fresh dates, he was gripped by a craving for them. He resisted it for several days, but it only got worse. Then one night he heard a voice: 'You must eat some dates and free your *nafs* from bondage.'

His *nafs* shouted with joy. But he told it not to be so hasty. 'You can have some dates—if you fast completely for a week.' The deal was struck. After fasting for seven days Malik went to the market and bought dates. But just as he was about to enter the mosque with them, a little boy shouted, 'Father! A Jew is going into the mosque to eat some dates!'

'What's a Jew doing in the mosque?' his father exclaimed, and ran over. Recognising the saint, he knelt and said, 'Forgive me, sir. In our neighbourhood we're always fasting, but our children see the Jews eating, so they think everyone who eats anything by day must be a Jew.'

Nevertheless, in the words of those who recorded the incident, fire consumed Malik ibn Dinar, for he realised that the child had been inspired to say what he'd said. 'Set your mind at ease,' he replied. 'That was the tongue of the Unknown.' And he never ate dates again until his death in 748 AD.

More than 1200 years later, one day on the second Turkey trip, Abdul-Malik got very hungry. When someone said, 'There's a pizza shop across the road,' he went in with two others. 'As soon as I got there I thought, "This is the wrong thing. I shouldn't be doing this." But I ordered a kebab.

'We waited what I thought was hours, and finally the bloke comes back. "I had the kebab all ready," he said, "and I dropped it. This was Allah Almighty's doing."'

So that message, too, found its mark. And although when the trio got back to the hotel nothing had changed and everyone was still sitting there, Abdul-Malik felt as if they'd been away for an age. Afterwards on the bus the Sheikh asked, 'Who was it that went and got a kebab?' On being told, he called the other two over and said, 'You know, I'm putting you on short rations here, and then you go and do that!'

'I thought, "I'm gonna be next," says Abdul-Malik. 'But he stopped there.'

As Sakina says, 'His mercy was greater than his justice.' In Australia she herself got into an argument with the Sheikh about needing special consideration because she had to have a car for work. 'It led me to answer back when he criticised me over it,' she says. 'He was furious, and he said, "I withdraw the *barakat* from you."

'I was standing up at the back of the room where he received us, and I felt something peel off from round me and fall down to my ankles. I think I just went home—but I was in shock and wondering if I was going to die. I didn't know what to do. So I did nothing different. I kept going round to the *zawiya* for meals in the evenings (as I was still doing at that stage), helping wash up and so on, and gardening every weekend. I felt like an outcast separated from the others, although nobody said any more to me.

'This must have continued for weeks, until one day as we left I noticed that the Sheikh included me in his farewell, *'Salaam alaikum wa rahmatullah wa barakatuhu'* ('Peace be upon you, and God's compassion and blessing'). Although he never said so in any direct way, I realised I must have been restored to his blessing, and I was very relieved.'

In Dalston, when the time came for everyone to leave, the Sheikh would always get up, go out into the hall and stand by the front door to bid them goodbye, one by one, with an embrace and those same words. In this he was following the *sunnah*. 'You could have had the shit hammered out of you,' says Muktar. 'You could have been through all that, and then on the way out he would embrace you, and you'd go, "What happened?!" It was a tremendous thing that he'd be prepared to do that.

'It's like there's two worlds. There might have just been some terrible conflict in the *zawiya*, but where he's at, it's actually not happening. He's still beaming at you, giving you a hug and loving you. I used to watch on the way out, and I saw him do it to people he'd been giving the shit to. They'd go up, and—It's as if it hadn't happened; or it wasn't the core of what was happening.'

One day in London the Sheikh dismissed Abdul-Malik with the words, 'F--- off out of it!' 'And then' says Abdul-Malik, 'there was a whole load of blankety-blanks. "Get out, you're not worth—You're a f---ing useless—I don't want to see you again." He was bringing up a number of things I'd done, and I was thinking, "I hope he doesn't mention such-and-such"—and he didn't. It was like the Day of Judgment: Allah will call us to account for actions we've done, and He may omit others. It's in His power. Anyway, I was doing a job there; and I stood and thought, "Well, I've got to come back to finish it." So I said to him, "When d'you want me to come back and finish the electrical work?"

'He said, "Oh, yes, yes. Come tomorrow. Come for about 11; you can join us for breakfast."'

Ahmed likewise outlines something he began to discern after four or five years. 'We were in Turkey, and because I could speak crude German, I had the job of conveying to the coach driver the Sheikh's displeasure when he missed a turning or arrived late. Although he did not understand all that was said, and I could only manage to interpret so much of it, he would grow sullen and I could see his mood darken. Nevertheless, each morning on pulling up at the hotel he would still alight from the coach and greet me by name with Turkish salaams as if nothing had happened. When I commented on that ability to wipe the slate clean, the Sheikh replied, "You have learned the same thing in the *zawiya*."'

His teaching went much further, however, because he taught the ability not to get offended in the first place. He said that in the process of being led to a knowledge of reality 'you have to realise that people's criticisms must have no effect on you. Hurts in everyday life as a result of slights and other encounters [should have] no emotional effect at all upon your consciousness.'

He condemned the bearing of grudges, such as Ahmed used to bear for Naima after she would attack him around the table. In such skirmishes Ahmed was always the loser, for the Sheikh's casting vote was never in his favour; but in any case, to try to win is to defend what doesn't exist—*the fundamental illusion that we possess something that is our self.*

'Mind is like a mirror reflecting all we have seen and experienced. The more we dwell on certain aspects of our experience or identifications, the more these facets are mirrored in our minds and uppermost in our thoughts. In fact they take over the control of our minds and we are in the grip of these patterns, passions and identifications. They are "ourselves", and we have been ousted from our kingdom.'

At that primitive, ordinary stage, he often explained, 'All your feelings are in your ego.' Such feelings are to be contrasted sharply, even scornfully, with the true feeling he endeavoured to develop in his pupils. And when he said he was teaching people to feel, he was not implying vagueness. He spoke of 'a feeling relationship which enables the right thing to be done at the right time' and added that it was lacking in modern people, whether Muslims boasting about their adherence to Islam or secularists boasting about the 'dialectical materialism' of Karl Marx (which was a little more popular when he spoke than it is now).

'Feeling is not simple: it's a highly complicated process. It plays its own tune—a different tune in accordance with each situation,' he explained, and cited the painted figure from the Tomb of the Leopard. 'Hermes, with double pipe and flowing cloak, represents this ability to go out and play the tune of the moment, as life is played. You hear it in your ear and respond. The microcosm is constantly at one with the macrocosm.'

We had all heard the Sheikh tell us, especially when travelling, 'You must be like a flock of birds.' The flock changes course in unison because each picks up what all the others are doing. Birds that don't learn the way of the flock may be stranded in the wrong hemisphere. When we set off at the invitation of the man in the brown suit that morning to visit the tombs of saints and other places, the Sheikh warned, 'Khidr's with us today: be especially vigilant and aware!' Even so, that was the day on which Walid hung back from the flock for as long as it took to buy the string of beads, and therefore missed everything that followed.

As you watch the Sheikh cajole, berate or just abandon stragglers like Walid, you may quiver at what you feel is the injustice of it—and your reaction will be exactly that of Moses, who berated Khidr for scuttling a ship, only to have it explained to him that the ship had thereby been saved from seizure by a tyrant. *People who judge by outward appearances are lost in a world of dreams and illusions. They can see the surface of a thing but never attain to its reality*—and in the Sheikh's words, 'Reality is beyond morality.'

Rumi himself wrote, 'When the sheikh has accepted you, take heed and surrender yourself to him: go, like Moses, under the authority of Khidr. Though he stave in the boat, do not speak a word.'

The paradoxes, inconsistencies, injustices and irrationalities can only be seen from the human standpoint.

'But then again,' says Zainab, 'completely the opposite would happen, where he would stop for someone because of a reason. And that's Sufism, isn't it? There's never a rule. And it was always the method of no method: "I teach the method of no method."'

No intellectual knowledge from your background can help you understand the processes of Sufism. You have to put yourself in the hands of the Sheikh and submit completely.

He could squeeze a particular pressure point, in the group or an individual, for weeks or mere seconds—yet AB recalls him sitting on the stairs on the phone for ages, counselling a pupil whose brother had committed suicide. So one gradually learned not to dwell on the lows or even the highs, but to try to follow a middle path.

'All that stuff in the garden,' says Farida, 'where we had to get up jolly early, no matter if you were tired, and work from daylight to dusk, and drag these heavy bags and filth whether it's rain or shine—it actually makes you very strong. It made you different. So now I don't mind the rain on my face. I think it's lovely.'

The Sheikh explained: 'We give you things to do which you don't like, and we break your heart. This is why the Sufi way is hard; but it's genuine, and it will transform you. Cultists go elsewhere. Those who see the value stay, and we burn them.

'Gold is produced through great heat. This inner heat is produced as a result of our exercises. *Tibetan adepts melted snow, and my people will tell you I can burn them like the sun.* Until you are burnt absolutely and completely you can't come through to the third stage, where you're cool and detached and nothing matters.

'Jesus said, "The house of mourning is better than the house of feasting." When you're giving way to your wants you're not getting anywhere, because they grip you like steel.'

Walid comments: 'If you could take it, then something was happening. He wasn't just beating up on someone to show off. It was like you were the bit of metal with the gold and the rubbish in, and the blows were coming down to get rid of all the rubbish.

'It's a very rare thing. In *The Pilgrim's Progress*,[26] when he gets through the Slough of Despond, there's a little wicket gate that looks almost natural, lost in the undergrowth. It isn't a big, grand wrought-iron ornamental thing, and people dismiss it—"This can't be the way!"—because it's so humble. But that's the way forward.'

'In Islam,' said the Sheikh, 'we talk of interrogative processes at death. One finds what one's real motives were, whether self-orientated or heaven-orientated. These attitudes and habit patterns go very deeply and have a meaningful impact on our lives and the hereafter. Now, hate or love or any other feeling is coming from you as the source, and it is easy to go to the source at the moment that you are angry or in love or in hate, because you are hot. It is easy to move inward, that is. When you reach a cool point within you, you will suddenly realise a different dimension, a different world opening before you.

---

26 The Sheikh considered John Bunyan's work a psychological rather than a religious one, and sometimes read from it at his lectures.

'Hot leads to cold, cold leads to hot. Most people project their feelings outwards on to somebody or something, and the whole of them is centred on that object or situation or person. They don't travel inwards. It is quite important in the early stages to become observer and observed. The average person is carried away by their own emotions or instinctual drives.

'Now you may say that when I ask people not to act out their emotions as modern psychologists encourage them to do, but to stay with the emotion, I am asking them to suppress emotion. Expressing or suppressing—either way, your thoughts are still centred on the other object, person or situation. They are projected outward.

'The whole point of my teaching is that being centred and going inward takes you to the source of both expression and suppression: that is, your self. When you know this, you cease to project it. Doing exercises, people encounter emotions not resulting from external stimulation: for example, sadness and then listlessness. You are the source of these feelings. The emphasis here is on knowing where the emotion arises. You have to move to the centre, the source from which anger or love, *et cetera*, all arise. Suppression is not a move to the centre, but a struggle not to express.

'When you are concerned about the energy of anger that has come to the surface, and struggle with it, your thoughts are still with the outer situation; but you are the cause of these emotions. They are contaminations of your energy. Forget the outer completely and just look at the energy of love, hate or anger arising deep down within yourself. Find the source, and just do *dhikr Allah*: remember.

'With anger, just use it as a path, going deep down into it to find out where it has arisen. When doing *dhikr* your mind will be in a receptive state, and in that moment you will find the source. Suppression doesn't find the source—it just struggles with energy that has come up, and sooner or later you will express it: for example, when you find someone weaker than you. You feel tense, heavy and ill at ease until you express it.'

Use the mood as a path as you go deeper down within yourself, changing one word for another. The opposite of hate is love. 'If you concentrate on the *dhikr* you are able to defuse the anger, which is different from struggling with it. Pause your feelings and change from one mood to another. These emotional feelings and instinctual drives are the barriers to a more harmonious relationship with the universe around.

'This is why we give basic techniques. If carried out as an inner discipline, slowly they make changes in the habit patterns, which if left in their chaotic state only enhance the strength of our ego, so that we face towards hell instead of heaven. These patterns are ingrained deeply on our soul. A soul is just the result of our attitudes and habit patterns. We came with something not contaminated, but once it becomes contaminated we judge things in terms of ourselves all the time.

'When we begin feeling, we dimly sense the unity which pervades the cosmos, and the feeling is endorsed more and more as we develop more. All the created forms, the projections from ourselves and collective projections held within the universe, form a framework—a heaven or hell where people of similar disposition are chained by their own identifications.

'*Reality is beyond all the heavens and all the hells; the complete abnegation of self.* A realisation that the true surviving portion is a drop from the divine ocean, not connected with our ego or personality. *You can merge with the divine ocean and time and space far away. You can see clearly for ever and ever: no past, no present, only the now*—because there is a depth of seeing in a way that blinkered intellectual or emotional or instinctual vision can never know.

'Intuition is the faculty contaminated by all the others, and its screened pictures are therefore completely distorted.' Instead, *you must encounter scenes as an observer, with no reaction and no conclusion drawn. The average person is carried away by their own emotions or instinctual drives.*

Enter Kalman Dede,[27] your average guy: a Turkish Everyman who stars in one of the stories which our Sheikh cherished and retold after learning them from Sheikh Muzaffer Ozak and his group on our visits. A dreadful epidemic was scourging the city of Istanbul—one of several waves of bubonic plague that invaded in the sixteenth century. At one time in the year 1567, 3000 corpses were removed from the city each day. On this particular occasion the citizens had gathered in the great mosque of Ayasofya to beseech Allah Almighty for deliverance, and the enormous prayer hall was so jammed that it was almost impossible to move at all, let alone enter or leave.

Very near the front of the congregation, Kalman Dede felt with horror a stirring in his guts. Perhaps it was the first sign of the plague itself; in any case, the sudden urge to relieve himself was all but unstoppable. Desperately he glanced around. He was many yards from any possible exit, and a solid mass of worshippers surrounded him completely. He could not take a single step—and yet he had to go.

Focusing on the man next to him, he saw something odd. His gaze was drawn into the stranger's sleeve. As he looked, the mouth of the sleeve grew

---

27 Pronounced roughly 'Deddy'.

bigger: and suddenly he could see, right there in the garment, a passage large enough for him to enter. He needed no further prompting, and dived in.

In a blink he found himself in the open air—in a park on the other side of the Bosphorus, on the city's Asian shore, where he saw the stranger hurrying away. Forgetting his bowels for the moment, Kalman Dede raced after him, calling out. The stranger took no notice. Speeding up, Kalman Dede caught up with him and grabbed him. 'Who are you?' he cried.

The man ignored him.

'Who are you? Tell me! Who are you? I want to be like you!'

'You can never be like me,' came the reply.

Kalman Dede persisted. But the unrecognised stranger was the great saint Yahya Efendi (1494–1570), whose tomb can be visited right now in the district of Beshiktash.[28] A second time he told Kalman Dede that his wish could not be granted. Still the supplicant did not give up, instead repeating his plea again and again.

'Very well,' said Yahya. 'Follow me.'

The pair arrived at a certain house elsewhere in the city. When they entered, Kalman Dede was overcome with awe, for he found himself in the presence of the Abdal—the Substitutes, part of the hidden hierarchy of saints who govern the world in obedience to God Almighty. They are forty in number, and so called because whenever one dies another is substituted. Furthermore Yahya Efendi himself was the Qutub: the Pole or Axis, God's representative on earth at that particular time.

Kalman Dede was sat down in front of a wall that acted as a screen and told that, no matter what he saw on the screen, he must not interfere. Then three successive scenes were played out before his eyes. None of our people can remember the third, or in which order they appeared, but let's say it was as follows.

First, a mighty naval battle pitted the Turkish fleet against the Christians. The cannon flamed and bodies filled the Bosphorus. Kalman Dede watched, mesmerised, until it became clear that the Sultan's force was flagging. Unable to contain his patriotism, he cheered them on—and then, when his countrymen suffered still greater losses, he leapt up and hurled himself at the wall in an attempt to enter the battle and reverse its course.

The scene disappeared, and he was told that he had failed the first test.

There then appeared a young couple in the open air, holding hands, embracing and exchanging soft endearments while a lion stalked them unseen.

---

28 The Sheikh referred to him as the Lord Yahya, a title also applied to the prophet John the Baptist.

It stole ever closer as Kalman Dede watched, appalled but still silent. It made ready to spring: and again he leapt at the screen, this time yelling at the lovers to run and save themselves, and meaning to wrestle the lion to the ground.

Thus he failed the second test; and he went on to fail the third in exactly the same manner. It was all over. Having wanted (as our Sheikh said) the ego trip of rescuing those who suffer, and having demonstrated that his impulses were in charge, he was shown out of the house and sent on his way.

Although the judgment had been passed on him, he thought he was still being tested. Many times he returned to the neighbourhood to look for the house: but always to no avail. As long as he lived, he could never find it again.

Yet as long as he lived, too, Kalman Dede never wanted for anything. It was ordained that he would be fed, clothed and housed in comfort until his death.

Occasionally the Sheikh would cite this story for teaching purposes, just as he would say chillingly that he would put pupils who could not learn out to grass, like horses, there to graze in contented unawareness of their situation even though their Sheikh was still in full view.

I will take you as far as you want to go—but you will all get off at your own station, and you will decide yourself which one it is.

Kalman Dede had followed in the footsteps of Moses, blowing his chance in triplicate just as Moses had done after likewise begging for companionship with Khidr. Sakina became only one among many who have repeated the mistake when she told the two pupils who were looking after the farm that the Sheikh hated courgettes (zucchinis). So he did; but they had been told to grow them, along with a beautiful array of other produce, because they were a good way to feed the pupils in town. The couple became concerned needlessly, because it had not been for her to say.

To quote the Sheikh again: 'In all alchemical literature the alchemists are depicted as in their laboratory watching an experiment: drawing no conclusions, not attached to the processes comprising that experiment. This is most important: there must be consciousness and awareness without identification. It is through identification with objects, humans and experience that we forge the links which shackle us in our minds to the person or object, and we cannot see clearly. Our perceptive ability is distorted.'

You can only be cured by experience of a different kind. Discussing alchemy once, the Sheikh placed his hand on his breast and declared, 'The only laboratory is here!' There was no doubt about who was conducting the experiment, and less mystery about the methods than one might imagine. 'We *tell* you what we're doing!' he said. Many of his explanations are quoted in this book; and for example he told Khalil, 'The Catholics use guilt; I use humiliation—it's more complete: humiliation and bewilderment.'

But despite that, he said with equal emphasis, 'You don't know what we're doing!'

The Sheikh had asked Dain to buy a car on his behalf. The commission did not go smoothly, and he left the group soon afterwards. One evening as the episode was still unfolding, the phone rang in the hall of the *zawiya*. Yaqub answered it, and there followed a long-distance conversation in which Yaqub, as go-between, conveyed ever-sharper comments from the Sheikh followed by Dain's ever-more-bewildered responses. Then Yaqub re-entered once more.

'Dain says, "What's going on?"'

'Tell him he's in the cauldron, and he'll either come out lead or gold,' replied the Sheikh.

Such an explicit answer in real time was rare indeed. But he plainly declared, 'We make an utter ruin of you,' and he left no doubt about the completeness of the transmutation he was trying to bring about. From his frequent telling, we knew by heart the story of how the ninth-century Sufi Abu Yazid (Bayazid) al-Bistami, another of his spiritual ancestors, had been sweeping the forecourt of a mosque when someone came up to him and asked, 'Where is Bayazid?'

'He went away twenty-five years ago,' replied the saint, 'and I hope to God he never comes back.'

The process is carefully calculated. 'For a long time,' Ahmed says, 'I could see that the Sheikh was withholding his full fire from me, instead criticising me only by implication when another pupil would have copped a faceful. At a certain point, that changed.' The Sheikh explained that too. 'Sometimes I have to build people up before I can knock them down.'

Yet even from the very beginning, like pans of water on a slow heat, those who find themselves in the kitchen are likely to feel an unaccustomed turbulence. 'We unsettle people,' said the Sheikh. 'We have our little ways.'

You'll start trying to figure out what's going on. Why didn't I get the sheepskin this time? Or is nothing going on? But why did he give me that Virgo cartoon? And should I be going to the strawberry farm—or not? The answers may not be clear. 'The whole of life operates analogously,' said the Sheikh. So what develops is a little uncertainty, a little tension, and a little more alertness. You cannot expect that condition to stop. Actually you can expect it to strengthen.

Abdul-Malik had just started driving for Uber, and already a passenger had posted a complaint that he'd started the meter too early. He told that to his stepson-in-law, a fellow-Sufi from a different background who had never met our Sheikh but had been an Uber driver for a long time—who replied that he'd done the same heaps of times with no complaints at all, and commented: 'Sheikh Abdullah's pupils certainly get put under a lot more pressure!'

That word again.

'When I moved into the *zawiya* I brought a pressure cooker,' says AB, 'because my flatmate and I would cook up stew and make it last four days or whatever. It was my pride and joy. I asked the Sheikh if the household had any use for it.

'"Fantastic! Ladies, Abdul-Barr's presenting this pressure cooker!" and I thought, "Oh, great, they'll like the old pressure cooker."

'Then he said, "And only Abdul-Barr's allowed to use it."

'So I'd be in the loft or on the roof or something, and they'd go, "Abdul-Barr, you've got to come down and release the pressure cooker!" Oh God. So I'd climb down from wherever I was and come and unscrew the thing. And he'd say, "Only Abdul-Barr! It's very dangerous, the pressure cooker. It could blow up."

'So I remember thinking: "It's gotta be one of them, surely. It's gotta be one of them lessons." But then I thought, "Was I really arrogant about the pressure cooker? I don't *think* I was."'

AB also relates that he used to bring in the afternoon paper to the Sheikh each day. 'I used to finish work early, come in with the *Evening Standard*, tap on the door and say, "There it is, Sheikh Abdullah," and if he wasn't there I'd just put it on the table. I thought the Sufi way, or the *murid*'s way, was to be like a quiet ghost, unobtrusive.' But one day after he'd quietly shut the front door, sneaked in and furtively opened the other door, there he was with Aziza having what was very obviously a private talk. 'Abdul-Barr!!' exclaimed the Sheikh in annoyance.

'But I thought, "I'm sure I'm doing the right thing," and I did it again. This time he was having in a very in-depth conversation with Sakina, and he gave me a right bollocking. "Can you make more noise? Can you just make a noise? Don't slam the door, but just close the door like everyone else closes the door!" When I looked back I thought the bollocking was because I thought I was being so clever.'

During the period in Australia when we ate dinner at the *zawiya*, with the Sheikh eating at around the same time, Ahmed made a work trip that took him to the seaside and brought home a giant crab. 'I gave myself a pat on the back for thinking of it,' he says. 'I presented it to the Sheikh, rightly assuming that the ladies would cook it. When he thanked me, I replied, "I'm looking forward to knowing what it's like."

'The following night we were served beautifully prepared crab, but the Sheikh was out of the room or away, and in any case not having any. I realised my blunder. Next time I saw the Sheikh I mentioned it. He didn't raise his voice, but just said: "You mustn't reserve things for yourself."'

Pupil after pupil; lesson after lesson. In London, Zafira used to organise the trips abroad because she was a travel agent. When the Sheikh was handing out presents at the end of one Turkey trip, she got a colossal string of bright-green plastic prayer beads. 'It was a joke present, and it was massive. Then he said something like, "Zafira, you always want people to thank you, so I'm not going to." And that's lived with me for ever.'

Encouragement is a different thing. Everyone likes it, but when and how do you get it? Abdul-Malik skipped work one day to help with a big job at the *zawiya* to which he had been summoned at short notice. The Sheikh made no comment, but next day, after arriving at the office, Abdul-Malik was greeted with, 'The boss wants to see you!' He thought, 'Oh, shit.' But they had decided to give him a pay rise. They thought he'd been off looking for another job.

At one stage Ahmed spent several weeks doing paperwork for the Sheikh, much of it against a deadline. 'Because I knew what a big deal it was,' he says, 'I made sure I devoted no spare time to anything else except eating and sleeping. I've got to say that that was unusual for me.' Then he answered the phone to Naima one day. 'The Sheikh wants to see you and he says you're to come round to the *zawiya* right this minute,' she announced in her sternest voice.

On arrival he was ushered in, heart racing. 'Sit down,' said the Sheikh, severe and unsmiling. Wordlessly he produced a package and gave it to Ahmed. It was a Harrods box containing a blue-and-white china teapot from Thailand in the shape of an elephant—a thank-you gift which Ahmed treasures to this day. Then they had tea.

In the words of a lecture: 'You must exhaust yourself for your Sheikh.'

Australia was hard. AB and Zaid had to use the little truck—a glorified pick-up—to get hay for the farm from 200 miles away. It took them five trips, taking turns driving all day and all night. 'We were so tired,' AB recalls. 'We were hallucinating. We were seeing things that weren't there. I thought we were driving through a town, and I'm looking at cars parked—but we're not in the town, we're in the middle of nowhere. It was unbelievable.'

Yet there was no other way, for as the Sheikh said, 'If you cannot be obedient, you cannot learn anything. Obedience is attention.'

Farida recalls: 'Even if it wasn't me on the spot, I learnt it from other people—not to be resentful about being ordered to do something. The resentment I've held against my mother for that! A human being doesn't like it: it's human stuff going on, and he made you rise above it.'

When a room in Dalston was re-decorated, Ahmed was sent with orders to buy four of a certain moulded neo-classical motif. He bought a different one he thought was better, the same height but wider. Next time he visited, the Sheikh had him taken upstairs, saying, 'This will be a lesson for *you!*' Sitting side-by-side in two pairs, each atop a pilaster, were the four mouldings he had been asked to buy in the first place. That had been the design, and the wider ones wouldn't have fitted.

We work through very banal things.

Again: the group had arrived in a Turkish restaurant and Abdul-Malik was wiping the Sheikh's table. 'There was a load of stuff spilt, and crumbs, and I sort of brushed them up with my hand. I stood there with my hand full of crumbs, and the Sheikh looked at me and said, "Eat it." I just ate it. Since then I've never had any compunction about eating things that have been on the floor, or been around.'

Muhammad Niffari, a Sufi of Iraq who died in 976 AD, heard a divine voice which told him: 'Do not wait for understanding: to wait to understand My imperative is to disobey the imperative and obey your understanding. Perform the imperative in the instant I make it imperative, and trouble yourself not to understand. Execute without question, and you will be of Me, and I of you. If I bid, and intellect intervenes, banish intellect. If your heart intervenes, dismiss your heart. Go alone, and you will go forward.'[29]

Obedience is attention. The wildness of survival, in which the whole of one's being is attentive to what is going on around.

Moving from the outer suburbs to the Australian countryside, says Sakina, 'he'd been gone maybe even a few weeks by the time we finished cleaning at the old house. We felt we'd worked hard to help out, but he was furious because, instead of doing that, he'd expected us to come and help him with the move to the new one—which we hardly knew was happening.' *I teach the method of no method.* And although for an appointment he would give people ten minutes' grace, once when we were on the bus awaiting stragglers as 9 o'clock approached he said, 'Well, it's 10 past 9. We've waited.' Everyone put their watches forward.

---

[29] The translation is abridged from that of Eric Schroeder in his anthology *Muhammads* [sic] *People.*

In Turkey there was no question of wandering about, shopping and doing what he called 'pissing against every lamppost'. For one thing, wearing a fez and with such a group of followers at hand, he was a natural target for shadowing by the rather obvious agents of the military government, although in the end they gave us no real trouble. The imperative was to stick close to him, for the flock could indeed change its course at a word, and in any case if you were too far off to know what he was saying or doing you were missing much of the point.

As we visited mosques, tombs (*türbe*s), Ottoman sites and classical remains, breakfasted in our hotel at one very long table, strode through the Grand Bazaar in a swift phalanx, sat with other Sufis, or spent the afternoon in a carpet shop, following his example and buying plenty while a pupil stood behind him wielding a huge fan and the delighted shop owner had tea brought for all (or in one case saw to it that we were served tray after tray after huge tray heaped with Turkish pizzas which had all to be eaten under the unbreakable rule of courtesy despite the apparent impossibility of doing so), the spotlight of the Sheikh's attention and commentary was constantly circling.

It fell on some more often than others. From a pupil's diary for 1 April 1983: 'Ahmed gets a double hammering, 1 for talking and 2 for taking us to a lorry drivers' café. I stumble and my ankle swells. I take my sock off in the hotel lounge to show Khalil. The Sheikh hammers me, Khalil and Walid—"all animals".'

On such trips the same mirror he used in the *zawiya* was held up to a larger flock of parrots, just as he would sometimes illustrate a point with reference to an audience member at his lectures. He never named the pupil concerned, but you knew when it was you.

Soraya had had a miscarriage. At the *zawiya* it had been suggested that the group send her flowers in sympathy. 'I'm ashamed now', says Ahmed, 'to say I spoke against it. I argued that people would get fed up with being levied for gifts such as this.'

Into his talk that evening the Sheikh wove bitter criticism of a certain type of person who was cut off from human feeling. 'You grudge—or you believe that others will grudge', he said, the sending of some token of sympathy to a person who has suffered a heavy blow, for which in the fullness of time Allah Almighty in His mercy may give them recompense. 'Such people [as you] are stunted! They have no feelings!'

Afterwards Ahmed went up to him and sheepishly asked if he should take the flowers round himself. Soraya lived halfway across London. The Sheikh dismissed the idea, saying derisively, 'It might be all right if you walked there.'

Ahmed recalls, 'Already he had told me, "One thing that is very marked in you is meanness." When I'd said I was careful with money, he had replied, "It's more than carefulness. You have to give without thought."' He also said you should give with one hand in such a way that the other hand didn't know.

Because Abdul-Barr owned a van he was constantly being asked to help someone out with it. The requests started to become a burden, or perhaps he felt they were diverting him from duties in the *zawiya*. Asking the Sheikh about it, he received in vehement terms the reply: 'Help people. Give them your time, give them of yourself. Because when you're gone, that will remain. That gift of your time and energy will survive your passing.'

The Sheikh gave vastly of himself and his time. Visiting Dalston, Samira was still a little girl with her colouring book, but she recalls, 'I remember the adults around me. I'd been around other adults, and on some level I'd have been well aware of how much "better off" the adults around the Sheikh were, and just how much people relied on him.

'Because to turn up every week and be sitting there, and sometimes obviously people wouldn't talk, and even if they did talk I wouldn't have understood much—I'd just be colouring in. But from a kid's point of view, to see adults do that, you'd make that link: "Holy—! It's obvious that this human being is vital: we need this person so tremendously."'

She felt what she calls a sense of productivity. 'Now as an adult I realise that people were just moving forward; that personal sense of progress. Obviously being around the Sheikh was just supremely constructive for so many people. And there was always something promising about the moment. Not on an intellectual level: "Oh, goody, I'm gonna find such-and-such." Just that productive, positive –' What Mansur calls 'that sense—of a very vibrant moving, rather than moving in circles. Sheikh Abdullah was consistently saying, "Wake up! The step, the step!" You could feel that he was supporting that step.'

For Asiya, 'the other thing was the sense of wellbeing. I didn't remember ever having had this sense of wellbeing, and almost an aura of—it wasn't happiness, it was just wellbeing and a protective feeling.

'I remember the "Allah-Hu" saved me too, because it kept me connected to something bigger than myself. That was the other sense I had when I met him. It was like I'd been let out of a terrible box of my own making. I'd been locked in my own selfishness, self-centredness, and this was like a door letting me out. Although I still had this suffering, all this grief and crying, the "Allah-Hu" connected me, and I could keep bringing myself back to something more solid and real. That saved my life, I would say.'

Every pupil has his or her own experience, and the men follow a different track from the women. It was part of the Sheikh's teaching to impart to women an understanding of masculinity, but if anything he emphasised even more strongly the need for the male to form a relationship with the feminine. 'Modern society is dominated by masculine ways of thinking. Sufism is taught through the feminine mode.'

When visitors were received at the *zawiya* the chairs were given to women first, so in Dalston at least some of the men usually ended up on the floor of the prayer room, behind the Sheikh. 'I would sit in that prayer room, trying to remain attentive,' says Ishaq. 'My behaviour was radically different to my normal day-to-day behaviour—but the Sheikh would say, "Show me someone who's shy and I'll show you someone who's got a big ego." I think I was behaving as if I was shy because the scale and power of my ego was under pressure a little bit there.'

We unsettle people. Yasin is another who regularly visited there, and he cannot disguise the fact that he is unsettled still.

'The men would sit on the floor behind the Sheikh. Weeks could pass and he'd seem oblivious to them. There he'd sit, conducting his chat and home affairs with the women around the table, and we'd just see his profile from the rear with the flames of a fiery red beard protruding left and right. Occasionally he'd seem poised to open up with some mystic knowledge, and the men would crane forward, but almost invariably a lady would offer tea, and through that or some other such innocuous interruption the subject was dropped.

'It's funny to think how such a low-key and benign scenario largely involving ladies serving tea can morph in our imaginations—perhaps, on a bad night, with all the knife-edged apprehension of a war zone. Either we'll be found out as not being quite the right stuff to mix in such demure, rarefied company, or we'll be addressed by the Sheikh and have to present a good account of ourselves, or something will be said that gnaws at some foundation of our ideas. Sometimes we'd have to combat boredom, alienation and a sense of being totally irrelevant. I'd heard him describe himself as "a master of monotony", and it's remarkable how he'd managed to keep a bunch of strong young men disarmed and enthralled in this way.'

The Sheikh counselled: 'People who travel the mystical way have to adapt to thinking and acting in a passive way so there is no aggressive exploitation of the situation. The knowledge and understanding is conveyed passively, not in intellectual terms.'

He alluded to one of the traveller's fears when he remarked, 'All my *murids* think that life is passing them by.' Yasin recalls that he would catch himself thinking something along the lines of, 'Here we are, at the very hearth within the mansion that lies at the end of the royal road—shouldn't it be a bit better than this?' On one occasion the Sheikh caught his thought and turned round, asking: 'So what's your heaven? Beautiful blonde wife? Beautiful blond children? Beautiful house in the Cotswolds?'

'But for us restless, confused young men it was rather like a cruel real-life enactment of the Monty Python sketch where the Spanish Inquisition had rounded up the pagans, witches and apostates and to their horror was meting out the worst of punishments: "Poke them with the soft cushions! Sit them in the comfy chair!"

'For the women, the men were as good as invisible, hidden behind one of those one-way glass windows that detectives use during interrogations, and from there we'd be privy to the most beguiling of revelations. We'd learn of the wonders of pot-pourri-bag production and design—night after night the same discussion in unrivalled exegesis. It seemed the weeks became months, and still it went on.'

The women were indeed sewing beautiful bags to hold pot-pourri made of rose petals from the garden. The work never progressed as a commercial venture, and in the end the samples were offered to pupils.

Sakina bought two: 'Like the design of the bags, the scent in them was devised by the Sheikh, and it was the most stunning rose and other floral perfume.' The promotional line that had been devised was 'A rose from the hand of the Sheikh'.

'Playful, light-hearted' is another phrase Samira uses about him. A photo taken in Dalston shows everyone wearing funny hats: Aziza in rabbit's ears, Yasin in a tea-cosy, and so on—all surrounding the Sheikh, who wears a sparkling grin and a splendid fur hat like an Orthodox Jewish *shtreimel*; goodness knows where it came from. In Australia one year, because the big garden's trees were full of possums and the dogs well knew it, when a birthday was celebrated for Besso (as the Sheikh called his beloved dog Bess) Aziza made up an exotic potion and filled a fine perfume bottle labelled 'Eau de Merde de Possum'[30] which then sat on the mantelpiece for several years.

Suhayla's two daughters were still very small by the time Sheikh passed from the world. 'That playful side of him certainly came out when the girls were there,' she says. 'One December Karima was four years old, and there was Santa everywhere in every shopping mall. She sat on the Sheikh's lap and pulled his whiskers and said, 'You really remind me of Santa Claus.' He laughed and said, "Except for my beard's red!"

30 'Eau de Possum Shit', in case your French is rusty.

'He bought them a scarf each. And when I saw them—no one should know more about my children than a mother, but they were the colours that I'd always dressed them in since they were babies: the blues, the greens with Afifa because she's cooler, she's more gentle, and for Karima vibrant orange and red, hot pink and so forth. "Karima's got a vibrant personality within her," he said.

'No one had even spoken to me about my children in that respect, not even my parents or in-laws. But he was reflecting something about the girls which on one hand I knew, but on the other I didn't really know.'

Some people ponder why Islam, like the other Abrahamic religions of Judaism and Christianity, refers to God in masculine terms. Once again the answer lies not in religious belief but in experience. The Sheikh explained:

'In Islam the active principle is Allah Almighty, containing the passive principle. The way to understand passivity is through the *sunnah* of the Holy Prophet, and in experiential terms the male principle is experienced at first by heat and the female by coolness. Those who follow the *sunnah* emanate this cool quality—the fountain of camphor: coolness of a penetrating kind at the base of the nose when you inhale. It's like going to the mountains where there is fresh, clean forest air and the scent of the resin of pine trees. [This is] the coolness of the Holy Prophet of Islam.'

You have to be cool within. He many times called Sufism 'the science of states'—inner states, or encounters with certain types of inner experience; and of course every relationship begins with an encounter. Sadiq describes an encounter in his diary for 22 June 1979, on a solstice trip in the Quantock Hills.

'As soon as we leave the main road at Combe St Nicholas the trees seem to draw in over us, the colours are more muted and a hush fills the air. We find a clearing in which to park, and the Sheikh is out first. He has something to show us. We all walk down a narrow path to a small village which has an ancient church almost bang in the middle.'

The Sheikh held that many old churches and other monuments had been built by people who still had the natural capacity to feel where currents of natural energy flow through the landscape, and had sited their structures accordingly.

'He takes us inside, where it's cool, and hushes us with a swift glance. We stand there as if sensing the very atmosphere itself. He opens his eyes, beams and asks, "Do you feel anything?"

'The silence grows deeper. The very air seems to be shimmering. As I relax, I feel the energy start to take form. It's like tiny fibrillations in the heart area, then lower in the navel, akin to clusters of power cells warming up. I tell the

Sheikh. "Did you get anything else?" he demands. It's coming to me now: I say, "A coolness around the eyes—a slight ozone effect."

'He breaks into a smile. "That's nearly it! A coolness around the eyes and a whiff of camphor: and when you develop further you'll perceive the sensation of falling rain inside the building. That rain we call the 'rain of camphor', and it's indicative of the harmonious coming-together of male, or positive, and female, or negative, currents that produces this effect at this particular spot."

'We go out and he speaks to a woman in the village. "The children are very quiet here," she replies. "It's sleepy." It's a village you wouldn't want to leave. He shows us how all the surrounds of the church are neat and in order, explaining that the villagers unconsciously respond in kind to the balanced energy.

'We follow him up a long wooded hill. At the top the energy is singing and zinging in the head—but he hasn't finished with us yet. He makes us walk slowly down and feel inside ourselves the changes in the energy currents. I amazingly feel this whole zingy mass move lower, into my heart zone, and become heavier and more negative. Then he asks us to stand under a huge oak and again asks what we feel. "Female you feel in the navel, male in the chest." I get sensations in the wrong areas, but he explains, "If you walk slowly from one area to another you feel the changeover better, and don't get confused."'

For Malika, a solstice journey from London by coach invariably meant that the motion of the vehicle and the effect of the Sheikh's energy would send everyone into a blissful doze. 'Then without warning he would suddenly shout at the driver to stop, and at all of us to exit the coach as fast as possible and run up some hill, double quick. When we arrived back panting and breathless he would command us to do it again with more effort,' she recalls.

Having raised everyone's energy he would ask them to stand and feel a certain spot or area in the landscape or, as in the Quantocks, the alignment of energy inside a church. 'These escapades were hugely enjoyable and at the same time a great experiential teaching in understanding our nerve plexuses, as the Sheikh called them, as well as feeling earth currents as male and female qualities. I still go into old churches and feel the cross of male/female energy the church has often been built on.'

One of the men recalls another solstice. 'We went to somewhere high up, where you get this very positive, driving energy, which I love,' says Abdul-Malik. The Sheikh called it the dragon current. 'He said, "Go down to the stream." We went down through the bushes and sat by the stream. I found my mind wandering, and I really didn't like it. He said, "That's the feminine energy"—and I suddenly realised I had no relationship with it. He was showing me something so obvious. You think, "How come I've never seen this before in my life?" It was so marked. All my life I'd felt those things but never noticed it.

'One trip we were going through a very old church with an overgrown graveyard, and he said, "See if you can find the positive current." We walked around and found this positive current. "You'll find there's a negative current too," he said. "See if you can find where they cross." We found it, and all stood at the spot.

'"Yes," he said. "It's moved." Using his hands, he cleared out a load of undergrowth about fifteen feet away and uncovered an old stone cross. "It's moved from here to there over the years. That's why they put the cross here—not like that monstrosity across the road!" He pointed to a modern village cross which had no relationship to anything. It just highlighted the knowledge that's within us all but had got lost.'

There is no top limit to sensitivity, the Sheikh told a pupil, who paraphrased his description: 'and you can be standing on a road, and you'll see a tree, and you can see it in another way in blossom, and then you can see the fruit, and someone pick it, and back in time—just from the impressions coming off the environment.'

In the Sheikh's own words: 'It's the seeing of the mind. And the dimensions of form are changed: for example, a tree is not just green with brown branches. You see the energy pattern of the tree vibrating as an energy cloud all around it. From the tree itself there are sounds peculiar to that particular tree. The atmosphere is either positive or negative. There is a whole range of colour which can be visible within this additional atmosphere. By means of this atmosphere the tree is signalling to other trees, and frequently is identifying with the atmosphere of certain animals. The tree knows when you can see its atmosphere, and will make signals to you. The tree knows that you are united in a new way, filled with *ishq*, a profound love which permeates the whole of the universe.'

When we visited the Quantock Hills and parts of the Peak District, the Sheikh remarked that fairies could be seen there. On one such trip Malika, who is more sensitive than many, experienced what she calls 'a change of dimension' in a small field the group was standing in. 'I felt very drawn to merging down into the earth. I could feel playful, laughing beings around me inviting me to go with them. When I spoke to the Sheikh about the experience, he admonished me and said, in a grave and urgent way, "You must remain human and not go into the realm of the dwellers in the earth. The fairies will take you and keep you in their world." He said the field we had been in was a portal through which the lower world was easily accessible.

'He then proceeded to make many jokes about my behaviour, and didn't stop until he had thoroughly marked me with the lesson, as was always his way. He showed me that to be fey with energy is not the right way. One must always keep integrity.'

Karima remembers him telling her and her older sister, when they were little, that they would be told that fairies didn't exist, but must remember that they did. Abdul-Barr is another witness to the truth of what he said.

'We were on a solstice trip near Glastonbury. We were in tents. In the middle of the night I had to go for a pee, although it was raining, and I thought I'd better go quite a way into the wood because I didn't want to bump into anyone.

'By the time I got there it had stopped raining. I'd reached a suitable tree when I looked round and went, "What the – !"

'I looked square on, and I can still remember to this day: all sitting on their haunches, sitting on the ground, were about seven or eight figures. All men with bony heads: you could see the shapes of their heads and their bodies. You could see their arms round like that'—wrapped round their knees. 'All sitting on the ground looking at me; and if they'd stood up they would have been at least seven foot tall—absolutely huge, muscular thin men; I can still see 'em.

'I looked at 'em. I thought, "Oh my God!" and I ran back to the tent.

'When I told the Sheikh, he said, "What did they look like?" and I described them. "Yes," he goes, "they were wood fairies."

'I said, "Pardon my ignorance, but aren't wood fairies supposed to be about two and a half inches tall, not seven foot tall?"

'"No, they can form any shape. And what you should have done is just stood there and spoken to them. They would have spoken to you."

'I said, "Well –"

'"Yes, I know. You shat yourself and ran off."

'It was unbelievable. You could see seven faces. You couldn't see their eyes, but you could see their heads—they might have had eyes, I didn't stare at them long enough; and all sitting like that—white shapes.

'And if anyone said to me, "Couldn't it have been the moonshine through the trees?" No, it wasn't the moon. You could see seven different shapes and you could see what they were doing; they were sitting like that.'

From the magic lamp in *Aladdin* there issues a genie that will carry out the possessor's every wish; and a genie, of course, is a *jinni*,[31] one of the usually unseen beings mentioned in the Koran along with humans.

As a matter of avowed policy, the Sheikh very rarely spoke about his own mystical or visionary experiences. He said, 'If you have ecstasies, you don't show them. If you have miseries, you don't show them. That is my teaching.' Yet his silence was not quite complete. He recounted how he had once been meditating when climbing in the Alps and suddenly became wide awake. In front of him, surrounded by an egg shape, was a Nordic *jinni*, with dark-blond hair, very blue and intensely cold eyes, and long earlobes. When the Sheikh smiled and spoke a greeting, six smaller ones appeared.

Another time he recalled how he had struggled to stifle his laughter at a high-level meeting in southern Africa when one or more *jinn* turned up and, unseen by anyone else, started crapping on the heads of the dignitaries round the table.

It can be testing to live in more than one world at the same time.

The towering Naqshbandi master Abdul-Khaliq al-Ghujdawani, who passed from this world in 1179, is one of the most famous of the Khwajagan and another direct spiritual forebear of the Sheikh, who often spoke of him. When Muktar impudently came up with some witticism about him, the Sheikh fixed him a with a baleful stare and simply said, 'Muktar, he's so heavy he would blow you away.'

Abdul-Khaliq listed eight tenets of the Sufi way.[32] The fourth on the list is given as 'Solitude in the crowd' and explained as follows: 'When Khwaja Bahauddin Naqshband [who lived from 1318 until 1389, and gave his name to our order, although he did not found it] was asked, "What is the basic principle of your spiritual path?" he replied, "It is solitude in the crowd, or loneliness in the community. That is, being outwardly with your fellow-creatures, but inwardly with the Lord of Truth." According to [another master], solitude in the crowd means this: "A person should reach the stage where he is

---

31 The Arabic singular is *jinni* and the plural is *jinn*.

32 These can be found in their entirety in *Beads of Dew from the Source of Life*, Muktar Holland's translation of a fifteenth-century Sufi classic by Mawlana Ali ibn Husain Safi, subtitled *Histories of the Khwajagan: The Masters of Wisdom*, from which this short extract is taken. This book is an important document of the Naqshbandi mystical tradition, and Sheikh Abdullah esteemed it highly. It records the lives, experiences and advice of numerous saints—many of whom, like Abdul-Khaliq, form links in his own spiritual pedigree. A similarly important and much longer work from the same translator, the magnificent *Breaths of Divine Intimacy* by the Sufi poet Mawlana Nur ad-Din Abd al-Rahman Jami, has been due for publication for several years.

so constantly and completely absorbed in *dhikr* that he could walk through the most crowded and noisiest place without being able to hear a sound."'

The fact that our own Sheikh had reached exactly that stage was illustrated, for example, by his perfect equanimity when working above his music shop. However, the exhortation to 'solitude in the crowd' further extends to cover the psychological challenge of pursuing Sufism in the midst of an indifferent, scornful or hostile community.

Even as a general principle he encouraged in his pupils the same discretion that permeated his way of life. Generous though he was with his teaching, with genuine help and counsel, and with many kinds of material support, he did not volunteer unnecessary information to us, let alone to others, and we all learned to moderate our questioning. Such discretion is general among Sufis, whether information is being sought or imparted, and the Sheikh's circumspection complements the Prophetic words which underlie his gift to Ahmed of a keyhole saw: 'Part of being a good Muslim is leaving alone what does not concern you.'

Beyond that, however, even a giant multi-ethnic city like London can afford trouble and embarrassment for the dervish who is visible, alone or in a group.

The *dhikr* ceremony that we performed every Tuesday night was led by the Sheikh and lasted for some two hours. At full tilt, the chanting was loud. That was never a problem except when we used a room in a little mews house—actually a converted garage—in up-market Knightsbridge. For a couple of weeks running we began to hear shouts from the flats at the rear. At first it wasn't clear they were meant for us, but on about the third occasion the yelling started as soon as we did: 'Shut up! Stop it!'

The Sheikh continued, but it was not long before the doorbell rang. He arose and went, in full black robe and turban, down to the front door, where stood a constable of the Metropolitan Police in full dark-blue winter coat and helmet. What was going on? the policeman asked.

'We are Sufis of the Naqshbandi Order...' the Sheikh began, and switched to dictation as the policeman took out his notebook and began to write: 'N—A—Q....' The Sheikh dealt with him soberly, and the interview ended with a gentle admonition from the law. We continued the *dhikr* in low voices and began looking for a new venue.

In Australia the tension was greater still, for we would have stuck out even more from our surroundings. Instead we were altogether incognito. The Sheikh did not lead a collective *dhikr* or teach publicly any more. Privately, his teaching was in many ways more intensive than before, for there were no holidays, and no spare time to speak of. Life revolved around work.

Ahmed says, 'I can't be the only one for whom the move to Australia has been the adventure of his or her life. Its challenges have been strangely invigorating. Standing by the veranda during our first summer, the Sheikh assured me, "We have a far better lifestyle here," and he has turned out to be wholly correct. There's no contest with the small, close-packed homes of Hackney and Stoke Newington, the dim winter days and the stifling Tube journeys.

'But it was very difficult at first, especially for those of us in or around the *zawiya*. Our skills were mixed, we had to take what jobs we could get nearby, and life for several of the blokes was a daily round of manual work followed by nights in a caravan parked in the garden.'

On the other side of the garden were the Sheikh's beehives. There's a lot of woodwork in a beehive, and much of it fell to Ahmed. But learning often still took place the hard way. The Sheikh said he needed, say, six new boxes for Friday. We made them, and he opened the hive and installed them with the help of AB. But then he told AB to get (say) four more. AB knew there were none; he returned to the shed, looked in for the sake of form, and took the bad news back to the Sheikh, who was soon berating Ahmed for not having grasped the simple need to be ready for anything. Ahmed had forgotten his advice: *You must be like a wild creature—fully alert to forces around you. You have to be, to survive.*

The Sheikh kept a beautiful flock of white geese in the garden too; but that was only a taster, for soon afterwards he bought the farm. It was almost 600 acres in a beautiful and quite remote spot with mountain views, partly surrounded by forest, and watered by two creeks. He chose it with enormous care and made clear that he saw it as a resource for his pupils in future years. He envisioned a new house there, although it was not built in his lifetime. You can gauge the significance of the project by the fact that he had initially thought of re-naming the property Medina, after the city to which the Prophet emigrated from Mecca with his followers to establish the new religion of Islam unhindered.

Sufi saints without exception affirm that they neither covet paradise nor fear hell, though both of those realms are real. Rather they desire nearness to the God who created the universe and for whom they are filled with that profound love. Nevertheless, the Sheikh remarked, 'Anyone who is close to nature will go to paradise.'

He devoted immense effort to establishing a cattle stud on the farm, which became extremely successful, but that was not the only activity by any means. At various times geese, chickens, turkeys and ducks were bred; there were sheep and a large vegetable garden, fruit trees and raspberry bushes. There were kelpie dogs, two of which were named Evil and Devil—'Evil' rhyming with 'Devil' because that was the way Sheikh Nazim had pronounced it when railing against the 'evils and devils' of the modern world.

A succession of pupils lived in the old weatherboard farmhouse as resident managers, and the rest of the men went there at weekends and on holidays to work, bunking down on the floor. The winters at their coldest and the summers at their hottest were both punishing, and many of the tasks (fencing, rounding up cattle, laying water pipes) were new to us. We got an idea of what it's like to be around livestock, and some became extremely proficient, grooming the finest beasts for agricultural shows and handling them in the show ring.

Surely you would not be wondering what all this has to do with mysticism? *If you've never seen clear soup before, it's not soup—it's water.* Yet it does not take much to identify loyalty, effort, resolution, endurance, adaptability, and the knack of learning without books. It was a further expansion of consciousness. If you or his pupils were still doubtful, the Sheikh gave at least one explicit answer. 'I am trying to give them a feeling for life,' he said.

That life was human as well, for he often repeated that a human being was only a talking animal. Over the years we had got to know each other very well. As we worked more and more closely together and shared various homes, we joked together and annoyed one another. The farm saw all the flare-ups you'd expect among the half-dozen or so men there. 'There will be times when you just want to knock the other person's head off,' the Sheikh had confirmed. 'But that's the way it is in a family.'

Like a blood family, we had been brought together not by friendship but by something else. Although some pupils did become friends, we hadn't chosen one another, and the only sustainable path was just to get along, if possible. Like a blood family, too, we gathered at festival time. Apart from Eid al-Fitr at the end of Ramadan, and some jollity at Christmas (celebrated in the *zawiya* with many of the usual trimmings and a naughty cardboard hanging Santa whose costume parted on the pulling of a tag, to reveal only an extremely long white beard covering what would otherwise have been his plump nudity), it was established custom to celebrate birthdays—in London for those who lived in the house, and in Australia for a larger segment of our smaller group.

During the first weeks in Dalston, Masoud came in one day and was asked where he'd been. At his mother's for his birthday, he replied. The Sheikh growled that he should never mind about his birthday: 'What matters is the day of your death!' Masoud answered a little lamely that he was looking forward to it. We all knew the injunction 'Die before you die' which the Sheikh so often repeated.

Nevertheless, on your birthday you would get your own choice of food, plus a present from the group, given to you by the Sheikh, with a card signed by every available pupil and the Sheikh himself, who alone would write his name in Arabic. In the case of the men, the celebration was part of the normal dinner. In the case of the women, it was done in great style at a special weekend meal, as Malika recalls.

'Each of us made an effort to put on our best finery. Every detail of the table, the gift wrapping and the food was created to the highest standard. As he presided over the event the Sheikh made it a delightful experience every time—for all of us, but especially for the one whose birthday it was. It gave us women the feeling of being loved and honoured, even adored, for a day.'

Sakina says, 'As well as contributing to the group present, the women would give the birthday girl their own presents. Each was checked with the Sheikh beforehand for approval, not always given. It was not necessarily expensive, but it had to suit the receiver, and it could be quite ambitious; clothes were the most highly prized and could be really smart. There were no joke presents. The idea was to express real love and care for each other.' The Sheikh always said that a gift was a reflection of yourself.

'There were jokes about *zawiya*-approved wrapping because, although the presents were always thoughtful and beautifully wrapped, it was no good if they took hours to open,' Sakina says. 'The ladies might each get seven or eight presents, and the Sheikh would get tetchy if it took too long—much as due appreciation had to be shown for each one in turn, and ripping them open was definitely not the form. He would start teasing, "Just rip it!" but one did not take that literally. Recycling the wrappings met with high approval, so they had to be preserved, and we learnt to use plenty of ribbon and bows but not sticky tape. If there was sticky tape it must not be parked on the tablecloth after removal.'

Again: *We work through very banal things.*

Muhammad's Companions are revered (though emphatically not worshipped) in every prayer and in the same breath as the Prophet himself. They are known as the Sahaba. They are not all saints, although the earliest Sufis are among them; rather, the term refers to all those who became Muslims in his lifetime and knew him personally. They started life as the ordinary people of Arabia and beyond, but by the time of his passing they had become infused, in varying degrees according to their natures, with the beautiful character of uprightness, thankfulness, firmness and unselfishness that was part of his legacy to humanity.

More than that, they all possessed the treasure of associating with him at first hand. That association is nothing other than *sohbet*, the word[33] from which *sahaba* comes, and their emulation of his qualities is the pupil's emulation of the sheikh. Such contact with another person enables what the Sheikh called a 'transmission' to take place. That term denotes, at its most sublime, the passing of definite spiritual secrets from the Prophet to one of his Sahaba and thence down the *silsilah* to the latest generation of Sufis. At a lesser intensity it denotes the imparting of personal traits, which if adopted from an ordinary soul are at best mixed and at worst hellish—the curse of a rotting apple causing further putrefaction in the barrel—but which in the case of the Prophet are all-embracingly constructive and indeed mirror the attributes of divinity.

So when the Sheikh told us in so many words, 'You are my Sahaba,' he told us something which even on its own should have re-dedicated us all to the journey ahead. Whether it did so is doubtful, and anyway something we cannot judge. But at the very least it accurately reflected a relationship that is like no other we have found in 'this short sojourn in the school of earthly life'.

When we celebrated his own birthday every year on 28 January, we were celebrating that relationship. We did so even more thoroughly in Australia, where the day fell in summer. In latter years a marquee was pitched on high ground at the farm, always at the same spot. Preparations had begun weeks and sometimes months beforehand. The decorations, flowers and food were intensively planned, but it was not expected that we would spend a lot, so ingenuity was needed. A collection of decorations gradually built up, but every so often a whole new theme would be started. One year the women made brilliant hangings in imitation of the marbles in the Taj Mahal, and the poles were wrapped in ribbons. Ahmed built the decorative surround for a fountain that played in the middle. Even some of the table decorations were hand-embroidered.

When all was ready at about 2 o'clock, the Sheikh would make a ceremonial approach past the assembled pupils as, following tradition, they chanted loudly and repeatedly, 'La ilaha illa'llahu' ('There is no god but God'), concluding with the single sentence, 'Muhammad ar-Rasul Allah' ('Muhammad is the Messenger of God'), in which he joined.

---

33 In Arabic *suhba*. A variant spelling is *sohbat*, as in the name of this series of books.

The feast itself was prepared by the women with enormous care. It would often include at least twenty different dishes, sometimes at least partly Middle Eastern or Turkish, but not always; elaborate French food was also a favourite. The entire celebration lasted for two or three hours including its usual sequel, which was an address by the Sheikh followed by the playing of recordings of much-loved Sufi songs to his replete and drowsy pupils.

One summer the occasion came round after weeks of drought had turned the poor remnants of pasture to a wretched brown straw and racked many of the country people with worry. The longed-for downpour arrived on the birthday morning, and as the celebration proceeded through the afternoon the Sheikh spoke of the unstinting quality of divine mercy while we gazed out of the marquee at sheets and waves of drenching rain that blurred the face of the distant mountain peaks.

Your impressions are your own harvest. To harvest well you have to sow well.

On Christmas Eve 1996 the Sheikh suffered a stroke that paralysed him on one side and deprived him of the power of speech. For almost four years after he had returned from hospital, Naima cared for him day and night, as he had many years earlier predicted she would, with constant help from Khalil. Until then his beard and hair had both been flame-red because of henna (which, like the beard itself, is the *sunnah*). Now the henna was relinquished, and they were soft grey-white.

He is buried on what remains of the farm, which he left to three pupils with instructions that it be used for the promotion of Sufism under the general direction of Ali, who was one of them. Another one died, the remaining two sold most of it, one exchanged her share for money, and Ali has ended up in sole charge of the remnant property, including the grave site. A small building was erected there in the mid-2000s. The family of pupils has scattered, and the Sheikh appointed no successor.

The alchemists are in their laboratory watching an experiment: drawing no conclusions, not attached to the processes comprising that experiment.

They are, in fact, *like the distant stars*. But while you have been reading, you have become our distant cousin. You are like someone attending the Sheikh's lectures for the first time. Never mind us: what will you make of the rest of your life?

Abdul-Ghaffar left the Sheikh in 1980 or 1981, along with his girlfriend Hamida, not long after he had told the TV camera that the framework of Islam gave him the discipline he needed to be free. He remembers Hamida crying, saying how much she loved and missed the Sheikh. What he says he doesn't remember is how he convinced himself it was a good idea to leave.

'In general terms it was because I found the rigours of the Muslim lifestyle difficult, but what that really means is that I was weak, and I was tempted by all the other things: the life of being a twenty-five-year-old young man in London.

'In the thirty years since I whirled off there have been plenty of times when I've wished I hadn't had that experience [of being with the Sheikh]—when I wish I didn't think and feel these things. Because life would have been a lot easier in some ways.

'I wish I hadn't known there was this absolute truth. I wish I hadn't known that I could be a better person if I wanted. I wish I hadn't known that there's the afterlife, and taken those vows of Islam, because I could have just done what everyone else does, and float along and get drunk and –

'For a long time I think I did try to forget. But you can't. Why would you?'

'**WHO ARE YOU?**'
Even the BBC producer interviewing the Sheikh asked him that same all-embracing question before any other.

You will also recall the pupil who looked into the Sheikh's eyes one day as the two sat next to a patterned wall. When he too asked, 'Well, who are you, then?' the answer did not come in words. Instead the wall throbbed with light and the room itself started to vanish.

'Those are pearls that were his eyes', declares Shakespeare's elegy.

All developed Sufis, said the Sheikh, 'are a fragment of reality, a drop in the ocean: but this drop functions in the same way as the mighty ocean of reality out of which the whole universe is composed'.

Rumi exhorted:

> Listen, O drop, give yourself up without regret, and in exchange gain the ocean.
> Listen, O drop, bestow upon yourself this honour, and in the arms of the sea be secure.
> Who indeed should be so fortunate?
> An ocean wooing a drop!
> In God's name, in God's name, sell and buy at once!
> Give a drop, and take this sea full of pearls.

4

BURNT

> And lately, by the tavern door agape,
> Came shining through the dusk an angel shape
> Bearing a vessel on his shoulder; and
> He bid me taste of it; and 't was—the grape!
>
> — *The Rubaiyat of Omar Khayyam*, by Edward FitzGerald

THE GOLDEN ASS is the only Latin novel to have survived intact since ancient times. The Sheikh cited it often in his teaching. Its author Lucius Apuleius told of a passionate, lustful man sharing his own first name who was accidentally turned into a donkey and had to undergo the resulting journey of humiliation and bitterness until his spirits had fallen so low that nothing mattered except, as the Sheikh put it, resurrection to a new level of understanding. 'Winter is over, and summer begins.'

Part of the journey you are on, said the Sheikh, is concerned with thieves and robbers in the mind that destroy your concentration. In other words the hard season of the winter caravan, the psychological leg of this longest of trips, calls for you to grapple with all your instinctive and egocentric processes until the mind can deal with them in peace—to change your habit patterns so that you become centred and your life assumes a new pattern, both disciplined and meaningful, which leads on to what the Sheikh described as a joyful, ecstatic communion with the life around you. At that point the summer caravan sets off, and the spiritual leg of your journey is under way.

Returning home from sessions with the Sheikh, Yasin remembers his younger self as having been infused with 'utter drunken joy'. He says the very route had all the glamour of an enchanted trip to a lover's door—the lover being the beautiful thoughts and feelings that ensued that night. 'The Sheikh's own words seem to apply: "Prayer in its real sense is . . . attuning the inner harp of one's being so that the strings of one's sensitivity soar upwards in this inner song of joy".'

It is true that Yasin there leaps from the journey's early excitements to a glimpse of its final stages, and that all the hard ground in between must nevertheless be traversed. *Many want to step into spiritual experiences and states while still blind and deaf to themselves.* A love affair does not necessarily become a marriage. The Sheikh drew a painstaking distinction between the state of being in love and the permanent condition of love itself. Like many Sufis before him he used the transformations in the human relationship to indicate those on the mystical journey, and like all of them he was clear that ecstasy is an experience and not a destination.

Nonetheless, the inner tuning can begin at the outset, and such glimpses can be caught as it steadily progresses. Asiya recalls that her view of life began to change right away: 'Because, first of all, I had an attitude of gratitude, which I hadn't had before; but that changes your relationship with the world and the universe and your own being, because instead of complaining and thinking you know, you're aware of your own relationship to the universe, which is very small.

'The big change for me was—instead of going around demanding, expecting, and being disappointed that I couldn't have life on my terms—just realising that I had to accept life on *its* terms: on Allah's terms. That was a huge change, because those things are not changes in philosophy, they're changes in experience. You experience things quite differently, and I think this is continued always.

'One of my favourite stories is the one about the fisherman whose boat is damaged in a big storm. The townspeople say, "Oh, how terrible!" and he says, "Is it a blessing? Is it a curse? Only Allah knows." Then two more incidents happen: I think his horse runs away for a time, his son breaks his leg. After that an army comes through. They take all the boats, but not his, because it's been damaged; they take all the horses, but not his, because they can't find it; and they take all the sons, but not his, because he can't walk. That story personifies the big change for me, which is seeing that some things that seem terrible may be not so terrible, because firstly they may have saved you from something much worse, and secondly they're an opportunity.'

You can hear the unmistakable echo of Khidr's lesson for Moses.[34] *The paradoxes, inconsistencies, injustices and irrationalities can only be seen from the human standpoint.* 'When we are united at all levels within ourselves, the constant, ever-changing drive towards balance and harmony within the universe can be understood because everything is apportioned, not in human concepts, but in relation to the ever-changing needs of the universe,' the Sheikh declared.

In time the reassurance may come, as it ultimately did for Hakim after he had arrived in Australia with his wife and brother, having sold up to follow the Sheikh in the knowledge that if he had not done so his life would have had no meaning, only for the three to be taken aback when the Sheikh offered them a series of choices: get a job, start a business, start a different business.

'Wow, this is frightening!' they thought, having expected a pre-determined slot. In confusion they went off and settled interstate, where they thought they could make a living more easily, but as a result they hardly saw the Sheikh from one year to the next. 'I took the wrong decision,' Hakim says now. 'We had a hard time.' Yet much later he received a personal message from the Sheikh, delivered in private by a fellow-pupil: 'He thanks you from the bottom of his heart for what you've done.'

'That was a relief of guilt after many years,' Hakim says. 'I was always in sorrow that I hadn't accepted the offer. I always thought what I did was very wrong to him. I always loved him, and even if I took a bad decision, he was still for me an achieved true and complete human being, and I was nothing. Maybe he saw some value in me. It was a big comfort for me.

'And in the end we did spend a few days with him. Once we were in the car and he was driving. He missed a turning, and then he said, "You know, that's what we all do sometimes—missing the turning." It's clear like yesterday. Brief but powerful. Those little moments, it will last forever.'

If you slip on a banana skin, all you can do is walk on.

'I've realised that you don't make fundamental stuff-ups; you make mistakes, but you learn by it,' reflects Abdul-Malik. 'We all want to learn by our mistakes without making them. When you beat yourself up—"Oh, I shouldn't have done that! Why did I let that happen? How did I get myself into this mess?"—that's really what you're saying. "I want to have learnt by this mistake, but I regret the fact that I've made it." Well, that's not right.'

'If only' begins Satan's work.

---

34 Khidr himself damaged a boat in order to save it, and rebuilt a wall to preserve the treasure beneath it.

'We don't have as much free will as we think. You just say, "This is the will of Allah Almighty, putting me in a situation where I can learn. I've got to look at the situation, accept it, and say, OK, what can I get out of it?" Whatever happens to you is there to teach you. What's important is how you respond to it inwardly.

'I was always an intellectual, probably still am—it's a part of my character—but it doesn't overpower me. There's much more relying on trust, on intuition, on feeling.'

Mansur was lucky enough to get that advice in writing. At the time, he was engaged to a girl in India, and they exchanged letters declaring their love. 'When I went there to get married, she'd suddenly changed: "No, I don't want to marry you"—and she just disappeared. That drove me nuts. If I have an issue I have to clear it up, so I kept insisting, "Why? Why?"'

That was when he wrote to the Sheikh, who once said, 'Mansur is like I was as a young man: filled with a great hunger for reality,' and who now administered a dose of reality. He dictated a reply telling his pupil he was chasing a fantasy. In Mansur's words: 'It's not because of what you've done or not done. It's simple: women have instinct. If that instinct says no, it means no. It's a natural thing. It won't work. Why are you insisting on finding out why? Move on!'

Mansur explains, 'That gave me closure to say, "Ah! It's only that! Now I know how it works, I switch off." And I carried on with my life.'

Two years later when the roles were swapped and the same girl wanted him again, he rebuffed her, telling her it was over and there was no going back. He took stick from his parents for it, but he says he'd understood that paradoxically the Sheikh's advice applied both times, and that once you've grasped the principle it applies across the board.

'Instinct can come at any point and say, "Look, we don't need sense." It has a separate sense. If the instinct says no, the mind can change and play games, but that initial instinct is the truth. You have to stick to it. I'd learned that there isn't logic here, there isn't a process; things can work or not work.

'That opens the whole door of a new world that exists beyond reason. It's the feel, the experience, the moment that gives you that gut feel—and all these things suddenly don't have to fit logic. In fact they defy logic. They will come to you when there is no logic, just that "Yes!"

'It hits a lot of areas. The Sheikh didn't give you a solution, he gave you a principle.' As he said, *I am trying to give you capacity*. 'So accept things as they are, because things work according to certain principles.

'That was one pointer I use in my life. He gave me the other when he wrote in his letter, "Your story is like the story of Joseph. Try to understand that story."' As a born Muslim, Mansur knew the life of the Prophet Joseph, as recounted in the Koran with much of the same detail as in the Bible. Joseph is thrown into a well,[35] sold into slavery, and later put in jail for something he has not done—trying to rape or at least seduce a nobleman's wife, when it fact it was the other way round. Yet ultimately he gains power and success (and the woman concerned),[36] while losing none of his uprightness or fear of God.

'That helped me understand a lot. Don't take it personally, and rather than fighting it, try to see there's a bigger purpose for things that you don't know. It's not necessarily your fault. It's not about you and your fault. It's about something bigger. It's meant to happen this way to learn something.'

Abdul-Malik concedes that intelligent people think about what they've done. 'But to a certain extent the wisdom is in asking the questions, not in looking for the answers. When I'm sitting down with a client—and this is something that's come from that teaching point through to everyday life—I've learnt to trust my gut feeling. I'll say things to people that there's no logical reason why I should say at all, and they'll say, "Funny you should say that, but –."

'I had a woman come in to my hypnotherapy practice with her son, who had dyslexia. We talked, and then I said, "Just sign this form, and read this part here;" and as I gave it to him I added, "It's in a different colour, so you'll have no trouble reading it." Then I thought, "What the hell am I talking about?" But his mother looked at me and said, "Just this afternoon I was at a seminar where they were talking about how dyslexics are often able to read if it's in a different colour."

'I hadn't known that. It had just come to me. In the past those things would have come to me and I'd have said, "Don't be silly," but now I act on things which are absolutely ridiculous. Sometimes you think, "Well, that didn't go anywhere," but often I'm finding I can just get this feeling about which way we should be going, and tease it out. This is very recent, and it's a huge thing. It's a kind of acceptance. You go into this mode where you say, "Every moment Allah Almighty presents me with something new; and it's not good, it's not bad, it just is what it is. What can I learn from it? How can I learn to love it?'

You can ask me a thousand questions, and I can give you a thousand answers. But you cannot penetrate mysticism by learning from books or talking. 'All the time questioners are trying to pin me to the wall,' said the Sheikh, 'and when

---

35 In the Bible, a pit.
36 In Islam she is Zulaika, though unnamed in the Koran. In the Bible she appears as Potiphar's wife.

I've answered them they are not satisfied. But when you've experienced these things in a slow-growing sense, there is a totally different form of knowledge obtained, like the seed growing into a child.'

He explained to Amira: 'On a great deal of Chinese porcelain, and on plates and saucer dishes in particular, during the Ming and Ching periods a dragon is frequently depicted amid clouds, chasing or encountering the precious pearl. This means simply that the instinctive energy flow within the central nervous system has been stimulated (raising *kundalini* in India is depicted as a snake, but in China it is a dragon—in other words, it is a strong, wildly uncontrollable surge of energy of a primeval nature).

'When the surge is felt within both body and mind as a joyful bursting-forth of this energy, the effects are finally registered within the brain, where the round pearl or TV screen of the mind operates as extended vision to enable the intellect to comprehend through imagery what the eternal mind wishes to reveal to that fleeting part of itself which we in our ignorance believe is separate and has a separate identity divorced from the pulsing life around us.

'The vision of the pearl is the realisation of the birth of new experience within ourselves. It denotes that the holy child is now within us, and will overshadow us in its own development to the extent that it engulfs us and transforms us completely in a new life entirely. It is true to say that it can denote, at a lower level of comprehension within us, the desire for a physical child, but this is only nature's way of bringing our attention to the surging flow of energy within us, which can and does in fact engulf us in an act of conception to sow the seed of new life within, so that mind can be born again in a bodily prison . . . to balance mind being given freedom from bodily prisons through the gates of death every hour around us.

'In giving this description of the ancient temple mysteries, such as the Dionysian cult of joy, embodying the growth, birth and death of the holy child within, I would point out that the early Christians understood this in exactly [the same] way. [Official] Christianity, however, in its long history of deception, has taught nothing of the holy child within, [but] has in its teachings projected on to the historical Jesus the holy child and holy man, instead of teaching that a common and universally shared psychological experience can be shared intensely and individually to give rise collectively in the mind to real religious joy and true universal experience.'

In the same letter he told Amira: 'In dreams or in visions the mind reveals itself to the mind (i.e. one aspect revealing itself to another aspect) by means of the senses, which are controlled by another aspect.

'In other words, the higher mind (high self) uses archetypal imagery to convey, or attempt to convey, information to the intellect (middle self) by means of stimulation of the central nervous system, which in turn acts on our senses (lower self)—causing them to be extended in character and function in order that they [may] be used as gates of understanding to enable the ego or limited aspect of ourselves to enter into the Kingdom of Heaven within ourselves [and] encounter there the King of the Universe or Heavenly King.

'In sharing His mind and experience we thus transcend the bounds of our own ego consciousness to share all knowledge and all understanding of the universe everywhere—which is the mind of God.'

Walid recalls the Sheikh's saying, 'I don't see things like you see them. Everything's undulating and giving off all the colours of the rainbow. It's all divine—it's not just something that you gain in the way that people want to grab things for themselves. Everything is emanating the glory of God: everything. All the time. But we're just cut off from it and we're not perceiving it.'

In the Sheikh's own words again: 'As we free ourselves from all our personal delusions we slowly begin to interpret the actuality around us in life in a totally different way. We see symbols all around us to which we were totally blind, and as we become aware of the synchronicity of experience, more and more things drop into place and we see the oneness and unity of everything in the universe.

'It's an awesome universe—a mysterious universe.'

The recorded lives of the Sufi saints teem with accounts of happenings far beyond the normal; or in plain language, wonders and miracles.

When someone told Abu Hafs the Blacksmith, who died in 879, that his pupils treated him with the obedience and respect due to a sultan, he replied, 'You are only reading the title of the book. However, it helps to indicate the contents.' Then he asked that his pupils be told to prepare a pot of cumin broth and some halva, and to get a porter to carry the food away on his head until he was too tired to walk any further—and to give it to the person who answered the door of whichever house he had reached.

He did exactly that, and reported back. From that house in a distant street had emerged an old man's voice: 'If you've brought cumin broth and halva, come in!' When the stunned porter had inquired how he knew, the old man had answered, 'Last night as I was praying it occurred to me that my children had been begging for those things for a long time.'

Again: the great Yahya Efendi was friend and counsellor to the Ottoman Sultan Suleyman the Magnificent, with whom he had shared a wet-nurse. One day as the two men were being rowed together in the imperial barge, the Sultan felt the impulse to remove the precious emerald ring he was wearing and give it to his friend. In doing so he dropped it into the Bosphorus.

The downcast Sultan and his party returned to shore. After disembarking, Yahya Efendi made his way to a spot where a boy was fishing, and stood behind him. A little while later the youngster hauled in a massive sturgeon. Yahya took it to the Sultan, reached into its mouth and pulled out the ring. He refused Suleyman's pleas that he keep it, saying he had no need for it: 'Allah Almighty has given me other gifts than this.'

Barring the odd inaccuracy that may have crept in over the centuries, such accounts are true.

'This is all part of the synchronicity of the universe,' Sheikh Abdullah explained in one of his lectures. 'You may not believe these stories—but you will, when you have practical experience of this for yourself.' And he told how he had been walking with Aziza in Soho market in London when he saw a 10p coin on the ground. 'One of the masters of the *silsilah*, Abdul-Khaliq al-Ghujdawani, was with me. I said, "It's strange I can find small sums of money, but never a large sum"—and he chuckled. That evening walking along, suddenly in front of me was a bundle of notes forming a large sum of money, and no evidence of ownership.'

Such things, our Sheikh said, were 'not just myth but part of experience based on processes I have been describing in this talk. Now these processes are the result of sharpening up the concentration in such a way that the energy and concentration act in harmony upon the basic structure of life.

'In the ordinary course of events everything looks like a series of accidents around us. [This is] the accidental character of the outside world, [in contrast to] the character of the inner world, which we learn to make constructive and ordered. But at the supranormal stage these forces become one, and as we understand how the "energy will" within ourselves operates, we can align it to the will which is outside ourselves.

'Sometimes we get gifts in advance and have to pay for them later. Sometimes we obtain gifts after we have helped others, but done it in such a way that there is no self-motive of gratification in us; their need has been understood to be greater than that of oneself or one's own family. When that true need is met (and it must be discerned as a true need), then the tide flows the other way, back in your direction, and there is a far greater abundance of distribution.

'This quality of mind has then got the ability to communicate with the needs of others, and it has the automatic ability to discern priority in these needs.

'This is all done by feeling and by the emotion of love, which has nothing to do with intellectual discernment; and the way to it is through ordered spiritual activity—the curbing of destructive qualities in one's being and the building-up of constructive activity.'

You go on living spontaneously, but a part of you is detached all the time. You are not surprised. You are directed towards the source of inner peace.

Zainab has often wondered how she would feel if she were told she had terminal cancer. 'I immediately feel, well, I would just trust in God. I would trust that that's what's to be. The power and the strength the Sheikh infused me with have given me a ticket for life to cope with whatever comes.

'I tried to model my faith on his faith, because I always felt that he absolutely, totally belonged to Allah. Everything he did was never for himself, and everything he gave me was for my benefit. It was never a personal thing. And I was very close to him at one point—very close: he would always give me a hug and a kiss when I went' (Zainab has always lived in the West Country), 'and always make me feel that I was loved, and always tried to help in lots of ways.

'He gave me such a sense of direction, and the ability to go inwards, and the ability to be strong inside "if you can keep your head when all about you are losing theirs and blaming it on you". He gave me the inner strength to cope with whatever came up in life. I could always go back to him mentally, or to my prayers, to cope. When something catastrophic happened, I could go there.'

Even though Zafira, in great contrast to Zainab, left many years ago and became a Christian, she and her husband Muktar still pay tribute to the Sheikh and his influence on their lives. In doing so Zafira cites a well-known hymn:[37]

> Speak through the earthquake, wind, and fire,
> O still, small voice of calm!

'It's the notion', says Zafira, 'that there's this wonderful central energy that is calm, and you just have to tap into this stillness, but it's a live stillness, not a dead stillness. It's something that we need to find within us: this still point of peace.'

Abdul-Ghaffar, over thirty years absent but recently returned to Sufism, is unequivocal. 'In those two years he completely transformed my life. My time with the Sheikh gave me a sense of what is real, and of something that could be trusted to be true—and a sense that such a thing could exist: which in itself is crucial, because most people don't have it.

---

37 Taken from a poem by John Greenleaf Whittier, who as a Quaker was attacking demonstrative Christian worship. In the Bible, the 'still, small voice' followed the wind, earthquake and fire, and was heard (I Kings 19:12) by Elijah, who has been compared to, or even identified with, Khidr.

'These things are hard to express. You read books, you talk to influential people, you think you learn stuff about yourself, but it's all floating six inches off the ground. It's not embedded in that sense of the truth. With the Sheikh, I always knew that he was real and true and had access to knowledge that was absolute and reliable.

'He also gave me the sense that I could access that myself. Not because I'm special, but simply because as a human being I have the capacity. He gave me a sense of there being something much, much greater than me which is true and real, and which I can become involved with.

'He enabled me to understand not only that I have something in me which is eternal, but that that's the important thing. Everything else is just ephemeral.

'He gave me a sense of purpose. Not even just what that purpose was, but that I could *have* a purpose—and that everything else in life is pale by comparison to the colour of Sufism. That's the real thing; that's what being human is all about. Nothing else matters in comparison to that.'

Our visits to Turkey, in particular, were infused with the colour of Sufism and with the sense that more was happening than the pupil's eye could see.

'Much can be learned there', wrote the Sheikh, 'both from the people in this life and from those who have passed into eternity. It is a land pregnant with spirituality and a love of the Prophet Muhammad. There is a wilful ignorance founded on anti-Islamic prejudices held by people in the West who do not understand Turkish culture and spirituality, which has been immensely influenced by Sufi teaching and the ongoing presence of Sufi saints. Contact with many of the spiritual masters in the hidden government of the world has already been made by [my pupils] on these journeys.'

In Istanbul he took us to encounter a little and very, very old lady sitting in the corner of a raised couch in a small plain room opening on to a garden. To this day no pupil knows where we were exactly, or who she was, but we had been drilled heavily beforehand: 'Control your thoughts, don't let them wander while you're in her presence, and don't try to shake or kiss her hand or make any contact at all.'

We remained with her for a short while as she repeated prayers and Koranic litanies in a low voice, eyes closed or half-closed, apparently near-oblivious to her surroundings or our presence—until she broke off to say something in Turkish with a sharp immediacy that belied the impression. 'She was fierce!' recalls Latifa.

The state of being caught in your own inner processes stops when you find wild alertness. You have reached to immortality, which is not altered by death.

Sadiq felt 'a powerful influence and sweetness' in that little room, and Malika remembers an energy emanating from the old lady 'that was deep and vast and came like waves on a seashore, engulfing one and receding, then engulfing again, washing over us like an ocean'. Afterwards Muktar said he felt that everyone in the party had received a blessing. The Sheikh replied that it would eventually become apparent just how great a blessing had been bestowed. He also remarked that in her youth she had been very beautiful: 'And in the next world she will be seen in all her great beauty.'

Reality is the complete abnegation of self. You can see clearly for ever and ever: no past, no present, only the now.

When the news of Lady Diana Spencer's engagement to Prince Charles broke in 1981, the Sheikh told Abdul-Malik, 'When she dies the whole of Britain will be in mourning.' He warned Aziza that she would not live a long life, and she died only in her sixties after being disabled by a stroke at about fifty.

Before he himself suffered a stroke not long afterwards, on his trips into town it had been his custom for many years to visit Brunetti's and unvaryingly order an ice cream and a single cup of coffee. In the final days, or weeks at most, before he was stricken, he made what was to be his final visit—and for the first and only time he ate two ice creams and drank two cups of coffee.

Earlier, weeks before a tall hedge in the Australian garden had caught fire, razing a large area and destroying scores of precious plants, the Sheikh had kept smelling smoke and sending people out to check.

When he several times disclosed the single detail of his discipleship that all of us remember, namely that he had been made to sit for hours at a time in front of a zenana window, a lattice screen made from small turned components, until he could count all the parts from top to bottom and corner to corner without moving his head, his point was that he was learning how to see with the eye of the mind.

Abdul-Ghaffar describes how, during his first visit to the house in Kilburn, the Sheikh began talking to him in a slightly different way from normal. 'He was seeing something. "You're going to go through a door near Regent's Park," he said. 'I couldn't make any sense of it whatsoever. But some twenty-seven years later I trained as a life coach. The course was an intensive period of personal development as well, and at one point I re-lived some of the connection I'd had with the Sheikh—in a way that's very hard to describe, but I knew I had to get back on that path. It was a seminal moment in my life, and one of the key reasons why I'm back as a Muslim. I did my training in a place near Regent's Park. I was going through a door near Regent's Park. He was a seer.'

He told us that 'the mind is a unity, a cave of treasures',[38] and that even designing and making things is a process of giving form to an idea that already exists in potential. He would lay his hand on his breast and say that all human technology was within. It was the same gesture with which he located the alchemists' laboratory. 'The reality of things is not in the created world.'

He was keen on new technology himself but had no training or specialised knowledge in the field. In the early 1990s he was sitting alone with Abdul-Malik, whom he had tasked with a computer project, and asking him questions about some detail of it. 'I couldn't quite grasp what he was talking about,' Abdul-Malik recalls. 'Then he looked up and said, "I think you'd call it a daemon." "Daemon" is a very technical term meaning a job that runs in the background of a computer.' It was a term the Sheikh could not have known in any ordinary way, and it immediately made sense of what he had been saying.

Abdul-Malik had also been near him on the bus in Turkey when our externalist escort had been on board. Whenever the Sheikh asked the escort a question, our Turkish interpreter would chat and nod to his fellow-countryman for several minutes before turning round again and saying baldly, 'Yes,' or 'No.'

'The Sheikh would reply, and the externalist bloke would reply—and then after a while the bloke said something, and before the interpreter could interpret, the Sheikh said, "Tell him this, this and this." The bloke replied, and again before the interpreter could interpret he said, "Tell him –!"

'The rattled interpreter asked, "If you understand him, why am I here?" And the Sheikh replied, "I read his mind, but I can't talk Turkish."'

It was not just the mind. One day Maymuna was next to the Sheikh, showing him something, when he suddenly leaned over and scratched her back. 'Ooh,' she said, 'That's exactly where it was itching!'

'Yes,' he replied. 'You don't really know somebody until you've literally stood in their shoes.'

He was well aware of what his pupils were doing and thinking, whether near or far—if not in detail, at least in essence. He was like Sa'ad ad-Din Kashghari, for example, who lived in Herat in the fifteenth century and told a pupil shocked by his teacher's accurate detection of his inner activity, 'By God, I have a disciple in Balkh, a grocer. He is busily at work over there, with his two feet in the mess of the shop, while from here [some 400 miles away] I know his heart better than he knows it himself.'

---

38 That cave also figures in the story of Aladdin.

In his lectures our Sheikh would tell how the famous master Junaid of Baghdad[39] had ordered his pupils to go off and slaughter a bird somewhere they could not be seen. All did so, each returning with a carcase—except one, who said he had been unable to follow the instruction because there was nowhere that God could not see him.

'We know what [man's] innermost self whispers to him, for We are closer to him than his jugular vein,' says the Koran. Junaid had known very well what each pupil would do, and achieved his stated purpose of demonstrating exactly how far the sincere one was superior to his fellows, who had been jealous of their sheikh's favourite.

Although our own Sheikh assured us, 'Unless you can behave at all times as if I am present with you, you cannot understand what I am teaching,' his pupils often did not act as if they believed him. For Ahmed, the Sheikh's capacity for perception at a distance took many years to become fully clear. 'I don't know why I was so blind to it, but the blindness must have been wilful. We not only got the occasional clear reminder, as when he told a group that he'd heard their screams of excitement the night before as they went tobogganning on Hampstead Heath, several miles away; we also had also plenty of proof.'

Several times, in a few words, he offered a startling insight into the character or behaviour of a family member, colleague or acquaintance whom he'd never met. Sometimes it confirmed one's own view; sometimes it supplied the essential clue. All such insights of his would have passed unnoticed by a sceptic, but we came to rely on this faculty when seeking advice, and even to take it for granted.

The evidence could be much more concrete, too. A few days after one party of pupils had called in at a pub on the way back from a summer solstice trip, the Sheikh recounted to them—unprompted and without having been told—the order in which they'd walked out of the pub door. They were not Muslims, unlike Yasin by the time he smoked a cigarette one day during Ramadan while working by himself on a roof on the other side of London.

'The next day I was at the *zawiya*,' he recalls. 'As we were leaving, the Sheikh turned to me glaring and said, 'In the Islamic world, fifty lashes for smoking during Ramadan!'

Zainab remembers a time when she lived with her two young children in a rented place in Cornwall, and in her words had got 'very, very lost'. 'It had all gone very wrong, and I'd sort of lost contact with the Sheikh—mentally, probably, more than physically. I thought, "I'm not going to be able to get

---

39 This story is also attributed to the Turkish saint Aziz Mahmud Hudayi (1541–1628).

sorted out down here; I've got to go to London," because there was nothing in London except the Sheikh.

'I left the children with my mother, and I remember travelling up. I didn't know whether I was alive or dead. I was wandering about in Hampstead, and I kept thinking, "I don't know where I am." I suppose it was a form of a nervous breakdown. I was stopping and sitting, and walking about and thinking, "I don't know where to go." And eventually I bumped into the Sheikh.

'He said, "I knew you needed me. I've come to meet you." He'd walked the mile and a half from Kilburn to Hampstead. I'd come up from Devon and I hadn't seen him for several years. "You've walked past me several times," he said, "but you're so lost that you didn't recognise me. Come on, we'll go and have tea."

'We went into a café and he said, "Now just keep looking at me. You've got to get your concentration back." I started to feel it returning, and eventually I was back inside myself.

'I'll never forget that. "I've come to see you because you needed me." I often feel that, alive or dead—wherever, the same would happen.'

This quality of mind has got the ability to communicate with the needs of others.

Mansur only once spoke with the Sheikh face-to-face. At the time he was practising the *dhikr*, 'Allah-Hu', intensively. 'I suddenly felt connected to everything. Time slows down, and you're just floating. I could see people picking up a cup of tea before they picked it up. But after going through that, suddenly everything went dark again. That's when I got scared.

'I ran to the Sheikh one night around 8 or 9 o'clock. I just sat down, spoke a little bit, maybe I mumbled—but he did the same thing as with [my sister] Rashida: he took me in the garden and he gave me a rose. When I left the house later he gave me a hug. There was no talk, no other interaction of any sort. I believe he gave me some pot-pourri, either then, or later through Aziza; I was in too much of a state of heightened love to remember details, but I remembered and still remember the feelings in the heart.

'It's beyond description and words: an experience I get when anyone and I have a connection in the same heightened wavelength. It's all communication between hearts, and no words are exchanged; yet all that ever mattered, or matters, or will ever matter is exchanged, as if in a timeless spot—Beyond words again. I keep not finding a way of saying it, yet I can express it even as I speak about it.

'The love feeling is towards a specific region, starting right in the middle of the chest (between navel and throat) and like a physically pulsating heart that gets expanded, though no physical organ exists, and gets a warm loving feeling which it sends towards the head and everywhere in different ways.

'It's more real than when feeling the touch or taste of something. It's what keeps me centred and in objective observation mode when under pressure in any circumstance, internal or external, and not "owned", as the kids say these days. It stays just beyond the highest or lowest emotional state, as if acting like a buffer—except that when there is a connection there are no barriers. It's like drops being made to flow everywhere, drowning all but itself.'

The old masters were quite clear that the word 'heart' in this context is not to be taken literally. It refers to a faculty latent in human beings, but quite outside the ordinary senses, that can be developed to act as a bridge to infinite knowledge.

'What is called the heart', wrote Khwaja Abdullah Isfahani some 600 years ago, 'is the centre of the comprehensive human reality, of which all the higher and lower elements of the universe are detailed particulars.'

You can merge with the divine ocean and time and space far away. You can see clearly for ever and ever: no past, no present, only the now.

Said Ubaidullah al-Ahrar: 'The real purpose of the heart is to be the centre of feeling and understanding, so that it inclines towards every direction, contemplates this world and all the concerns of this world, and explores every place, the heavens and all the worlds, in the twinkling of an eye. . . . Just as the kernel of every nut is ripened according to the essential nature of its own tree, the whole universe has been ripened in the heart.'

The Sheikh many times referred to the following unforgettable anecdote by Bahauddin Naqshband's son-in-law, Khwaja Ala ad-Din Attar, who was the teacher of Abdullah Isfahani:[40]

> At the time when I had recently been attracted to the venerable Khwaja Bahauddin, a certain Sufi asked me: 'What, according to you, is the nature of the heart?' When I said it was unknown to me, the questioner then offered his own definition: 'In my opinion the heart is like the moon when it is three days old.'
>
> I mentioned this to the venerable Bahauddin, who was sitting in the corner of a garden. 'That dervish has described his own condition,' he said.

---

40 The following passage combines two accounts of the same incident, both translated by Muhtar Holland: one from Safi's *Beads of Dew from the Source of Life* (see note on p. 138 above) and one from *Masters of Wisdom of Central Asia*, by Hasan Shushud.

Then he placed his blessed foot on my foot, whereupon I experienced a great exaltation, in which it was as if I witnessed the entire universe within myself.

When I returned to my ordinary state, he said, 'That is the heart—the central point of connection, not what that dervish imagines it to be. How can you comprehend the nature of the heart unless you have witnessed its true greatness?

'To know the heart is to know one's purpose, and to find the heart is to find one's purpose. In the words of the sacred tradition:[41] "The whole of My creation cannot contain me, but I am contained in the heart of My faithful servant." As this subtle statement makes plain, if someone understands the heart he has understood the goal.'

Sitting with our group by the beach in Turkey, near the site of Troy, the Sheikh told this same story, and then said to Muktar, 'Just put your hand on the table.' Muktar did so, and the Sheikh placed his own hand over Muktar's. They stayed like that for two or three minutes. Then the Sheikh took his hand away and asked, 'What was that like?'

Muktar said, 'That was better than an acid trip.'

It was also in Turkey that the Sheikh one day said to Khalil, 'Come here,' and then told the same story to the group while Khalil knelt by his chair and held his hand. Suddenly Khalil got up and hurried out of the door. Among those watching with curiosity was his roommate, who asked him later, 'Khalil, why did you shoot off like that?'

'Because he was doing the same thing to me as he was telling the story,' Khalil replied. 'It was just like overwhelming love, and I couldn't—I was going to burst into tears, and I ran out of the room.'

'So', the Sheikh explained, 'I am trying to tell you that [Sufi training] is not a psychological process understood in intellectual terms like reading a book. It's an experience which changes one's whole being and eventually brings about a quality of immortality in the spirit and eventually the body, which remains incorruptible after death.'

Those who knew the Prophet Muhammad testify that he naturally smelt of the most glorious musk. One of them, his servant Anas, said, 'A sweet

---

41 A *hadith* or 'tradition' is one of the enormous number of oral accounts, later written down, in which Muhammad's Companions recorded in meticulous detail his words and actions. These words and actions constitute his *sunnah*, or way. A 'sacred tradition' *(hadith qudsi)* is a *hadith* in which the words of God are reported by Muhammad although they do not form part of the Koran.

fragrance was naturally emitted from [his] blessed body. I have never smelt anything more fragrant.'

The point of visiting saints' tombs—a practice shrilly condemned by externalists, who have bulldozed the resting places of the saintly Companions in Medina—is not to worship their noble occupants, but to benefit from their presence.

'Building your subtle energy levels helps you in the next world,' said the Sheikh. 'The most important thing is to die well.' He was shockingly clear that most people die (as he put it) like a dog, oozing or dribbling out of their bodies. By contrast, he said, Sufi masters leap out, and leave behind bodies which remain infused with energy for the benefit of others.

Malika had that confirmed for her in Turkey. 'We experienced first-hand the amazing and beneficent energy pouring out of the tombs of several Sufi sheikhs who had died hundreds of years earlier. At one site a sheikh was buried unmarked beneath a large paved area, and our Sheikh asked us to find the spot—which I and others did by relaxing, focusing and feeling until we could sense the place from which a wonderful, fresh and serene energy was emanating.'

It cannot be emphasised too often that Sufism is as much a physical process as a psychological one.

One evening Ahmed was sitting on the floor in Dalston while the Sheikh was at the table with others. 'Ali was on the floor next to me,' he says, 'The Sheikh was five or six feet away. He got up and left the room for a few minutes, and when he re-entered he had a closed safety pin fastened through one nostril. Otherwise his appearance hadn't changed; there was no blood or any other disturbance. He sat down and the evening continued as before. Neither he nor anyone else made reference to the pin, except when Ali murmured in my ear, "Has the Sheikh got a safety pin through his nose?" and I replied, "Yes." Later on the Sheikh returned to his own quarters, and when he re-appeared it had gone.'

Bahauddin Naqshband's own sheikh had been Amir Sayyid Kulali al-Bukhari, a potter by trade. Both men are links in the *silsilah* of our Sheikh, who would tell how Amir Kulali had left instructions with his pupil to fire a batch of pots that had been placed in the kiln. But Bahauddin soon afterwards fell into contemplation of the divine beauty and majesty, in which he became so utterly absorbed that he forgot to do as he had been told. He was still lost in contemplation when Amir Kulali appeared and demanded, 'Bahauddin, have you fired the pots?'

The School of Celestial Fire

As our Sheikh remarked, 'the anger of the sheikh is something that the *murid*s do not like to feel.' *Fire has to be felt within one's being, and it has to burn.* The unlit kiln was opened. Every vessel had been fired, and on each one was emblazoned the name of God Almighty.

'First I was raw; then I was cooked; then I was burnt.' When Amira dreamed that she was told the heart was a fruit which must be protected from getting burnt, the Sheikh replied firmly, 'This has no spiritual significance, because you have to be burnt so that all your desires are consumed and the dross is burnt up to leave only gold.' *If you only have gold coins in your purse, you can only give out gold coins.*

In his own words again: 'The male principle is light, which when not experienced enough by people is felt as heat. In a cold country the hot sun is pleasant, but in a desert it burns and consumes you. This energy experienced as light and heat is that process which goes on in the retorts of the alchemists. It burns away that illusion you believe to be you and provides a new form of consciousness, neither conscious nor unconscious.

'Even at highly developed levels there are some who have this quality of male and some of female. For example, Rumi had the coolness of the *sunnah* of the Prophet. Shams-i-Din Tabrizi[42] had the searing brilliance which is like the sun, which is part of the reflection of the positive quality of the universe. I am more akin to Shams than to Rumi—even [in] my name, Sirr-Dan al-Jamal.'

He translated that name in several ways: 'The one who penetrates (to the hidden view)', 'The piercer of the outward qualities of beauty', 'The piercer of the outward appearance of His beauty', 'Piercer of the secrets of His beauty', 'Seer into the secrets of His beauty'.

It is well known that Muhammad said that God has ninety-nine names. These appear both in the Koran and in his own sayings, and denote attributes of divinity. Among them one pair in particular is often cited as representing two complementary principles in the universe: al-Jalal, the Majestic, and al-Jamal, the Beautiful.

Sheikh Abdullah espoused the principles of sacred geometry and encouraged their study by those of his pupils who were called on to design buildings or other things. He identified Majesty with the mathematical constant *pi* (π) and Beauty with *phi* (Ø), long known as the golden ratio, which latter he said enshrined the proportions of the universe. Both are irrational numbers. Despite the majesty—and it is not too strong a word—that was apparent in his presence, he said that of the two he represented *phi*, Beauty.

---

42 See pp. 262–4. 'Shams' means 'sun'.

Malika bears witness: 'The Sheikh was a man of exquisite and sophisticated taste, loving items of great craftsmanship, good proportion and genuine beauty. He was also wonderfully charismatic. He exuded vivacity and generosity of spirit. He was witty, hilariously funny, very astute and enormously kind, and he emanated great love, although he was not in the least sentimental. He was also singularly fiery and spectacularly fierce; he could undo you in a second. At the same time he taught us constantly, and by example, how to be magnificent and robust about every aspect of life.'

Sakina was with him for the last nineteen years of his life. She records: 'He was a living illustration of *jasbet,* charisma. His smile and approval were so attractive that we would do anything to get it—and it was the force which drove the jealousy between the women. His disapproval or anger were terrifying, and it was like being shut out from the sun. I once said in front of him that a hammering from him was worth a thousand sweet words from anybody else, and he was approving. I meant it.

'He had a genius for turning your world upside-down. Something you thought was one way was suddenly shown in a totally different light.' It's the experience of Moses at the hands of Khidr. 'This was unique to being around him, and it has hardly happened to me since he passed to the next world.

'We were as much afraid of him as we loved him, but either way he was the centre of our world, and he still is. He made an impression which I could never forget and will never be replaced. I pray that that will guide me to him by the power of my own attraction to him in the next world, so that I will not die rudderless.'

Questioningly, hauntingly, the Sheikh would repeat a famous line of the great Sufi Farid ud-Din Attar, who was revered by Rumi: 'I am in love, but with whom?' On one occasion he gave an answer: 'With life and the Giver of life.'

He taught that the essential nature of God Almighty was love. 'Intellectual reason is a blight on the development of humanity. Love, which is longing for the beautiful, is the guiding lantern.'

During the lecture he delivered in London on Thursday 8 March 1979 he said: 'Experience leads to attaining an inner harmony between the individual personal unconscious and the infinite knowledge in the soul of humanity. This union is not achieved in intellectual terms at all. It is a process of love—a love soliloquy.

'When you have been in love you project so much of your notion on to the other person that thoughts of yourself disappear and the form of the beloved disappears as well. You are in love with a notion. This is related to surges of energy in the central nervous system which lead to a pleasant excitement and wellbeing.

'In love there is a feeling relationship. There is nothing intellectual about it. The madman, the lover and poet are all akin in this sense, as Shakespeare points out in *A Midsummer Night's Dream*. The reality of going towards the centre of your being is a love affair between two parts of your being, positive and negative. They are brought together as lovers, not criticising each other—relating in a passive way ("passive" in the feminine sense of being receptive); so all the ancient mystery cults refer to this state of passivity as being like pregnancy, when a woman does nothing active of herself. Pregnancy is an act of love, and she takes part in an act of creation, but passively. The child grows within her.

'In this love affair the positive and negative elements within come together to produce an entirely new range of conceptions about life, which lead to a new reality where there is "I am", neither conscious nor unconscious. Where the two are too much separated, they seek each other.'

The lecture was unusually long, and the Sheikh spoke for perhaps as much as another hour before ending with these words:

'Self-control frees one from the bondage of self, and the process I have just been describing is a form of passive self-control. The seven heavens and hells cannot hold the one who is self-controlled. Remember that they are all a reflection of yourself. Those [who get] through to reality are not identified any more with form. They are in eternal ecstasy. Theirs is the summation of this love affair—like two lovers who begin cradling each other in their arms, and end as one mind, one body.'

Jamal is one of a dozen or so pupils who has never cut his inner connection with the Sheikh despite having last seen him many years ago, and he remembers their parting still.

'It was as if he knew we weren't going to see each other again,' he says. 'The last thing he ever said to me was, "It's all love."

'I didn't need any more.'

THE END POINT of the Sufi path is *baqa billah*—subsistence in God. The Sheikh was never more awesomely serious than when he told the following story, more than once.

Although *baqa billah* passes normal human understanding, the pupils of the Naqshbandi master Baqi Billah Berang[43] (1564–1603) were insistent in their request that he explain the meaning of his name.

He told them they would receive the explanation after his death.

When he died he was prepared for burial. As his pupils stood before his body, ready to perform the funeral prayer, they saw in the distance a horseman galloping towards them. They waited as he came closer and closer, pulled up and finally dismounted, his head covered and his face veiled.

The visitor stood in front of the congregation and led the funeral prayer for Baqi Billah. As soon as he had finished, he strode away and mounted his horse again.

One of the master's pupils ran over, seized the bridle to prevent his departing, and cried out to him, 'Who are you? In the name of God, tell us who you are!'

There was a moment's pause as the pupil repeated his plea. Then, without saying a word, the stranger pulled aside his veil: and the assembled pupils clearly saw the face of their master Baqi Billah.

The rider spurred his horse and galloped away.

---

43 Baqi Billah Berang of Kabul (incidentally an almost exact contemporary of Shakespeare) is a member of the Sheikh's *silsilah*. 'Berang' means 'Colourless'—a reference to 'the complete abnegation of self' (and see p. 212–3). A similar story is told of Sabir Kaliyari (1196–1291).

5

EPILOGUE

ON HIS PASSING from this world, the Sheikh left frozen embryos of fine Murray Grey cattle to Zaid, whom he had involved very closely in the work of the stud and to whom he had delegated much of it. Eventually born, these cattle grazed beside others on a farm owned by Zaid's brother Martin in New South Wales, where they stood out from the rest. A flood swept away much of the fencing, and when the stock were rounded up afterwards, these particular beasts—the Sheikh's personal legacy—were missing. The neighbouring farmer was suspected, but a search failed to find them.

Some time later, Martin answered the phone to a stranger who introduced himself as a psychiatrist. The man apologised and said he would never normally make such a call, but had been able to see no alternative. He was treating Martin's neighbour, who had come to him very depressed and quite unable to sleep because he was being tormented by a recurring dream in which a red-bearded man was commanding him in the most fearsome manner to return to their owner the cattle which, as he now confessed to the psychiatrist, he had indeed stolen in the flood.

Ashamed to go straight to Martin, he had enlisted the psychiatrist as a go-between. Once the cattle were returned, Martin realised that he had seen them while searching, but had not recognised them because the thief had gone as far as changing their ear tags.

Immortality lies in the process of consciously controlling your being. Death becomes a chance event which cannot shatter the essential nucleus. Death to the

Sufis is only a transition,' said the Sheikh. 'Death is just like changing your coat.' The group's letterhead carried Abraham's words of calm acquiescence to the angel who had come to remove him from the world: 'Friend, now take my soul.'

The Sheikh had told Zainab at their last meeting, in the 1980s, 'You'll see me again—but that'll be at a much later stage.' As for Ahmed, he was asleep one night, due to rise very early for the long drive to a crucial and difficult meeting, when he had an almost terrifyingly vivid dream. 'The Sheikh was yelling at me to get up, get my act together, not be late, turn up on time and so on. I mentioned it to him later. "It'll be even more vivid when you're dead," he said.'

It was quite clear that he knew both the process of dying ('The last thing you hear at physical death is the sound of your blood trickling to a halt in your ears') and what lies on the other side of it. He spoke of how those who have recently died are helped to travel further by their children and the people who love them. 'Their love, good thoughts and happy memories are like wings that lift the person's spirit,' he said, and mentioned in particular that forty days after dying was a very important time for the deceased—a fact recognised in Orthodox Christianity as well as Islam.

Malika recalls that he spoke often about death. 'It was very real when he did. At the age of twenty-six and a young mother, it was not something I thought much about. He never softened the reality of dying, and spoke with skilful timing to create maximum effect. Initially my mind would somersault, creating a gap in its activity, which of course was exactly his aim. His words made deep and lasting impressions that have acted as a meaningful and present guide.

'After the initial shocks that broke through so much conditioning and sentimental religious upbringing, I felt awake to the finite reality of death and the immediacy of living. This would create a gratefulness and joy for life itself, and I understood what a great teaching he was imparting.'

He succeeded in pulling at least one pupil back from death. We were on a trip to the Carcassonne region, where he later said he had taken us because the area still possessed a spirituality placed there by the Cathars, who had been so cruelly destroyed by the French king at the bidding of the Pope. We camped in the Gorges du Tarn, and a few went swimming in the river. That was when Imran got into trouble. He was dragged out unconscious, and the alarm was raised as he lay on the ground. While some of the men tried to help him, everyone else rushed over. Although nothing like it had ever happened before, without a word they linked arms in a circle around him and started chanting,

'Allah-Hu!' The Sheikh was in the centre with him, loudly shouting words to the effect of 'Wake up!' The paramedics arrived and tried to shut the Sheikh up, but as he explained later, he was stopping Imran's soul from leaving. He survived.

The whole idea is to make the journey before you leave. As he spelt out again and again, if you don't make it while in your physical body, you will face a much harder task after death. You may endure a second drowning.

'When you die it's like being inside your dreams. You cannot affect them; they continuously replay. You are at the mercy of your impressions. You will go into [a] world of fantasy where you are swept along like in the current of a river. I am teaching you how to make the hero's journey and have conscious control over your activity all the time.'

> While you live,
> Drink!—for, once dead, you never shall return.

Those are the *Rubaiyat*'s words. It is Abdul-Ghaffar who says, 'I think that we are alive in order to prepare ourselves to die—to be dead.'

Nevertheless, even if you know the journey is there to be made, the Sufis warn that if you lack a genuine guide you can get into bad trouble and never reach your goal. If you want to travel an unfamiliar road on a foreign continent, you have no good option but to attach yourself to someone who has been that way already. As for finding who that person is—if they speak wisely about things you have some knowledge of, perhaps they are also right about things of which you have none.

At least take the Sheikh's advice. Strive to observe yourself, your habit patterns and attitudes, as others often do with you, and as you do with others: because those patterns and attitudes make your destiny. And think it possible that there are other ways of sensing and feeling than those you know. Believe there are forces you don't know about, and worlds you cannot see.

> I swear by the afterglow of sunset,
> And the night and all it unfolds,
> And the moon as it grows to fullness,
> That you will journey on from stage to stage.

So declares the Koran, before asking: 'What then is wrong with them, that they will not believe?' No human voice is talking.

You have heard the Sheikh often use the word 'lord'. It has nothing to do with Jesus, and in this book it is almost always spelt with a small L. Besides repeating the words of the Prophet, 'He who knows himself knows his lord,' the Sheikh gave further explanation. *In order to know your lord you must know yourself. The innermost nucleus of your own being is an immortal creature.* 'This being is the humanity in each of us, the divine mind. It is not God. It is not the face of God, but the mirror of God—the divine within each of us. This leads to knowledge of all things.

'Sufis show you how to create your lord out of nothing. When dying of (say) lung cancer, you are then whining for your lord, but it is too late. Few people survive the shock of death. There is no continuity, no bridge. A bridge has not been built. Then [it becomes] a long, arduous process.

'Those who are so angry that they have done murder or rape are in all-consuming fire. But hell is not all hot—parts are cold. There are fearful caves, wet, slippery, dank, dark and stinking. There is a whole range of experience.'

Even so, fear is not the only reason to hurry. Another is wonder. You must understand that real diamonds are being handed out. If you advance on the way, said the Sheikh, 'you'll find it's even more incredible and fantastic than you could ever have imagined, and you'll wish you'd tried all the harder.' *The vivid qualities of the inner world outshine the qualities of our physical capabilities. They enhance and expand our physical capabilities so that we see the objective universe with new eyes, and see things in it that ordinary people cannot see. Intuitive experience is a wonderful, startling form of experience.*

'[After] rigorous training in which the body and mind are affected via . . . the central nervous system, not the senses and intellect, the central nervous system becomes aware in another way. This process enables some of the energy of ourselves to travel out so that it acts as a beam of light, so we can use it to focus on a scene. This is not a separation but a projection, [and] is seen as another body. We can appear present to people—as dense corporeally as a physical body, but that body is only an appearance, like the hands and face of a watch reflected on a wall. It is done as a result of the diffusion of energy into areas where concentration is.'

The juggling of a circus performer is achieved with the same quality of concentration, the Sheikh added. 'The ability to do this in your soul depends on losing the conceptions and fantasies that prevent you from being simple': from regaining what he called the 'Adamic simplicity' of the first human being, the trait with which we all came into the world.

'This process of understanding how one obscures oneself is a long, long process'—one during which, as he warned, knots that you tied with your hands you must now undo with your teeth. 'This understanding has to be guided by the sheikh.'

EPILOGUE

The companion of wonder is strangeness, and the secular Westerner in particular finds many things strange. For example, it was the hidden hierarchy of the world who rejected Kalman Dede's clumsy application for membership. Many Muslims know, though not all believe, that the head of that hierarchy at any one time is the living person known as the Qutub. The Qutub can be found in Wikipedia. But few indeed know who he is, and in fact the matter has nothing to do with religion.

The Sheikh stated that in earlier decades the position of Qutub had been bestowed on Padre Pio (1887–1968), the great Italian Catholic mystic; and he told how after the battle of Caporetto in 1917, while Padre Pio had been in Gargano some 400 miles away, the losing general Luigi Cadorna had gone into his tent and already put a gun to his head when he saw and heard a Capuchin friar in front of him, warning sharply: 'General, that's very foolish!'

'– And it is!' added the Sheikh as he told the story.

Cadorna lowered the gun, and the friar left. The shaken general immediately went out and grilled his subordinates, but they assured him no one else had entered the tent. He remained bewildered for many months before eventually discovering Padre Pio's existence, and finally travelling south to visit him incognito. He was told to wait in the corridor. On seeing Padre Pio approaching, he immediately recognised the same friar, who shortly drew level and exclaimed, 'Hello, General! We took a big risk that evening, didn't we?'

The Sheikh explained that those who kill themselves are forced to repeat the act again and again. 'When people commit suicide they give themselves such a shock that they are stuck in the place they were before the act, going over and over and over their deaths like a broken record stuck in a groove. That is hell.'

No ordinary person knows what other shocks may await them. A pupil recalls the Sheikh also saying 'that if your mind has been accustomed to running riot and thinking about this, that and the next thing—and you haven't gained control over your thoughts in this world, when you have intellectual control—in the next world they just run riot. He said you could find yourself in a room, suddenly thrust in there after death, unfamiliar surroundings, and you start word-associating: "What's this? I'm scared!—scared"—and then, word association, a scarecrow will appear in the middle of the room and start advancing towards you.'

He observed that in the physical body people cultivate busy, preoccupied minds, and that the pattern continues after death: the mind of a ghost is interior, and therefore the ghost always seems preoccupied, as indeed any number of sightings testify. In particular he lamented that so many people have songs going through their heads all the time. In the next world, he explained, it can take years to get rid of just one piece of music.

Immortality is concerned with acquisition of conscious control over the mind's activity. That's all it is.

Doubling as ringmaster and juggler, keeping all the balls in the air at once, the Sheikh exerts just that control. As far as we know, none of his pupils have ever come close to matching his proficiency. Nevertheless, they have all found a place in the circus, and spent part of their lives in the big tent. He set out to give them all the skills they needed by direct transmission, and never wrote a manual. Because he said we were the only book he would ever produce, that book has no title. Yet it has plenty of illustrations, and when some particularly astonishing or instructive scene enacted itself he would sometimes say with a kind of detached amusement, 'You can put that in the *Tales of Piss and Wind!*' Such is the imprimatur for this work.

Proverbially, after the main act has left the ring, the clowns are sent in. In that capacity it only remains to hear once more from two of the pupils themselves.

Ahmed says: 'When I came to the Sheikh at the age of twenty-five I had a young person's view that death is a long way off. What's more, even though I was looking for experience which by definition was completely outside my understanding, I had a deep-rooted belief that everything I did was OK. Maybe I had some idea of duty, but it was subservient to my view that if there was a problem in or around me it could not be my fault.'

You cannot understand anything outside yourself, and you cannot understand your lord, until you understand yourself.

'I don't think the Sheikh managed to shatter that smug self-satisfaction, but he showed me there is no place to hide. He awoke in me a sense of responsibility for my time and actions, and he was right when he told me I had no shame. Now I try to take to heart the last words spoken in public by the Prophet. After repaying a man who said he was owed three coins, he declared, "It is better to blush in this world than in the next."'

Sakina says: 'I now believe absolutely in the life after death, and that it is more real and important than this life, but this life is our chance to prepare for the next, and in that way this life is vitally important too. What you sow now, you will reap then. You have to be constantly worried about the deeds you are sending before you. You will be held to account for every bit of good and every bit of bad that you did here, and as the Koran says, you "will not be wronged by so much as the hair on a date stone".

'We were taught that our individual identity is still distinct in the next life, but everything is very, very different otherwise. We will have no capacity to learn by intellect, and it is our automatic attractions and habits which will determine what happens to us: so we have to watch out for how we train ourselves here.' *To harvest well you have to sow well.*

'Although I try to look at myself from a distance and see what I look like without all the personal narrative and excuses, *et cetera,* the need is to do this constantly, not just sometimes. Our total responsibility for everything we do is frightening. There are no excuses in reality: you did it or you didn't. But we are also taught that the mercy of God is greater than His justice, which is our great hope of being forgiven for our constant failures.'

It will have become clear to you, as an attentive reader, that the sense of profound responsibility that haunts, or should haunt, every pupil prefigures the account that must be rendered in the next world. In the words of the Sheikh: 'Our life consists of dreaming until we awake at death'—when the departed, now newly arrived, is given (we are told) his or her book. The transgressor must take it in the left hand, others in the right; and each stands clutching the unalterable record of his or her time on earth.

Whether you take your warning literally or otherwise, you must take it; and so the Sheikh strives to makes sure that every pupil is brought to book, and brought to consciousness, while the opportunity still exists. This utterly necessary, unavoidable process has never changed. It operates today just as it did in the late fourteenth century, when a namesake of Ahmed's was a pupil of the great Khwaja Ala ad-Din Attar, another direct spiritual ancestor of our Sheikh.

The former Ahmed lived in a time when young men could not so easily feast on the sight of young women as they can today. Having gained his master's permission to go and visit relatives,[44] he was on the way back when, passing a fountain, he caught a glimpse of the desert girls who had gathered there to collect water. He tried to control his urge to get a closer look at them, but lost the battle. He walked up and watched them for a moment before turning away and resuming his trip.

When he got back, his sheikh was holding a great assembly. Though already surrounded by a crowd, the Khwaja hailed Ahmed and said: 'On the path of the Masters of Wisdom, we practise accountability! We keep account and render account. You must therefore recount everything that has happened to you since you parted from our company.'

---

44 This story is adapted from Safi's *Beads of Dew from the Source of Life* (see note on p. 138 above), where the disciple appears as Mawlana Ahmad.

Ahmed reported in detail all his experiences, both going and coming back: with a single exception. He said nothing of the desert girls.

Khwaja Ala ad-Din spoke again. 'There is still one event that you have failed to mention. If you do not recount it yourself, I shall do it for you in front of all these people, and I shall put you to shame.'

Ahmed had no escape. The pressure on him was such that he doubled up and staggered about as he described what he had done at the fountain.

The Khwaja listened. Then he stared straight at his pupil as he instructed the crowd: 'Let everyone take a hard look at this shameless young man!'

When Ahmed later recalled the incident he said: 'I was so humiliated by terror and degradation that no trace of my existence remained intact.'

Few people survive the shock of death.

NINE DISCOURSES

by
Sheikh Abdullah
Sirr-Dan al-Jamal

THE FOLLOWING are the only extended pieces of the Sheikh's writing or speaking available for publication. The second, third and fourth are samples of the several hundred weekly public lectures he gave in London until 1985.

It should be emphasised that his lectures, conversation and letters embraced such a vast range of subject matter and reference that these nine items, while authentic and perhaps representative, cannot be regarded as at all exhaustive or definitive in terms of the themes he addressed in conveying Sufi teaching. In fact they are only a minuscule fragment.

He quoted from many authors in the course of his talks, usually adapting the original to his purposes, and it was often unclear where such quotations began or ended.

1

THE INNER JEWEL

This undated essay was transcribed from one of Sheikh Abdullah's notebooks. Its title has been added.

BISMILLAH ir-Rahman ir-Rahim—In the name of Allah, the Most Compassionate, the Most Merciful:

Surah Fatiha, the opening chapter of the Holy Koran, commences with this sonorous, rhythmic cadence. Following the example set by this glorious revelation, all sincere Muslims repeat this most holy phrase to regulate their lives and conduct.

Islamic culture in all its magnificence owes its growth and beauty to the fact that everything comprising it has been made an offering to God Most High through the use of this phrase. Thus scholars, writers, poets, artists, musicians and architects have made their offerings to embellish and adorn the exterior jewel of Islam.

No matter how magnificent and how glorious are the facets of this shimmering cultural jewel, they pale into insignificance in comparison with the fire of the well-guarded beautiful and glorious secrets contained within the jewel at the mystical interior of Islam. The mystics who find and enjoy the beauty of the inner realms of Islam have gained endless pleasure by exchanging the ephemeral beauties of this transitory physical life on earth for eternal beauty of a kind that cannot be described in sensory terms.

Nevertheless this hidden beauty has a separate reality which all prophets and teachers have come to share with mankind as part of the heavenly peace and knowledge of absolute beauty they endeavour to transmit. Their companions and contemporaries are shown that man originates in the heavens of this star-encrusted cosmos, and that true peace can only be found by searching for the endless beauty contained within the place of our origin.

In Islam those who are successful in this search are designated by the term *awliya,* which is the plural of the Arabic word *wali*—a friend; for they have become Friends indeed of God Most High. In Islam they are the true followers of the pattern set by the Seal of the Prophets, Habibi Muhammad Mustafa,[45] on whom be peace. Such spiritual masters are regarded by Muslims as the nobility among the sons and daughters of Adam, and are pictured sitting upon the thrones reserved for the prophets. In this way they are given honour and respect within the heavenly realms. In fact they differ from mankind in general because they have been awakened to the knowledge of reality within the universe. This achievement results from wise control of instinctual urges combined with detachment [from] the emotional identification which the human mind makes as an automatic bond with people, places, objects and events. By this means rational knowledge is married to intuitive knowledge. In other words two distinct branches of knowledge are unified by merging the experimental, rationalising function with the contemplative, intuitive function of our minds.

The mission of the *awliya* or Friends of God, like that of their precursors the prophets, is to awaken the rest of mankind to experience and appreciate the inner reality of life pulsating at one and the same time at the heart and throughout the essence of all creation. The *awliya* are therefore the custodians of the knowledge of the eternal reality of the universe. These mystics regard humanity as occupying a place in the scheme of creation between the grade occupied by animals and the station of angels. Indeed they have always taught that life is not static as we understand it in intellectual terms. They have always underlined the fact that life is a vibrant continuum, or an ever-changing, continuously evolving process where, on earth for example, a self-perpetuating resonant harmony links mineral, plant and animal life in a unity containing all the secrets of common communication and transmutation.

Stemming from the fact that we contain in our bodies a mirror of the whole evolutionary process life has undergone during the existence of our planet, and that the basic energy permeating our bodies is the same energy that motivates the stars in their courses, we possess duality of nature and outlook as a result of our inheritance. This has introduced both animal and angelic qualities within our being, and these are as equally manifest in the cells of our bodies as they are encountered in the patterns of our everyday behaviour. The Friends of God teach that a process of complete reorientation of mind and body must take place before the problems resulting from this duality can be dissolved in the harmony of unification of our whole being. When the character and power of our angelic being, representing the forces within the universe, overcomes

---

45 'Habibi' means 'Beloved', and Mustafa is one of the names of Muhammad.

the animal nature and perverted egocentric views of life we have developed haphazardly within ourselves, we gain God's peace—the Islam of Muhammad.

The path to such peace is through self-discipline, concentration and love, and is a re-forming of habit patterns and attitudes. In other words we submit ourselves to a process which brings order and harmony from the chaos and disharmony caused by the destructive elements in standard human behaviour. Muslim mystics, who are known as Sufis and dervishes, have always understood that this process of submission is identical with the process of submission to the will of Allah in Islam.

We can establish an angelic spirit within ourselves which these mystics call the *ruh*. This is accomplished through the aid of God's grace and by complete submission to the guidance and direction of the Friends of God in the way that they themselves have submitted their minds and bodies to the pattern or *sunnah* of Islam established by God's Messenger, Habibullah (Beloved of God) Muhammad.

Sufis and dervishes follow this path, known as *tariqat*, and the most highly evolved among them become *awliya* or Friends of God. These emperors of *tariqat* are dedicated to preventing humanity from descending down the evolutionary scale to the level of animals. Their aim in life is constantly directed towards raising the spirit of humanity towards the angelic level of detachment from instinctual and emotional identification with the experiences we encounter as humans.

All religions have contained both commandments and prohibitions, and when these cease to be practised by their followers, the religion itself ceases to be an effective force in guiding the lives of the people involved. Such commandments and prohibitions were inaugurated as a means of preventing humans from returning to the animal level. [As long as] we observe the commandments and act within the prohibitions, we safeguard ourselves and the rest of humanity who may be influenced by our attitudes and beliefs. In Islam the *awliya* maintain and reflect the high standard of human behaviour contained in the divine wisdom set by the Prophet—may peace and blessings be upon him. In this way these Islamic saints, who are the Friends of God, have moulded their natures to be examples for humanity to follow. Because they have refined all the dross from their characters, the attributes they reflect consist only of those which humanity has always regarded in the past as being archetypally associated with God. Consequently their hearts are free from the attachments to the material values held by the majority of humankind. Therefore when it is stated that they have renounced everything except love for Allah and that they are engaged in contemplating the beauty of His Face, they are in fact engaged in contemplation enjoying the ecstatic bliss contained within the inner reality of Islam.

As living examples of the *shariat* (Islamic law), by following the *sunnah*, or pattern, set by God's Messenger Muhammad, the Friends of God reflect the love of God. This love is experienced in states which are just as real as the state of mind experienced by human lovers, but infinitely more intense. This divine love is a product of training both mind and body to respond equally to the impact of the Divine Presence in the universe. Because two similar kinds of love cannot co-exist in the human heart, the Friends of God have eliminated from their hearts all false love aroused by illusory conceptions, which in Islam are called *dunya*. In turn the Friends of God seek to detach humanity from the *dunya*, or world, of false and distorted conceptions, and they accomplish this by filling a pupil's whole being with this experience which they call the love of God. The *awliya* know that humanity in general is in love with the *dunya* and therefore the love of the *dunya* has to be replaced by the love of God. They undertake this task by being a living example of the truth they advocate.

To find their state of peace it is necessary to seek them out, associate with them and emulate their example. By means of such close association they teach a pupil how to develop and expand the volume of energy within the body. Contemporaneously they teach how to adjust the mind to deal with [this] expanding volume of energy. . . . This inner power produces physiological as well as psychological changes. When the volume of energy is eventually great enough in the individual under their guidance, a radiance which they call the *nur* illuminates the mind, affecting and expanding the visual capacity of the pupil. Experiencing this light is no mere flight of fancy. The validity of the experience is as real as an encounter with ball lightning or experiencing the discharge of electricity from an electric eel.

Special centres which Sufis call *lataifa* are opened in the body and are expanded to relate to vital plexuses within the sympathetic nervous system. By this means the *awliya* develop a relationship with the heart which enables them to use it as a visualising area called the *qalb* or centre of the *lataifa*. This results from direct transmission of energy from master to pupil. Specially designed exercises are used and revolve around the practice of *dhikr*, or remembrance of God. This consists of a resonating process which in fact is responsible for 're-membering' or reforming body and mind, bringing about the physiological and psychological changes mentioned above. Direct association with the master and submitting absolutely to his guidance introduces a pupil to new areas of consciousness by gradually understanding the experiences undergone in states of contemplation. Eventually a relationship with the Divine Presence is constantly enjoyed in which there is continuous peace of mind, coupled with the bliss described as the love of God.

When Muhammad the Messenger of Islam was asked the shortest way to Allah so that the relationship with the Divine Presence could be enjoyed, he recommended the inquirer to follow a Friend of Allah as a shadow follows a body. This is the way of perfect emulation within Islamic mysticism, and at the first stage of the *tariqa*[*t*] or path of spiritual knowledge the *murid* (student) is gradually absorbed into the way of life practised by the *murshid-i-kamil* or perfect spiritual instructor. A second stage occurs when the pupil is taught to emulate the way of Habibullah (Beloved of God) Muhammad, on whom be peace. At this stage the knowledge contained in the *hadith*[46] (sayings and traditions of the Prophet) are incorporated in the pupil's behaviour patterns so that he emulates the complete lifestyle of the Holy Prophet of Islam.

The third stage is reached when the pupil is accepted into the Divine Presence. At that point the pupil's heart has been cleansed from all attachment to all creatures and created things. Only a burning love for Allah motivates the pupil, and the state of peace and ecstatic bliss [produces] eternal pleasure in which God is seen in all things and all things are seen to flow from God. This everlasting pleasure is a direct experience derived from feeling the love of God in practical terms through the pursuit of the spiritual science imparted by the master as knowledge of his energy and emulation of his actions and mode of life. This spiritual science is the inner jewel of Islam: and as its inner secrets are gradually absorbed, the pupil is drawn more and more to God, and is finally absorbed in the Divine Presence.

---

46 The Arabic plural is *ahadith*, but *hadith* is often used for both.

2

THE JOURNEY TO REDEMPTION

This is the transcript of the slightly incomplete recording of a lecture delivered on 8 December 1977. Its title has been added. The lecture incorporates material from Martin Lings' What Is Sufism?, *quoting Frithjof Schuon's* Understanding Islam; *from* The Masters of Wisdom *by J. G. Bennett; and from Muhammad al-Misri, as quoted in the* Dictionary of Islam.

'HE IT IS who has sent down to thee this Book of which there are some precise verses, which are the fundamental part thereof, and others which remain mysteries. Those whose hearts are prone to pervert everything cling only to the various interpretations which these verses might induce, craving for controversy and disorder, whereas God alone knows the true interpretations of them. The real learned men will say, "We believe in it. It is all from our Lord;" and alone those with sensible minds will profit by them. This Book, full of wisdom and superior to all, derives from the prototype, which is near Us.'

Thus it describes in the Koran the true source of the revelation. It is a revelation from God. The Koran is not of an intellectual character; it is, in fact, quite different from all other books because it is divinely inspired, and the prototype is with God.

It is a miraculous quality of the Koran that one never grows weary of reading and hearing it, so that the tribe of the Qureysh at the time of the Prophet Muhammad used to come secretly by night and listen to God's Apostle while he was praying, and marvel at this recitation. One of the most eloquent—and at that time, and still today, eloquence among Arabs and in the speaking of Arabic is considered to be very, very important—[was] Nadr ibn al-Harith. [He] and Utbah ibn Rabiah were bewitchingly eloquent, and Abu Jahl ibn Hisham was a wondrous orator. One night Utbah swooned on hearing the Apostle recite a chapter of the Koran, and said to Abu Jahl, 'I am sure that these are not the words of any created being.'

The *peri*s also came and listened to the word of God. Now the *peri*s, or the *jinn,* are beings who are not human. 'Verily we heard a marvellous recitation which guides to the right way, and we shall not associate anyone with our Lord.'[47] This quality that the Koran has when it is recited, when it is sung, [is] a resonating quality which is of tremendous importance. Now the whole of life is resonated here on earth, and the influence of the galaxy is used by Mighty Allah to stamp, on all the creatures of the earth, one stamp. It is extremely curious that life, from microbes to whales, from the giant redwood tree to the meanest, dirtiest alley cat, from the humble peas and beans that you grow in your garden, from polar bears to pumpkins, sparrows and humans, all share the same genetic code, the double-twisted helix. If evolution by random natural selection and adaptation to environment is true, the creatures of this world should have thousands of different genetic codes. Each one should have evolved at different times under different conditions. Instead the curious and, to the intellectuals, the unexplained fact is that all life on this planet has one genetic code. In the Koran, among the ninety-nine Names of God, who are aspects—what could be called archetypes—of the divine, there is one very important one: al-Qahhar, the Dominating One. He is the One who breaks the back of His powerful enemies. He dominates them by killing and humiliating them. Everything in existence is subjected to His dominance and power and is helpless in His grasp.

This aspect of Mighty Allah is this powerful, dominating effectiveness which transcends all duality, and in fact transcends reality itself. This transcendental effectiveness includes both creative and destructive aspects. It places the stamp of being, which is effectiveness, on all. It is through this mighty aspect of Allah, al-Qahhar, the Dominating One, that we possess in common with the whole of life the same simple genetic code. As I have mentioned in other talks, this genetic code intrigued the scientists who became aware of its existence by the fact that its potentiality is almost limitless: that the code itself can be altered on the framework to an almost limitless degree. This framework is the work of one of the mighty organs that we have knowledge of—our galaxy. This is one of the mere mechanisms of God.

Among humans the one who dominates his enemies is greatest only when he can dominate himself, and the stage of al-Qahhar, the ability to relate to al-Qahhar, is only possible after the stage of the Perfect Man has been reached. In the Naqshbandi orders[48] there were three *qayyums*[49] who were in a relation-

---

47 Koran 72:1–2.
48 The Sheikh here uses the plural.
49 A designation of rank derived from the Name of God 'al-Qayyum', the Self-Subsisting. It may be rendered as 'maintainer of the cosmic order'.

ship with this aspect of divinity. Man's greatest enemy is himself, his own inner being. He is even a greater enemy than the opposite in our conceptions of God, that is, Shaitan or Satan, the archetype of evil. When man has dominated his own carnal appetites he actually dominates this archetype that we call Satan. It is impossible to imagine that one who has dominated his own desires can be caught in the snares of this archetype.

Now, when you have gained dominion over the desire for all that is connected with wants and egocentric expression, you can be in a position to dominate all of mankind. Certainly [you cannot] be dominated by any other human. The aim of an enemy, in the final summation, can only be to destroy the body. The purpose of dominating one's carnal desires is to revive the spirit. The one who puts to death his desires during life gains immortality and freedom from delusions and the dreams that one's wants impress on one's innermost thoughts.

The *dhikr*, or repetition of God's name and appropriate verses from the Koran, resonates the being in such a way that physically and psychologically one is totally changed.

Now the recitation of the Koran is the most widely spread rite throughout the Islamic community as a whole. In Sufism the Koran is like the world: at the same time it is a unity and yet it is a tremendous complexity, embodying multifarious themes. The universe is a multiplicity which disperses and divides. The Koran is a multiplicity which draws together and leads to unity. The multiplicity of the holy Book, the diversity of its words, sentences, pictures and stories, fills the soul and then absorbs it and imperceptibly transposes it into the climate of serenity and immutability by an inbuilt wisdom which it contains.

The soul, which is accustomed to the flux of phenomena, yields to this flux without resistance. It lives in phenomena, and is divided and dispersed: and in our culture, due to our intellectual attitudes and our intellectual fixations, we have fragmented our souls into a tremendous multiplicity of chaotic thoughts and impulses. The revealed discourse of the Koran has the virtue that it accepts this tendency, while at the same time it can reverse the movement, thanks to the celestial nature of the content and the language, so that the fragmented portions of the soul can learn to swim like fishes, without distrust and with their habitual rhythm, in such a way that they are caught up into the divine net.

The Name of Allah and the Book, the Koran, are two poles between which lie a wealth of possibilities of implication and litany, some being nearer to one pole and some to the other. The recitation of the *shahada*,[50] for example, and

---

50 The profession of faith.

the invocation of the two Names of mercy,[51] are nearer to the Supreme Name, whereas certain long and complex litanies are more comparable to the Koran, and as often as not they consist largely of extracts from it.

I have said throughout all my talks that there is a mathematical synchronicity within the universe: that every event and every experience is interdependent upon every other event. Even intellectually, at the mathematical level, we recognise that the future can be forecast with some degree of accuracy by using the probability theorem. This is only an understanding of the fringe of this synchronicity, because synchronicity relates not only to space and the events in space, but to the timing of these events.

Now, the divine revelation [has the quality of being] strung together in certain harmonics which the human voice is capable of repeating so that the frequencies and the resonating effects can be felt again and again as they were intended. Such a construction is contained throughout the whole of the Koran: and the construction relates in feeling quality, and in the resonating impact it makes, to the subject matter concerned. When somebody has spent a lifetime in relating to *dhikr* and so gradually coming towards an understanding of God, the ability to continue this recitation without drawing breath becomes built in to their being. At a certain stage pupils begin to understand that they needn't draw breath so quickly or at the rhythm at which they have been accustomed to draw breath in the ordinary way. They find that their being becomes imbued with energy as a result of the resonating process; and this energy keeps them sustained.

The great Swedish mystic [Swedenborg] described this as a spiritual breath. When the energy is flowing freely and one is relating to a tide of high energy in the universe outside, all this can be felt within the heart. I used to say that Sufism is seeing a lark in a field above golden grain, hurtling skywards in a paean of praise. The Sufi who beholds this can feel the lark's song in the heart, and at the same time he can feel the lark's tongue in the heart as well as the resonation of the song.

This is sensitivity of a degree that seems quite beyond the average person's powers, but it is brought about by the ability that one achieves through constant resonation—the singing of praises of one's Creator. Prayer in its real sense is not a recitation in praise of God strung together intellectually, nor is it whimpering and whining for one's wants. It is attuning the inner harp of one's being so that the strings of one's sensitivity soar upwards in this inner song of joy: these beautiful inner psalms of praise to the God within, to that Divine Presence that permeates our whole body and influences our minds.

---

51 Al-Rahman and al-Rahim, the Compassionate and the Merciful.

Now, many say, 'We see God.' Is it possible for any to say, 'We see God?' No, this is not possible. Those who talk in this way are asserting that they know God, that they see His power. As it says in the Koran, 'No sight reaches Him. He reaches the sight, but He perceives men's sights—the Subtle, the Knowing.' Now the blessed Prophet of Islam knew this, and commanded, 'Adore God as thou wouldst just *as though* you see Him; for even if you do not see Him, He sees you.'

This permission to adore God is a divine favour, and the Sufis are God's servants by divine favour. The fourth Caliph, who was concerned more with spiritual things than temporal or earthly things, said, 'Should the veil fall from my eyes, how would God visit me in truth?' This saying confirms that no one really sees God: that even Ali, who was close to the Prophet, and was his cousin, never saw Him. We say that you can see the traces of God. When any person sees the brightness of the sun he may safely say that he has seen the sun, though indeed he has not really seen it. If you hold a mirror in your hand you see a figure in it, and you may therefore say that you see your own face—which is really an impossibility, for no one has ever seen his own face. You see a reflection.

By this process of resonating, inner feelings are brought about within the being. Eventually these feelings become visual experiences, and these visual experiences are the reflection of God's face. But this is a metaphor. These are the reflections of the influence of all the aspects of God which compose our being in the areas that we know nothing about within ourselves. It's the area of not-you, or not-I—that vast area, which is quite limitless, in our minds that contains the aspects, these archetypal notions which humanity has, of divinity. There, reflected in terms of contemplation, their influence can be seen. These reflections start in dreams and end in contemplation.

Now, one of the things that we cannot do is to bring the full content of what we are unconscious of into the area of our consciousness. But we expand our capabilities in such a way that we are able to penetrate consciously into this area, which remains completely dark and unexplored to the average human being, and there vast panoplies of splendour are revealed to us. Untold numbers of worlds are explored. All these have a meaning.

Now those of you who were with me when I went through *The Golden Ass* of Apuleius in some detail will remember that Lucius was first led astray by Fotis. Now Fotis in Greek means 'light' or 'reflection'. This feminine image led him astray because his habit patterns were of the kind that [meant] he treated women only as objects of sex: and he turned into an ass, as all men do who remain at this level of understanding.

Within the story of *The Golden Ass* there is the story of Psyche and Eros, as a little story within the main story in order to illustrate the whole theme. Now, Psyche is what the psychiatrist Jung later called an anima. Psyche is a familiar type of feminine figure, to whom one can relate in dreams without being overwhelmed by the numinous awe which the greater archetype, the goddess Venus, can engender.

In all human relations, the relationship is circumscribed by the position of the parties. To give you two opposites, the king and the beggar man: the beggar man can be overawed by the magnificence of the king. Where one projects energy from one's being in relating to deep and awesome things that one is not normally conscious of, there is a tremendous feeling of numinous awe. That would relate to the goddess Venus. To a lesser degree, at a more humble and domestic level, one can relate to the psyche, what Jung called the anima, in the way that one reacts when one falls in love. There's the same 'Ahh!'[52] There's the same reaction. Now this is simply a surge of energy through one's being: but the surge of energy is contaminated by a process of conceptualising and habit pattern, so that one discriminates emotionally in a certain way when one is exposed to certain stimuli.

In other words, when a man falls in love he projects something of his own innermost unconscious on to the person to whom he is attracted. This attraction is brought about because, to the man concerned, that woman epitomises in her atmosphere something that he has not developed in his conscious mind. There is an immediate appeal of the strange, of the mysterious, and with it there is this surge of energy plus the emotional feeling of being in love. This idea of Psyche epitomises that.

The great love goddesses like Venus and Hathor, Astarte in the ancient world, [also] epitomise that feeling; but it's so profound that one can swoon away with the impact of it. The impact of the energy is so great that one swoons into unconsciousness. Now in order to learn, people have to relate at a level which they can understand. So the experience has to contain a surge of energy sufficient to make its impact, but not strong enough to cause you to leap over the abyss into unconsciousness: because in unconsciousness you can learn nothing. Unconsciousness is the unresolved. When you are in that area you are unredeemed. When we redeem you from these influences of being in the control of the unconscious, and [make you] independent individually, we redeem you from that area where there is no distinction. Consciousness is the ability to distinguish and to discriminate. That is individuality.

---

52 A thrill like a sharp intake of breath.

Of course, egocentric behaviour of the area that we call the *nafs* is the perversion of that for the sake of your whims, your personal pleasure, your self-esteem or your own sensual delight. What I am talking of—this individuality, this power to discriminate—is to show you the emotional links which are made with energy, and the instinctual links which are made with energy, so that certain symbols [are] strung together in the form of a story in which you take part in terms of experience, in the way that you can read a book, watch a film or be befuddled by TV. It is of the same quality. But the mind projects this story so that you are either an observer or a participant in it. This is the essence of beginning to dream coherently or to contemplate. You have a certain individuality and an ability to discriminate.

When my pupils start to tell me of their dreams where they are doing *dhikr Allah* with me and relating to certain experiences, they are going towards this area of knowledge and control and individual participation. Ordinary chaotic dreaming is where people are swept along in a sequence of events where they have no control. This establishment of the individuality through processes of concentration and resonation in one's waking states brings about an individuality which leads to immortality. Immortality is simply being distinguished as a unit and being able to move freely within the totality. This is all part of the inner journey, and this is why the Koran is so important and why resonating through the *dhikr* is so important.

Now I talked last week of four stages. What we call *fana al-ahkam*—this really refers to the external world rather than oneself—[is] the stage where one becomes terribly disillusioned by one's life experiences and by what one thinks is the outside world and its influence. The ego or what we call the *nafs* (the ego and the passions comprise the *nafs*) is very closely bound up with the external world; but we don't understand how the inner world of our being constantly intrudes upon the outer world, just as the outer world intrudes into our being.

We gain experience through our five senses. That experience is conveyed into our being, and we start to conceptualise about our experience. This is a subjective undertaking; each of us has an individual model of the world, our interpretation of what we think is reality, and at one time or another in our lives we become disillusioned. Many become embittered. Some are carried off by this, and many commit suicide. But there is this stage which comes, sometimes a number of times, in a person's life.

Just before I pass on from this point, I must emphasise that we intrude on the external world. I was at pains earlier to talk of falling in love, and to talk of this numinous experience which we project into the external world or on to the subject matter of our dreams. The feeling can be so strong that we can be overwhelmed by the archetype: we can be carried off. So we have to take people through relatively banal experiences in their dreams and slowly lead them to more and more strange experiences. At the same time we slowly get them to permeate the whole of their beings with energy, so that they become accustomed to the inner energy and to the surges of it [and] are not carried off in swoons so easily.

I have emphasised that the Blessed Prophet of Islam, on the night of the *miraj* [his celestial journey], went up through all the heavens and went beyond the lote tree. In other words he went from the world of forms—that was the last form—to the worlds of force, and he saw God face-to-face. Now you can't literally see a force. You can't see the wind. You can only see its effects. The tremendous currents within the universe can be felt. Our impressions of them, our notions of them, can be seen. And when these mighty forces manifest at God's command in our presence, then we feel overwhelmed by them, and we gain a vision of the particular being. This is like looking in a mirror. It is not the reality: it is the mirror. When we come to reality, of course, we understand that we *are* the mirror.

The mirror, of course, is only a metaphor. It's this ability to reflect, not only in the inner worlds of our dreams but out on to the external world, in terms of the forces of our own energies. And when you fall in love with somebody you project some of the force of your own energy on to what you consider to be strange, mysterious, captivating in relation to this person: but this is a projection, and may not be in the person concerned.

So we are bound up with our dependence on the external world at the ego level. Egoism is the fundamental illusion that we possess something—our selves, our ego—that is our own. This is the greatest lie by which man cuts himself off from his destiny. There *is* no ego within. Man turns to the outer world, the world of bodies, which, being outside, allows him to feel that in some way he exists. The energy lets you feel certain things.

Now let us return once again to the exotic poetry of the Sufis, and to a very good illustration that Christians know of: the Song of Solomon in the Bible. This is full of exotic allusions to the Beloved. These are feeling qualities. When lovers touch each other's hand, a slight pressure, a pressure in the dark, ensures that there is a communication, a feeling communication. Now these pressures stimulate feelings inside the central nervous system, so that plexuses behind the navel are stimulated, or there is a quickening of the heartbeat. The mystical path is of the same quality. By orderly and disciplined stimulation the sheikh arouses in every pupil certain spasmodic feelings in the central nervous system. These are of a sporadic kind. They come and go—little quivers now and then. By constant stimulation and by the correct guidance, and by the force of the resonation, these feelings begin automatically to respond to the stimulation. When this takes place the responses become more orderly and gradually develop a life of their own. It is an inner life of feeling, which takes over from the feelings which are normally concerned with your ego and your wants. These feelings become separate from your ego. This is the birth of a new individuality: what is called in the Christian Bible, by the prophet Isa, the Son of Man. The Son of Man had no place to lay his head: simply because the Son of Man is within one's being, in terms of feelings. These feelings are of the same quality as those of lovers, but they can be made to [be felt] at a heightened level: an ecstatic, numinous type of feeling that would cause the ordinary person to swoon off.

It is not uncommon for certain sensitive women to swoon under the impact of sexual intercourse. This is exactly the same process: that they have been subjected to a surge of energy which drives them into unconsciousness. Whether a person comes to us with blunted feelings or highly sensitive feelings, we can slowly bring, from out of the chaos of their own feelings, a consistent pattern of development which enables them to reach heights that are not normally experienced in average human contact. At these levels they are relating to the aspects of God, the ninety-nine Names of God incorporated in the Koran, and I've said that these are in no way exhaustive of the attributes of God. These feelings are extremely important to relate to, because they are the instrument, as it were the thermometer, of your progress. The greater the feeling, the deeper and more meaningful will be the visual imagery or the audial impact at a later date, as feelings evolve into other impacts upon one's senses.

So we return now to this point that the ego is the great lie which cuts you off from your destiny: and I have shown you how we bring about an individuality in you which lives alongside the ego in the beginning. The two function [together], and can function quite harmoniously, for some time, because most people compartment their lives into thousands of fragments.

Somebody came to me the other day who had just accepted Islam, and I was told that, for social reasons and in order not to offend anybody, pork was eaten. I explained that apart from being the foulest *haram*[53] that could take place, this came about from fragmenting the way of life—and this is typical of the West, and typical of the self-deception which occurs with everybody here: that in one context they do one thing, in another context they do another thing, and in a third context they do a third, and in another context they do a fourth; and they are all over the place. They have compartmentalised their lives

---

53 *Haram*, 'forbidden', refers to things forbidden in Islam.

to suit themselves in their own self-selecting manner. They have arrogated to themselves the ability to select, instead of following God's law.

When you submit to the yoke of Islam, then you must be the same person in all situations; and those who have come into Islam recently will find that they are tested again and again and again in circumstances of this kind, so that they have to stand up and declare what they are. They can't make it public in one instance and a secret in another.

Now the whole of development is of this character and kind: that you have to be the same being at all times, and not an actor on one particular set and then another actor on another set, and another actor on another set. Remember you are on one bare stage: and that's why, in the theatre of Shakespeare, there was little backdrop, there was little scenery. It was to show that everybody was on a bare stage, performing one role.

So when people become tired of all their play-acting and all the work that the ego does for them, it allows them to feel in some way that an inside world exists. And when a person awakens and becomes aware that the world of bodies supports his own body but does nothing for his ego, this is the first liberation. It brings him face-to-face with the need to find within himself a reality that he can't find out there. And we all relate to what is out there, and keep projecting our feelings on to what is out there.

Now the second stage is the great and awful stage that not many are able to make. It comes with the realisation that this inner life consists of dreams within dreams within dreams. This world of spirits, or the world of ghosts— the world of the dead—is here within yourself. People mistakenly call it the spiritual world, and believe that it is the other world promised by religion. The world of the spirits is here and now. We live in it, because we exist in a dream state with rare moments of awakening. We exist as ghosts in our bodies, because our conceptions, our dreams, eventually take us to where all the other ghosts, all the other spirits, are. We go to our own place—but you are living in it now: all of you.

This dream state is the second stronghold of your egoism. It is exceedingly hard to accept that we are no more real persons in our waking state than in our sleep state. This is very difficult to swallow. You see, we dismiss our dreams at night when we sleep: 'Oh, it's only a dream.' But what we *can't* realise is that we are in dreams now. You're all ghosts in a dream. The acceptance comes only with repeated experience of waking and seeing; and we do this by means of *dhikr*. We gradually bring you, we shake you, awake; and in these moments of wakefulness, slowly there dawns this awful realisation that you're nothing at all: you're just a dismal, wandering ghost in the realms of your own unconscious.

The third stage is a very great step, because it opens the way into the real world. This is the world where free acts of will are possible. When you come and tell me that you are performing *dhikr* with me, and that you hear and see me in that *dhikr* and that you are performing particular acts of the *dhikr*, then this is a step forward. When you come and tell me that you are praying while you sleep, then this is taking a particular habit pattern into your dream state, so that you are controlling it and no longer being controlled by it. This is the inner world that we lose contact with when we believe in our dreams; and believing in our dreams consists of participation in all the haphazard things that we dream about—and, under the fickle jade of hope, looking forward to the fulfilment of the particular will-o'-the-wisp that is the current whim in our lives.

All spiritual paths must lead to this vital step, which is the real world, the world where individuality becomes apparent in the dreams and in daily life. This is why you must become the observer and the observed; and when you are observing what you are doing, you are having a control and a direct and true influence on your life. You are distinguishing yourself from the content of your unconscious, which takes you along like a slow-moving river. You are not aware of flowing downstream. When you start to swim upstream, then your individuality becomes apparent, and this individuality is concerned with the process of discrimination. You start to be redeemed from the area of the unredeemed: the ghosts, the spirits, those who are carried away by the dreams within dreams. Conquerors spend their lives dreaming of fresh countries, fresh worlds to conquer. Misers spend their lives in the acquisition of wealth. The whole of human dreaming consists of wasting time in feeble and impossible aspirations.

Now those who reach this third stage don't find it easy to convey their inner state to others, because they are being affected by this quality that brings you near to swooning; and you have to bear more and more and more of this inner pressure of energy, contaminated with emotion, so that, by being accustomed to the greater pressure, you can gain in depth of experience. But all who meet those who are in this state can see that they are aware and in touch with, or in the presence of, real being. Their individuality and their centredness is conveyed.

The fourth stage consists in the complete liberation from the self that enables this divine love, this overwhelming feeling of numinism, to take possession of the whole of one's soul. All separateness is overcome, and the creature becomes the creator. Now this does not mean to say that the creature has become God. The creature has become the creator, because then you are the creator in another way, and you are doing it by means of the divine presence within you.

In the process the *murid*, or the pupil, learns to create a mental image of his sheikh, his teacher, and holds on to it until he is able to feel that the sheikh is really present. He represents his teacher as possessing all the qualities to which he aspires, and models his behaviour on him. When the sheikh perceives that the power of creating a mental image has been acquired, he directs the attention of the *murid* to the *pir*, or the founder, of the brotherhood to which they both belong. Thus somebody of the Mevlevi Order will concentrate on Jalaluddin Rumi. A Sufi of the Bektashi Order will concentrate on Hajji Bektash Veli.

These beings live outside time and space. In the inner reality you live outside time and space. The average person is away in the future in hope, or away in the past in nostalgia: they don't live in the present. We teach people how to live in the present; and through that present they come into contact with the present of the universe, which is outside our time and outside our space.

There the other immortals are. They are not in the world of the ghosts. The ghosts and the spirits are in their own place, carried away by their dreams, continuing like mice on a treadmill. The enlightened are separate, and can penetrate into all the worlds and be anywhere at any time. They are the redeemed—and we introduce you to the redeemed.

The head of each order is one of the redeemed. Through association with him we bring you to the Holy Prophet, and we show you how the world is governed and influenced in ways that ordinary people have no conception of.

Sufis who are properly developed have strange powers, and these strange powers have been written of and sometimes experienced. They are not things of the past; they are of today. My own pupils can experience strange powers of the Sufis.

[*The ensuing words, 'But here is a description . . .', are the last before the end of the tape on which the lecture was recorded.*]

3

THE CENTRAL KNOWLEDGE

This is the probably incomplete transcript (described as 'rough' by the pupil who made it) of a lecture given around early 1977.

GNOSIS is the knowledge on which all knowledge rests. We call it *marifa*. This knowledge is real and demonstrable, but in other ways than those of our intellectual culture. Other knowledges do not illuminate their knower. They do not remove his anguish, nor do they give him judgment in every sense, nor do they invest his presence with light and radiance. The man of knowledge remains in need and dependent, whereas the man of gnosis does not remain in any need, except his dependence on his Lord, who gives him what he requires from creation. Other knowledge is without foundation and is therefore baseless.

Gnosis, the central knowledge, *marifa*, is the knowledge of the reality of one's being and is a proof to the one who knows, and this is its glory and supremacy over all other forms of knowledge. By its use its possessor knows the universe, how it is set up, and its underlying laws, actions, qualities and essences. His knowledge of the universe is based on his knowledge of his own being, while his knowledge of his own being is direct knowledge of his own original reality, that reality which we identify with the Prophet Adam.

Everything that he has comes from Allah; he never sees anything except he sees Allah in it, before it and after it. There is only Allah in his eyes and in his heart. Whoever has gained this knowledge has gained the sulphur of the wise, in the words of the alchemists. But he can transform the hearts of those who come to him, for his presence alone is a guidance and a reminder. He guides by Allah to Allah.[54]

Now for Sufis the object of contemplation is the absolute beloved; everything else is purged from their minds. The contemplation of the *arifin*,

---

54 The foregoing three paragraphs are quoted from Abdul-Qadir al-Jilani (1077–1166).

the true mystics, is of this kind. It can be summed up in the words of the great Sufi mystics and Sufi sheikhs.[55] 'Contemplation is the heart's grasping of the meaning of objects for the sake of comprehending the subject' [Zainuddin Abu'l-Hasan Jorjani]. 'Contemplation is to be effaced in the remembrance of God' [Shah Muhammad Darabi]. 'The one who prays and fasts is near the people while the one who contemplates is near to God'—and this was said by one of the great saints of my own order, Sheikh Abu'l-Hasan Kharaqani. 'Whosoever contemplates properly can neither speak nor act without sincerity' [Abu Amra Najid]. 'Sitting in contemplation for one hour in the state of witnessing is worth more than a thousand accepted pilgrimages' [Farid ud-Din Attar]. 'Speech without wisdom is a plague, and silence without contemplation is lust and negligence, and the noblest action is to contemplate with self-abnegation' [Hasan al-Basri]. 'One hour of contemplation is worth more than a night of prayer' [Hasan al-Basri].

'The apostles asked Jesus if there was anyone like him on earth. "Yes," he replied: "anyone whose speech is invocation, whose silence is contemplation, and whose perception is opened by awareness"' [al-Ghazali]. 'Thought for the ordinary man is plunging into the sea of illusion, while contemplation for the elect is being immersed in the ocean of understanding' [Ruzbehan]. 'Contemplation brings you to God, while prayer brings you God's rewards. That which brings you to God has more value than that which brings you to something other than God' [Fakhr-e Razi]. 'At the beginning contemplation directs the attention to the needed understanding, while at the end it turns one from knowledge to inquiry, from form to meaning, and from the created to the Creator' [Shah Nimatullah].

The *arif*, the true contemplative, contemplates his own being, and contemplation on one's own being is referred to in the Koranic passage in which Allah says: 'And do they not reflect upon themselves?' In this kind of contemplation the mystic ponders on the purpose of his existence. This is in accord with the Koranic verse: 'Verily, it is from God we came and it is to God we shall return'. He considers how he may go towards God and what he should do to please Him. He may concentrate on the meaning of the sacred tradition:[56] 'I was a hidden treasure. I desired to be known. Thus I created the world so that it might know Me.' As Sheikh Jalaluddin Rumi, the founder of the Mevlevi Order, wrote in his poetry:

> Day and night my only thought
> is why I am ignorant of the states of my heart

---

55 The following quotations are from Javad Nurbakhsh's *The Paradise of the Sufis*.
56 See note on p. 162 above.

> Whence have I come and wherefore have I come?
> Where am I headed? Will you not show me my home?
> How rapturous is the day when I fly towards my Friend's abode,
> Beating my wings in the hope of reaching that hope.

Man belongs to both the inner and the outer worlds, and therefore humanity must participate in both worlds. Western civilisation is capable of creating mental illness, tensions and exhaustion in all its areas of endeavour. Conversely, of course, a person who pays attention only to the inner states and is forgetful of external reality may become lazy, inept, inactive, unable to continue even in contemplation. Sufism is effective because its long tradition and its great experience of balance between these two extremes is used to bring harmony in both worlds. The Naqshbandi Order has a long history of realism, and this realism came into prominence particularly in the time of the Moghul emperors. It was then that Naqshbandi masters, known then as the Khwajagan, the Masters of Wisdom, advised the rulers of the time.

In the Indian subcontinent at a later date the Chishti Order in particular had a tremendous influence due to its emotional impact. The Chishtis play music, and to a mystic whose heart has been opened, this type of *dhikr*, or remembrance of God, is extremely meaningful at an emotional level. The emotions and the instincts are carried away in a frenzy of love. The Moghul emperors up to the time of Shah Jehan [were] influenced by Chishti masters. Shah Jehan's own daughter was buried simply, and on her tomb was written the fact that she was the daughter of Shah Jehan and the pupil of a Chishti master. At this same time the Suhrawardi Order influenced the subcontinent of India in its doctrine of love and in its vivid imagery, which was brought about by ecstatic processes.

Like the great Sheikh Junaid of Baghdad, the Naqshbandis have always emphasised that the outer exterior of their saints, their *walis*, their *arifín*, should not reveal the wild exultant ecstasy which is taking place within them. We are careful not to get carried away by the exultant quality of the inner burning love that we experience. We are careful to use the rational side of our being, which is part of the positive aspect of being, which could be called the masculinity within the universe—the positive aspect, as against the experiences of the feminine that are emotional and wildly exultant in their spiritual joy. So if we meet some emotional fakir who wants to devote himself entirely to what he considers contemplation to be, with marijuana, the first question we ask is: 'Have you got a job? If not, get one.'

Now when Western people ask what they should be, a Sufi would tell them: 'Be human.' Sufism represents the real purpose of Islam, and Islam is concerned with the middle way. Every human being needs to participate in both inner activity and external activity in order to understand divinity. Both are indispensable. One must be *for* God with one's total being. If one of these human functions is not working, he or she cannot be a real person, for to be truly human one must be completely dedicated to the absolute, which is in divinity. A fakir type of mystic who is carried away by his inner states is not working for Allah Almighty and can never reach perfection.

The intellectual culture of Western man has made people in the West forgetful of their true being, and much of their activity is concerned with making money to serve the interests of business and technology. Westerners who become dervishes need to be instructed in inner activity, and we do this even when we know that they are still seeking the inner activity in the same way that they seek material aims. Most people come to us because they want power of some sort or another. They want to exploit some power in themselves or they want to exploit other human beings. It may take many years before the sense of inwardness spreads its roots.

To dominate the weed of Western culture, Sufism has two levels: a public aspect, and a deeper level reserved for the elite. We prescribe the outer or public aspect for the West and hope that this will help to eliminate the disease of the West. But the deep and secret aspect of Sufism we bring about in the elite. They are the elect because they have had the ability to overcome all obstacles, and the sheikh is constantly trying to trip them up on the way to test their endurance. They endure to the end, and in enduring to the end, they discover the deep mysteries of life within themselves. No pen can write adequately about these mysteries. No tongue can describe them in full. But the Naqshbandis are very careful to guide their pupils so that they are not carried away by these overwhelming inner forces that at times cause them to suffer from inflation, causing them to make egocentric statements that they are the reality, that they are the truth. They are a fragment of reality, a drop in the ocean, but this drop functions in the same way as the mighty ocean of reality out of which the whole universe is composed.

And so the inner journey is a journey towards their own lord, and they relate to their lord by negating their ego and egocentric drives at many levels—intellectual, emotional and instinctual. In negating the egocentric behaviour patterns with which they came into the world, they approach the inner living reality. That inner living reality can only be attained by experience, and cannot be found in books. The pupil has to come to the sheikh to have it explained at every stage or phase. In the Naqshbandi Order we are careful to apply rationalism and the yoke of Islam. If we did not do this, people would be carried away in self-inflation and believe that they are incarnations of divinity. The emotional inflation can lead to megalomaniac notions. We bring people down to earth; we teach them to have their feet firmly on the ground whilst soaring to the heavens in their hearts.

Real meditation is used in Sufism to draw the traveller's whole attention from the external world to concentrate his senses inwardly on the lord. All forces, all faculties, are channelled in one direction, one path, towards the absolute and away from the relative. Now the so-called meditation of so-called gurus and occultists in the West—all these popular cults [that] have arisen—is no more than a mental escape from the noise of the world: a numbness, a sleep, that started with the notion of nirvana. I can assure you that we are not asleep, and even after hundreds of years the bodies of our great saints are as intact as they were when they were first buried.

Sheikh Nazim, who often comes here to visit us, told you about a great Sufi sheikh of Aleppo who died over 500 years ago, and the Aleppo council wanted to re-plan the city in the way that modern town planners do, gripped by the passion of the bureaucrats to straighten everything out. And this Naqshbandi sheikh's tomb was in the way, and on paper it was written off: it had to be bulldozed. So a number of bulldozers continually attempted to break it down, but without success. Eventually the bureaucrats approached the living descendant of the sheikh, and said, 'You must visit him in his tomb and try to persuade him that he must come out.'

So the living descendants went with a group of people at the request of the bureaucrats. When the cotton shroud was lifted and the body was taken out, the sheikh slapped one of them round the ear and they all fled. Eventually they plucked up enough courage to return, and the relatives asked the sheikh why he had done this. One of them . . . quoted a passage from the Koran where it is said that you should obey your sovereign master, and the sheikh became quiet.

But you see that even in death we are not asleep. We do not go in for transcendental meditation. Our form of mysticism expands the consciousness and makes you vividly aware.

Now to us the mosque represents the outward aspect of Islam, and Sufism does not oppose this; it is part of it, and in fact protects it. Throughout history, wherever Sufism has found its way, Islam has been established and advanced. There is a good reason for this, but it is very difficult to understand until you have actually experienced the Sufi way. We do not rant about religion, we say, 'Taste and experience it for yourselves.' We use a lot of psychological methods and we have our own psychological terms. I referred to one of these terms tonight: the *arifin*, the mystics, the performers of miracles, those with hidden powers, those who function (in modern terms) at the paranormal level, a level that modern psychology does not understand.

Now many mystics have talked about the treasure, and Sufism brings about a ruin within us so that you may find the hidden treasure in the grave. I quoted the *hadith qudsi* [sacred tradition], a saying placed in God's mouth: 'I was a hidden treasure. . . .' This treasure is the discovery of the *arifin*, those who attain to the level of paranormal experience. Alchemists refer to it as the gold, and it was a mysterious substance consisting of body, soul and spirit. In many cultures it appeared in winged and even in hermaphroditic form. On Greek vases it is so depicted. In ancient Egyptian mythology it was associated with Baat, the man-headed bird, which was also associated with the phoenix, the symbol of immortality. Many mystics who have attained the level of the *arifin*, those who function at the paranormal level, have so much energy that their bodies continue to radiate it after death, and this energy kills all the bacteria so that the body is completely preserved. This is only one form of energy that is contemptuously dismissed by modern psychology.

4

THERE ARE THREE STAGES IN THE JOURNEY TO REALITY: THE MINDLESS FLOCK, OBSERVATION OF ONESELF AND THE FLOCK, AND DETACHMENT FROM ALL IDENTIFICATIONS WITH LIFE. IN OUR PATRIARCHAL CULTURE WOMEN ARE LOST IN THE FLOCK BY BEING DELUDED IN THE MASS MALE ILLUSION.

This is the incomplete transcript of a public lecture given in London on 11 February 1982. Its title would have been added by the Sheikh. He was in the habit of dictating the title, usually long and explanatory, either immediately after the lecture to his pupil Saifuddin, who had usually been the person recording it, or later in the evening to whichever other pupil had brought the tape cassette back to the zawiya *for him. It was written on the cassette label.*

FROM THE KORAN: *'Bismillah ir-rahman ir-rahim'* ['In the name of Allah, the Compassionate, the Merciful']—saying about the Holy Prophet (may God honour him and grant him peace): 'Say: "Truly am I a warner, no god. No god is there but the One, Allah, Supreme and Irresistible, the Lord of the heavens and the earth and all between, Exalted in might, Able to enforce His will, forgiving again and again."

'Say, "That is a message, supreme above all, from which ye do turn away. No knowledge have I of the chiefs on high when they discuss matters among themselves. Only this has been revealed to me: that I am to give warning, plainly and publicly."

'Behold, thy Lord said to the angels, "I am about to create man from clay. When I have fashioned him in due proportion and breathed into him of My spirit, fall down in obeisance unto him."

'So the angels prostrated themselves, all of them together. Not so Iblis.[57] He was haughty and became one of those who reject faith.

'Allah said, "O Iblis, what prevents thee from prostrating thyself to one whom I have created with My hands? Art thou haughty, or art thou one of the high and mighty ones?"

'Iblis said, "I am better than he. Thou createdst me from fire and him Thou createdst from clay."

'Allah said, "Then get thee out from here, for thou art rejected, accursed, and My curse shall be on thee till the Day of Judgment."

'Iblis said, "O My Lord, give me then respite till the day the dead are raised."

'Allah said, "Respite then is granted thee till the day of the time appointed."

'Iblis said, "Then, by Thy power, I will put them all in the wrong, except Thy servants amongst them, sincere and purified by Thy grace."

'Allah said, "Then it is just and fitting, and I say what is just and fitting, that I will certainly fill hell with thee and those that follow thee, every one."

'Say, "No reward do I ask of you for this Koran, nor am I a pretender. This is no less than a message to all the worlds, and ye shall certainly know the truth of it all after a while."'

There was a rich and generous man of Bukhara. Because he had a high rank in the invisible hierarchy he was known as the President of the World. He made one condition about his bounty. Every day he gave gold to one category of people—the sick, widows, orphans, etc. But nothing was to be given to anyone who opened his mouth.

Not all could keep silent. One day it was the turn of the lawyers to receive their share of the bounty. One of them could not establish himself, and made the most complete appeal possible. Nothing was given to him. This was not the end, however, of his efforts. The following day, invalids were being helped, so he pretended that his limbs had been broken. But the President of the World knew him and he obtained nothing. The very next day he posed in another guise, covering his face so that people thought him to be of another category. He was again recognised by the Commander of the Invisible. He was recognised and sent away.

Again and again he tried, even disguising himself as a woman, but without result. Finally, this lawyer found an undertaker and told him to wrap him in a shroud. 'When the President of the Unknown Aspect of the World [comes], he will perhaps assume that this is a corpse. He will throw down some money towards my burial and I will give you a share of it.' This was done.

---

57 Iblis is another name for Satan (Shaitan).

A gold piece from the hand of the President fell upon the shroud. The lawyer seized it out of fear that the undertaker would get it first. Then he spoke to the benefactor. 'You denied me your bounty. See now how I have gained it.'

'You can have nothing from me', replied the generous man, 'until you die.' This is the meaning of the Sufi phrase, 'Man must die before he dies.' The gift comes after death and not before, and this death is not possible without the help [of] those who are truly guided.

Once upon a time there lived a poor goat-herd.[58] Every day he took some goats to a hill overlooking a village where he lived with his family, to seek fresh grazing. He was deaf, but this did not matter at all to him. One day he found that his wife had forgotten to give him the bundle containing his midday meal. Nor did she send their child with it, as in the past when it had been forgotten, even when the sun was high overhead. 'I'll go home and get it,' thought the goat-herd. 'I cannot stay out here all this time until sundown with nothing to eat.'

Suddenly he noticed a man cutting shrubs on the hillside. He went up to him and said, 'Brother, please keep an eye on the goats and see that they do not stray, for my wife has stupidly forgotten my midday meal and I must go back to the village for it.'

Now the shrub-cutter was also deaf, and he didn't hear a word of what had been said and completely misunderstood the goat-herd. He answered, 'Why should I give you any of the shrubs which I'm cutting for my own animals? I have a cow and two sheep at home and I have to go far and wide for food for them. No, leave me. I want nothing to do with the likes of you seeking to take what little belongs to me.' And he waved his hand in derision, laughing harshly.

The goat-herd did not hear what was said, and replied, 'Oh, thank you, kind friend, for agreeing. I shall be as quick as I can. Blessings be upon you. You have set my mind at ease.'

He ran off to the village and went to his own humble hut. There he found his wife sick with a fever with his neighbour's wife in attendance. He took his bundle of food and ran back to the hill. He counted the goats carefully and they were all there.

The shrub-cutter was still busy at his task, and the goat-herd said to himself, 'Why, what an excellent person this most trustworthy shrub-cutter is. He has seen that my animals have not strayed and seeks no thanks for this service. I will give him this lame goat which I meant to kill for myself. It will make a fine meal for him and his family tonight.'

---

58 The following story is taken from *The Way of the Sufi* by Idries Shah.

So, putting the undersized, lame goat on his shoulders, he bounded down the hill, calling as he ran, 'Ho, brother! Here is a present for looking after my goats while I was away. Unfortunately my wife has a fever and that explains everything. Roast this goat for your evening meal tonight. See, it has a lame leg and I meant to kill it anyway.'

But the other did not hear his words, and shouted in a rage, 'You vile goat-herd! I never saw what happened while you were gone. How can I be responsible for the leg of your infernal animal? I was busy cutting these shrubs and have no idea how it happened. Get away! Or I will strike you.'

The goat-herd was amazed at the man's enraged gestures. But he could not hear what he was saying, so he called to a passer-by who was riding a fine horse. 'Noble sir, please, I beg you—tell me what this shrub-cutter is talking about. I happen to be deaf and do not know why he has refused my gift of a goat with such annoyance.'

Both the goat-herd and the shrub-cutter began to shout at the traveller, and he got off his horse and came towards them. He was a horse thief, and was also as deaf as a post, and he could not hear what they were saying. He had lost his way and meant to ask them where he was. But when he saw the threatening gestures of the other two men, he said, 'Yes, brothers, I stole the horse, I confess. But I did not know that it belonged to you. Forgive me, I pray, for I had a fleeting moment of temptation and acted without thinking!'

'I had nothing to do with the laming of the goat!' shouted the shrub-cutter.

'Get him to tell me why he will not accept my present,' urged the goat-herd, 'I merely wanted to give it as a gesture of appreciation.'

'I certainly admit to taking the horse,' said the thief, 'but I am deaf and I cannot hear which of you owns it.'

At that moment an old dervish came into view, walking along the dusty road towards the village. The shrub-cutter ran to him and pulled at his robe and said, 'Venerable dervish! I am a deaf man who cannot make head or tail of what these two other men are saying. Please, in your wisdom judge and explain what each of them are shouting about.'

The dervish, however, was dumb and could not answer; but he came to them and looked searchingly into the faces of the three deaf ones, who had now stopped talking. He looked so long and penetratingly first at one, then at the other, that they began to feel uncomfortable. His glittering black eyes bored into theirs, seeking the truth of the matter, trying to get a clue to the situation.

But each of the others began to feel that he was going to bewitch them or gain control over their wills in some way. Suddenly the thief sprang upon the horse and rode it furiously away. Immediately the goat-herd began to round up his animals, driving them further up the hill. The shrub-cutter, lowering his eyes from those of the dervish, packed his shrubs into a net and hoisted it on to his shoulders, bounding on down the hill towards his home.

The dervish continued his journey, thinking to himself that speech can be such a useless form of communication that man might just as well have never been given it.

Al-Sheikh al-Akbar—'The Greatest Sheikh'—Muhyiddin Ibn Arabi wrote hundreds of years ago:

Now there is a thing one should know, and that is that the person following the mystical path should know his place of beginning and his place of return: where he came from and where he is going. This knowledge is tied to three journeys. Therefore we shall explain these journeys. Naturally it is understood that these journeys have to do with the spiritual development of an individual. There is no beginning nor end to this journey, nor can it be numbered, but these three journeys we have chosen include them all. Unless a man has travelled through these three journeys he cannot understand his own being and cannot find in himself the necessary feeling of knowledge towards his Creator. Neither can he ripen within himself in order to grow to maturity. Nor can he lead others.

Each person has a real place in the universe. When the Ruler of the universe desires that reality to appear in relation to that person in the immanent world, He delineates the form of this in His own knowledge, which is total. The totality of it is the divine mirror, the universe of the knowledge of Allah Almighty. That form remains in this state as long as Allah Almighty sees fit. Then he descends through many levels, traverses the seven spheres and comes down into the globe of fire, then into air, then into water, and then falls on earth. After that . . . the life force is related to minerals. Then it changes to plants, then it relates to angels and then it relates to mankind and the *jinn*.

Until the life force reaches the degree of a human being it passes through many tribulations at every level of this descent. It meets with great difficulties. Sometimes it rises, sometimes it ebbs. Half a circle of the whole is completed before that life force is lodged at the level of mankind, and this is the point of its lowest ebb before the journey of return. For [a] man without understanding whence he comes and whither he returns, this appears to be the beginning. In a verse in the Koran it says, 'We created man in possession of all the beauties of the creation, and then We brought him down to the lowest of the low.' All these levels and degrees we have mentioned before—until he reached the human degree.

This is the first journey, and in [?] a man who has no understanding from whence he comes, [or] whither he is returning, joins the journey. He occupies himself only with motion and belonging. If he finds only the point of beginning he still remains very far from finding the universe of joining up. Such a person is in separation, and as an indication of this it has been said, 'Any person who is separated before finding the universe of union is a polytheist.' In other words, he is in direct opposition to the true law of Allah Almighty.

[In] the story I have just read you about all these deaf people, [they] are at this stage in the journey. They are so concerned with their own affairs that they interpret them in the stupid, intellectual way that this culture promotes. They have no way of relating to the real world. They are deaf, they are dumb. As the dervish went on his journey musing, at the end of the story: speech is no real means of communication. In the vast world of inner sensation, inner feeling, unless people are trained and taught how to be discriminating, speech is absolutely useless to them. They are blind and deaf and dumb and they are incapable of discriminating in relation to their own actions and activities. They are incapable of observing themselves and seeing the prison that they live in. Therefore, although they are [?endowe]d with speech it is not a means of communication, and so they are cut off from each other and from the true world of reality. In the Koran it says they are like flocks. Or perhaps they are even more addled, more bemused, more confused; and they are returned at the Day of Judgment belonging to the same group.

Most people live their lives thoughtlessly, stupidly, and projecting all their own notions about the world out on to people and situations in such a way that they are incapable of seeing beyond their own noses.

The second journey is also known as the journey of observation and education. In this second journey one must hang on to a source of knowledge because it is necessary to fly to the complete mind. This is found in the reality of Muhammad (may God honour him and grant him peace) through his way of life, which has been recorded in infinite detail by those who lived with him, who were intimate with him—all his Sahaba, all his Companions. At . . . the time of his death he had converted [about] 140,000 to the truth of Allah Almighty. Most of these people had direct contact with him. After his death, in what we call the *hadith,* sworn statements were taken about the guidance he [had given] to them all and about his attitudes to life, so that a comprehensive guidance exists in which one obtains an observer's view of life.

Muhammad lived totally unselfishly. He didn't project his notions nor his interpretations on to life. His personal servant said at his death that he had served him for most of his life but he [had] never questioned anything. He just accepted what was given in terms of service and love. He observed the servant but he voiced no criticisms of him. The whole of his life was spent observing and making a commentary on it, and he taught his Companions to be observers of themselves in order that they could deal with life objectively.

The people in the story who were completely confused because they were blind to reality because they were deaf to each other and dumb to each other—these people did not observe themselves. They could only relate to the world in terms of their notions about it: their whims, their interpretation of it. All the time they were at the mercy of their instincts or their emotions. They did not stand back and they could not see themselves as an observer would have seen their actions.

Most people on the first journey, which I've already described to you, are so self-obsessed that when you are in conversation with them they are not even listening to you: they are busy thinking up what they are going to say, or tell you they feel, so there is no communication. They haven't the ability to stay still within themselves and allow a communication to take place.

[In] this state of travelling as an observer, Ibn Arabi goes on to say, until man has reached his own position he has acquired on his journey of descent many [*omission in transcript?*]—what one could call impurities; what I have described in my talks as identifications: personal identifications at many levels—intellectual identifications, emotional identifications, instinctual identifications with the world as they have experienced it. This is not just in relation to the one earth life that they believe they have lived. At the instinctual level there are instinctual likes and dislikes which have very little to do with having lived as an ego, as a personality in the world from birth until the point at which their life is being considered.

Such a human being has acquired from each level—the intellectual, the emotional and the instinctual level—a useless or hindering quality. It is because of these that he has got lost in the multitude of the false journey and has become, as it says in the Koran, lower than the flock—like a flock of sheep. When he has held on to a complete teacher he will have to let go of most of these characteristics that he has acquired on the way down and he will return to that state which was his primordial state. He will need to return to the guidance of his instincts, but his instincts have to be purified from all the false identifications which have been built up in them since childhood.

The primordial state is like the state of a wild animal that is compelled by the seasons to act in certain ways. Its instincts respond to forces beyond its control, and these forces are built into the seasonal life which governs the growth [and] coming to fruition of plant life and then the dying and eventual decay and the resting period until the new cycle comes about. Animals are subject to this cyclic process, and human beings are subject to this cyclic process but know nothing of it consciously because they think intellectually on the lines that the culture has fed them. Later I am going to point out that women, who are really built to be closer to their instincts than men, have suffered even more from the false intellectual culture than men have.

When I say that the primordial state is like that of an animal I don't mean that people should live at the level of animals, but they should be rightly guided by their instincts. Most people deduce, from insufficient facts, assumptions which they make about life, its situations and their relationship with other people, and they develop opinions about things which they hang on to tenaciously, blindly and stupidly.

Ibn Arabi says [that] unless [a man] is purified in this way it is not easy for him to reach the area of the total mind, the area of instinctual knowing. Imagine a man who has started on the way: unless he has a mystical understanding of the real mind he will never be [on] the same level as the people of truth. To become properly evolved, it is necessary when you are still on the way to reach this level of instinctual guidance. This is what the Sufi saints have achieved: the *awliya*. Those who have reached the guide—what we call al-Hadi—this guiding aspect of Allah Almighty—are pure. Those who have not reached this level of guidance are impure. A man who is on the way becomes a real man when he reaches this level of understanding. This we equate with the reality of Muhammad (may God honour him and grant him peace), and that which is mentioned in a *hadith* about him applies to such people: 'First of all Allah created my mind.'

The man of the mystical way at this station is colourless and finds unity. What is meant by colourless is that the identifications are lacking: they have become detached. Those who can see with the eye of the heart see an atmosphere around each person. This is coloured, and its degree of intensity and its actual range of colour is as peculiar to the individual as . . . individual fingerprints. A number of people have the same general background colour, but within that there is a tremendous variety of additional colour.

For those of you who know about art, [among] the French Impressionists a lot of the *pointillistes'* paintings appeared to be comprised of a lot of dots in the way that the printing of photographs evolved. The dots were composed of a whole range of colours which go together to make a comprehensive whole. This is a rather poor simile for the atmosphere around each individual, and the points of coloured light all represent aspects of identification. These aspects of identification change as the lifestyle changes and as the habit patterns change.

Sometimes people adopt constructive courses, sometimes they adopt destructive courses. Those who are rudderless and don't know where they are going fluctuate between these two areas of acting. As this fluctuation takes place it is recorded on the light points around them. Even although they change, the marks of the former state are left there. It's rather like hammering nails into a door. You can take the nails out but the marks are left there.

So the people with the eye of certainty can see what you are, and when the two angels come to you in your tomb to question you about your life, they look at this record. This is what the Tantric people call the [Akashic?] record. We know that it is the colouring of the pure colourless light which Allah Almighty has given to each individual, so that the one who is at the station of colourlessness is in this state—that 'the colourless imprisons even the colour. Moses makes war with Moses. One who does not enter a colour finds a sweet way. Moses and Pharaoh become friends'. In other words, all the opposing forces—the positive and negative complexes which bind the energy of one's being and maintain them locked up in certain ways—have to be married together in an harmonious way to create the clear light of understanding. The mind, the expanded mind of a human being, then finds the total mind, and his identity merges with the vast Identity that controls the universe. His spirit finds the holy spirit.

This station is known as union after separation. This is the station of the people who are attracted to Allah Almighty. Perplexity, remorseless distraction and [?]intellect are at this level, while many get irrevocably lost at this stage of the way. That is why they say, to look for union whilst still separated is madness, and if this madness happens the man of the way of truth remains at this stage. He can never go forward and can never reach perfection or completion, and cannot find truth in itself as it is.

However, this state is an extremely pleasurable one, and it is the station of journeying with truth in truth. The one who has started on the journey—the *saliq*, the traveller who desires the journey for its own sake—has thrown into the ocean the atom of existence inside himself. He is now non-intellectual. He looks at life not from the point of view of the intellectual consciousness, and he is not obsessed with himself, so he's not constantly aware of himself nor of the universe nor of anybody else, and from this moment on he cannot take refuge in any one aspect of religious relief and cannot subject himself to regulation by means of dogma.

He must not loiter in this state, however. It is absolutely essential that he must go forward. With the help of Allah Almighty in this station finding the state of non-existence, it is necessary for him to reach the universe of subsistence with Allah Almighty.

The third journey is what we call *baqa* or *baqi billah*. This is subsistence with Him. It is the journey from reality to the many—from *haqq* to *khalq*. That is to say, having found the universe of the unity he passes back into the state of separateness. The man on this journey is in the state of helping others to know. He has to clear a way [for] others with a spiritual descent, and he puts on the cloak of manhood and comes down from his spiritual estate [to be] among the people, and mingles with them. At that stage he is all things to all humans in that he is only observing them.

There is a *hadith* about this which says, 'I am also a human being like you all,' and this the Holy Prophet said to his Companions. It is necessary at this stage to eat, to drink, to sleep, to marry—in other words, to perform the human functions as Allah Almighty intended them to be performed, and to be aware of every function, to experience every function and to be complete as a human being in experiencing all these functions, but not to be identified emotionally or intellectually or instinctually with any part of life, any event or any association, so that one is not bound to them.

Many people are the slaves of a cigarette. Others are the slaves of alcohol. Others are the slaves of their mortgage. Others are the slaves of their pension. People are all slaves of one thing or another. Complete balance and knowledge of the direction—travelling along a straight path—is essential.

As Ibn Arabi describes it, 'neither excess nor deficiency must there be in him: that is the right way in the midst of this. The person who reaches that state is therefore of the level of being above reproach, and he knows his real direction. Outwardly he agrees with religious law and accept[s] it, but he never gets involved with extra ritual other than that which is absolutely essential'; and all the great masters of the Naqshbandi Order, to which I belong, have made this one of their ruling principles. Many of them refuse even to lead the prayers. They always had, in many cases, a deputy, from among their followers, to take the prayers.

When you are at one in the way I have been describing it is not necessary to be part of the mechanical processes which are used to discipline those who are of the flock. This doesn't mean to say that we don't pray, and we insist that while people are being trained . . . they do pray. 'To understand this person is very difficult, because people think and judge a person by his visible devout attitude and his exterior actions, and they think it is the devout man who is evolved.' Devotion to religious matters is excellent in itself but it is not necessarily a mark of real spiritual evolution. This is judged in terms of the spiritual science, and at that stage the person is psychologically complete in a way that our culture does not even begin to understand. As Ibn Arabi says, 'the perfect man's development cannot be seen with the eye of the normal senses. To be able to see him you have to have eyes that have reached him.'

When we come into contact with people of our own kind we do not have to use the so-called communication of speech. Our own kind make their presence discernible to us afar off and we feel them in our being. As they approach, our mind becomes calm and still and we are listening for their words, and when they have said the words without speech they become listeners for our words.

The three stations that I have described are the meaning of the totality of the properly developed human being; and this descent into the world, where we are in the world but not identified in feeling terms with it—this doesn't mean that we are cold and hard and lacking in love and compassion, but sometimes we distance ourselves in such a way that we appear to have no feeling. This is sometimes necessary, because to show compassion when it cannot be understood is a worthless gesture. You can give to a charity, and there are international charities dedicated to feeding the starving masses in other lands. To give to such a charity does not necessarily mean that the intended recipients will receive the aid you believe they are going to receive. Many of these things are completely misguided, so we detach and see the reality of the situation.

The world as people see it is a collective illusion at any one time in history. I have said in talks frequently that the Graeco-Roman period is totally different from that of Norman England [or the time] of the Medicis in Italy [or the time] of the Prince Regent in England, and our time today is divorced completely from any of these. Each time has its collective illusion: its own outlook on life and its meaning. For a very long time—literally for thousands of years—this has been a male, patriarchal outlook in which men have manipulated the world to suit themselves and where they have imposed their will on women for their purposes; and this was brought about by the spread of warrior, discontented peoples in and around the Mediterranean area several thousand years ago.

All the times of the world are controlled by hidden forces, and each has its own appointed life. You have probably heard or read that creatures like the lemmings suddenly mass and travel for long distances and can sometimes be seen in their thousands swimming straight out to sea towards their own destruction. They are influenced by forces in just the same way that the hare displays a strange madness—the madness of the ecstasy of spring: the mad March hare. This ecstasy makes it run about in unaccustomed ways because it is feeling the vernal energy within itself, and it leaps about in patterns that are quite distinct from its patterns throughout the rest of the year; and when people pour out of land masses in the way that the Mongols poured out of Inner Mongolia and spread out into the world in warlike conquest, they are subject to forces which we teach people to feel and understand and make a relationship with within themselves in respect to the impact which these hidden forces make upon their central nervous system.

These warlike peoples in the Mediterranean took over a settled society which was based largely upon agriculture. It was the society that superseded hunting. It's what historians call the time of the Bronze Age, when weapons of war made it possible for certain tribes to conquer other tribes so that they obtained their wealth from the land and made them captive in terms of slaves.

During the agricultural times an understanding of femininity was greater in the minds of people than it subsequently became, because the slow cycle of the year's progress from winter into spring and from spring into summer and from summer into autumn and back into winter would appear to be the governing aspect of life, and this cyclic round was related to growth and related to the deep forces of life and the forces of the moon's phases, in which sowing was undertaken on the waxing moon, and the waning moon was known to have a diminished energy area. People in this settled area of activity were much influenced by femininity, and the role of women was much more equal with that of men—and in many cases dominated the area of human life, because it was understood that women were the recipients of the life force and enabled life to carry on, and that their role was not subservient to men: it was more important than men, because they were the instruments of life itself in the way that the earth is the instrument for promoting growth.

There were two aspects of this understanding of femininity. One was the bright moods which the women felt and the other was the dark moods that they felt. Part of the feminine initiation process was an understanding of the dark moods and what they really meant. One had to journey down into the deep interior of one's being, and women knew that they were equipped to do this better than men because cyclically, once a month, when they had their period, they were close to a sensation understanding of the deep nature of their own being, and they had to understand the cyclic ebb and flow of their own internal energy.

More and more people in our modern culture are training women to do highly intellectual, competitive jobs with men, and they ape the way of life of men and so they become lost in the male illusion of what they think the world really consists of. We know that the women are even more lost in the flock, as it says in the Koran, than the men, because the men have tried to carve a role for themselves and can see a destiny because they control most of the financial and social aspects of life. At present there is a female rebellion, but it's due to an inner dissatisfaction, and there is no true understanding of what motivates this rebellion. It is in fact a backlash within the consciousness of women, who are being motivated by hidden forces within the universe which are making themselves [manifest] at this time.

These forces are only slowly emerging. It's what people call 'entering into the Aquarian Age', and the Aquarian Age is only a description of a new range of forces making themselves felt on the earth which have not formerly been felt. When people encounter new forces they enter into a state of inner confusion because they have no previous experience by which to relate to these new factors, and they try to interpret the things in terms of their previous cultural experience.

In ancient Sumeria the dark side of femininity was described as 'the lady of the great place below'—this alien place which was outside patriarchal consciousness, outside that male-dominated world. She symbolized the great round of nature: grain and its growing, the seed below and the dying of the seed to sprout again. This area of a woman's consciousness represents the continuum in which different states are simply experienced as a transformation of the one continuous form of energy, but at any one moment this continuous form of energy is experienced in what Ibn Arabi calls its colourings.

Masculine rule over conscious cultural life, and over agriculture itself, relegated feminine power and fertility to the inner world. Women were driven in upon themselves. They could no longer take part in the exterior aspects of life. They were made into a certain type of flock by men, who said, 'Your role is domestic. Your role is that of a mother. Your role is this or that. We will dictate to you what your role should be.'

Women are in a position of being a transformation, like the grain which grows into the sheaf of corn which the reaper cuts down, and in this way instinctually women surrendered to seasonal forces which prevailed. In Sung times in ancient China, when this feeling relationship with the universe was understood, they called it the *dao* [the Tao]. The ladies of the court made beautiful embroidery, and they did not embroider if the feeling of the day was not right. They had to be at one with the feeling of the time. Their eternal feelings had to accord with the forces outside themselves: then they were in harmony with them.

Among the Sufis there is a particular order, the Mevlevi Order or 'whirling dervishes', founded by Jalaluddin Rumi, and this is [?]controlled by what is called *sema*, in which music plays a very important part. This music is laid down for each particular ceremony and there is no variation from the general theme, but at the beginning of the ceremony there is always provision for a ney or flute solo to be played by the solo master, the *neyzenbashi*, who feels the atmosphere of the day and unites with that atmosphere from within himself so that he sets the feeling for the ceremony; and my own pupils know that what we call *dhikr*, which is a special ceremony of the remembrance of Allah Almighty—each *dhikr* has its own individual feeling, has the stamp of the day placed upon it, and the Sheikh has not only to convey what this is but has to balance it if it is strongly positive or strongly negative, so that a certain climactic point is reached in which people concur with the feeling of the particular time.

Femininity at the level of which I've been speaking is the place where potential life lies motionless. It's like primal childhood experiences, like the darkness of the moon, like the places of oblivion. These are the perilous states on which daylight consciousness treads. It's the primal matrix of our understanding. There's a wisdom about this—a feeling wisdom; strange isolation, and even a bitterness. This dark side has to be explored, and a woman is close to exploring it. She sees what she is really like at that time in the month when she is menstruating, because she is different—quite different. But most women are taught nowadays to ignore all this and to live in their intellects and to neglect their feeling consciousness at a deep level.

This area in which women have to learn to feel is so much neglected by our culture that women interpret their role to themselves as fulfilling themselves in a man's eyes or in the eyes of men, and career women are now apparently trying to fulfil themselves in the various intellectual and social areas which have been devised by men for men.

The process of suffering that women undergo, for example, in childbirth teaches them to remain detached. If she is caught up in and identified with the pain it becomes extremely painful and unbearable. If the mind can detach from it and can submit, the pain is less. The suffering is part of the deep experience of femininity at a deep level. A lot of this is unconscious, and people have to awake and become aware of not only physical pain but emotional pain [where there] was formerly a silent numbness. Where there is no awareness of suffering, pain is numbly endured, and many women are placed in a position of suffering by their fathers where they numbly endure, either mentally or physically, certain male reactions. These condition them in such a way that their whole attitude to men and to life in general is affected.

At the instinctual level, femininity has the reality of constantly recurring childbirths attended by real deaths: a natural cycle that kept women at the instinctual level focused on the harsh process of reality in terms of the cyclic forces of nature—a sense of living on the brink of the abyss.

Women in their creativity have been concerned with births and the arts and the sustenance of the household, and all these things are subject to wear, to destruction, to devouring forces; but these are not appreciated in the wider conscious male culture. These may be the basic civilising force of certain cultures, but the wounding for a woman is part of the feeling brought about by her inner experiences and often by her physical experiences. Birth and death are intimates in a woman's experience, because in ancient cultures—in ancient Egypt, for example—due to fly-borne diseases infant mortality was extremely high, so they bore children and they saw them being carried away, and they became inured to the heartbreak.

This has gone into the feminine psyche at a deep level, and in all the ancient cultures the great goddesses suffered. They are wounded by separation from the child, or the separation of the mother who had a lover. They do not avoid suffering, but steer into it and express its reality. Many become impaled or eliminated by it. A terrible passivity can result, an inertia can take place, a hopelessness and a coldness within the heart can take over, and this becomes a sacrifice of activity which, if it is gone through, in time can lead to a rebirth and an illumination when it is accepted as a way of learning to be passive.

When people obtain my exercises, the men have to learn to be passive and the women have to feel the inner activity of the positive forces working upon them, and sometimes these positive forces can affect them very strongly because it brings out the suffering within them which they have endured at the hands of their fathers in childhood and the impact that a poor relationship with the mother has had upon them—and when women have had no real feminine guidance from the mother, because the mother has also been caught up in the web of male illusion and is trying to perform a feminine role in a male-dominated world, and cannot relate in feminine terms to the daughter, [this] produces certain male symptoms, and these male symptoms, when energy is applied to them, come bubbling up in terms of male patterns; and these male patterns can be at a physical level as well as at a psychological level. All the male type of impatience and irritation can come out. These irritations can be physically experienced.

This is part of the psychological transmission from the father to the daughter, but it's experienced at a physical level of irritation once again, in order that the memory of the original experiences can be understood, and how certain patterns of wild, emotional uncontrol came about in the woman's life. When she gives way to these unconsciously, she enters into destructive phases. These phases become part of what I talked about in terms of being coloured in a certain way. You have to experience at a feeling level all the heat, all the impatience, or all the cold, frustrating agony that you endured in childhood or at the hands of certain men.

Suffering has to be encountered in a detached way so that you draw back from the particular area of impatience or irritation or back from the cold, enclosing darkness of sheer desperate loneliness. This is suffering in a detached and primal way. It's a sacrifice of activity which can lead to a rebirth and illumination when this is accepted as a way. It's the presence of energy at the very darkest level of the mind, and you have to have a loss of all activity—the capacity for action—and you must be able to say, 'Well, nothing matters. It doesn't matter at all.'

When you have grieved deeply you come to a point where the sobbing and the grieving and the sorrow just goes on and it no longer has any meaning. It's just absolute desolation—and so a strange detachment from the sorrow takes place. The calmness of desolateness is encountered. You endure—barely conscious, barely surviving the pain and the powerlessness: suspended out of life itself, stuck until an act of grace takes place within you where a new wisdom arises.

These raw, impersonal, deep, destructive experiences are necessary in order to find other aspects within yourself. Many women can say quite truthfully, 'There's pain because I was abandoned by my mother. It's like a knife in my heart, and all my life I've been dead.' It's the bereft state of the child of the death [or ?dead] mother. It's a life of mortification. A woman can speak of her sense of being deprived: it's so raw it cannot even be touched, so it's an empty craving. This is felt so acutely that the whole of the human realm seems to be only ugly and terrible.

In this way women develop an antipathy to men because, although they think like them and are conditioned in a male society, at the instinctual level they dislike sex and the sexual act. Women can feel very desperate at times in their lives until they can stand back from their own moods, which come about psychically because they have been programmed at deep emotional levels in relation to summer, autumn, spring and winter. Each has its own emotional memory.

The recurrence of the cycles of nature and the recurrence of similar areas which are felt in the way I was describing animals as being guided by their instincts, these forces of the outer universe are felt in emotional ways in a half-recognised way, in a semi-conscious way, particularly when a woman is having her periods—there are many regressions back to earlier [times] in her life. Many women regress even to childhood memories at this time. Such women can spend the major part of their lives hoping finally to be mothered, hoping to be acclaimed in their womanhood by some knight on a white charger who will redeem their passivity.

Women have to be able to sacrifice their habitual emotional dramas, the frantic unconscious activity that goes on within themselves—and they have to withdraw from these things and see how they were started, and realise that the force within them is not aggression or rage or bitterness or recrimination, but really the forces can be felt in terms of force. There's the buzzing activity which, if it's separated from all the things like aggression or anger, is just like an inner 'zzzzz'.

Then there is a tremendous heaviness, and then there are other periods where this heaviness exists but there's a certain lightness such as you feel in the spring, which sits on top of the heaviness [and] makes it less heavy, but makes the buzzing less aggressive, and when people irritate you you are not so quick to react. You've got to learn to stand back from all these aspects of force, the forces of the universe within you, and see them for what they are.

The destructive, awesome character of the energy which rushes through women and provides [or ?provokes] their aggressions has been carried out of their normal consciousness by male domination, where they play the passive role of fitting into the male-dominated society. But these things abide in the depths of their unconscious.

This aspect of femininity is not antagonistic to masculinity, but a woman is surrounded by male judges—her concepts, the people who serve her. She gives birth to sons. She also has her own notions of how a man should relate to her. She doesn't understand that men have their notions of how they should be relating; and this is like the language of the story. Speech is an impossible form of communication, because neither speaks the same language. They interpret the forces of life—intellectually—in totally different ways. The real deep forces of the mind are not in antagonism in relation to each other, but the split-off infantile impulses which people carry into adult life and sometimes retain for the whole of their lives refuse to be recognised, because they control the person, and therefore true wisdom can never be found.

If a woman is playing a part, like an actress, in the male-dominated illusion of what culture should be, today she will become more and more aggressive and more and more unfulfilled. More unhappiness will be experienced, and she will reject out of hand in many cases the role she is forced to perform, and in many cases she will turn away from the dominance of men. These things produce paranoid behaviour patterns which lead to ever-more-destructive effects within the culture.

Women have to find what I described last week as eroticism within themselves—and I don't mean sexuality when I'm talking about eroticism. I described eroticism last week as a feeling relationship with the tides of life, [with] the tides imposed on the whole of life on earth by what scientists call the auric wind: the electromagnetic atmosphere of the solar universe. This relationship has got to be found by both men and women. Men have to learn to be passive, to be patient, in the way I've been saying that women have to learn to be patient to deal with their inbuilt suffering.

When women have had a bad relationship with their mother and have had an inbuilt suffering through a dislike of male patterns in their fathers, they frequently, at times when they are passive . . . encounter male voices or male images.

[*The last ten minutes are not recorded.*]

5

MAKING COMMUNICATION AN INTERNAL AND EXTERNAL PROCESS FOR FINDING REALITY WITHIN THE INDIVIDUAL MIND IN ORDER TO DISCERN WHAT IS FALSE AS WELL AS WHAT IS TRUE IN HUMANITY'S CONCEPTIONS OF REALITY

This essay is dated 7 October 1994. Again the title would have been the Sheikh's own.

SUFISM, unlike religion, depends on being constantly aware of what you are doing from moment to moment. This process of monitoring one's activity enables the Sufi to be in control of his or her being and therefore [have] the advantage over people in the world, who remain in a state of dreamlike reaction to the events that they encounter. The Sufi has the ability to choose or not to choose what he or she does at any one time. Most people in the world are carried along like flotsam on the surface of the river of the events that they encounter.

In religion, people participate in ritual or devotion of a spiritual kind for long or short periods, mostly in specialised places or positions. When the religious devotions or religious mood [are] superseded by other thoughts or demands upon their time, people switch off in order to give their attention to other things. Whether they are in religious devotion or giving their attention to secular subjects, most are not aware in an alert sense about what they are actually doing, simply because most of their activities are the result of habit patterns and therefore their minds are performing the activities concerned in a mechanical way and they are not alert to what they are doing from moment to moment.

The aim of Sufis is to realign the mind in such a way that the ego, [with] all its attachments of a habitual kind, is eliminated in the process of reorientating the attention of the individual towards becoming an objective observer of all experience and people encountered. For most of this century humanity in the Western world has devoted its attention to furthering the cause of individualism, and in this way the cult of personality has been fostered—to the detriment of character building. People's characters are created from their habits, and these habits influence both the conscious and the unconscious aspects of their thinking. In this way they determine whether they are ineffectual or effectual in the world.

In today's climate of consistent apology for individual and collective mistakes, where something or somebody else is always used as a cause of blame, and where the individual is lulled into believing that their individualism has a right to make consistent excuses for misbehaviour and failure, society in general has become hypnotised into believing that it can only react defensively in every situation.

Sufism has always taught that bad habits cannot be eradicated easily or in a short time, because the habits have been ingrained over the course of the years of an individual's experience. The culture in which we live today has reached such a peak of intellectual control over everything, and the individual's trust in that control leads to beliefs of such an erroneous kind, that beliefs and opinions are confused with reality. For example, people regard science and what scientists say in exactly the same way that they regarded religion and its priests and teachers in previous centuries. What is not understood is that scientific research and the information related to it is about fifty years ahead of popular scientific belief, which had been previously disseminated to the masses as fact. In the real world . . . the so-called facts of popular belief are all too frequently being re-aligned to comply with the latest information available as a result of experimentation in a whole range of fields, to which the average person in society cannot possibly gain current access.

With this trend in mind, priests and religious teachers are also consistently revising their opinions and their theology to take account of the so-called modern world and modern thinking. In this way original ideas are abandoned in favour of constantly renewed modern views which give rise to the obliteration of concepts which were held as tenets of faith for guiding people like milestones on the road of life.

These two factual trends alone should show that people are living in such a way that they are using assumptions as a veil for reality, and because they do this mechanically they can never check them, because the views of the society in which they live have been formed just as mechanically from the same or similar attitudes and behaviour patterns as they themselves are [immersed] in.

Alternative ways of seeing are therefore extremely difficult to convey in such circumstances, because people are living in a state of individual and collective self-deception.

The way in which Sufis think and act is not at the level of any contemporary set of social ethics. The thought patterns of the Sufi are based on the development of character, and this is opposed to the modern notions that it is expedient to live life by adopting a set of personality characteristics which people, using them to deal with problems or encounters, have adopted from their experience in order to carry them through each different situation as it arises.

When religion played a greater part in the lives of ordinary people, some at least among them occasionally thought about their actions and weighed them in their minds against the fact that one day they might have to account for them to God Almighty. Fewer and fewer people are doing this today. The Sufis, on the other hand, know that death is always at their elbow, and they verify this by looking around at the multiplication of perils in the modern world. For example, death in the public street by a car accident or by shooting, death in aeroplanes and at sea, where due to human negligence more and more accidents are occurring as a result of carelessness of the mechanics or inspectors of the vehicles concerned.

Sufis begin each day, or any project they may undertake or any problem they may encounter, with the appreciation in their mind that death is at their elbow. This enables their actions and responses to operate in such a way that they do not transgress certain principles which they hold to be the guiding milestones on the road of life. In this way, they can look down this road and understand just where they are at any one point on it and whether they are deviating from its straight path into some other field of semi-conscious wonderment.

Nowadays, people are taught that time is pressing upon them from all directions, and some become so trapped in their mechanical activity that they run instead of walking in the corridors and offices where they work (in some factories they even leap on a bicycle to get to another production point instead of using a telephone to check the interruption in the production process), and sadly are less efficient in the process.

Sufis are taught to produce effective work, and they can only do this because their minds are clear and alert and therefore they are aware from moment to moment about what matters most in relation to any undertaking. In other words, they are consciously thinking from moment to moment and never lapse into mechanical semi-conscious behaviour. In this way their attention is rooted on what they are doing, and because the mind does not wander from the matter in hand, the problem or the encounter is dealt with in a more effective way than in the case of people who perform activity bodily whilst their mind is in a state of inactivity in relation to the matter in hand, and instead their concentration has been directed to some other field of thought. In the inner space of their mental screen their whims or desires are dominating their attention and sapping it from the real object of their intent, [which is] directly in front of them in the physical world.

In any project, anything which is produced has its existence initially in the mind as a concept, and depending upon the skill and experience of the operator the concept becomes a physical reality, slowly after many stages or much more quickly through one or two trial runs. Most people in undertaking their daily commitments have no plan or idea about what they want to achieve. Until the mind is very clear and a strong inner vision can be seen, no concrete plan can be drawn up. Nowadays clever computer plans are capable of producing what an operator requires, but this is only another detrimental blow to the thinking ability of an individual, because these plans cater for and accord with the general trend of mechanical behaviour in today's humanity.

When craftsmanship still played a part in human activity the craftsmen consistently checked the plan or the idea, and as alert attention was brought to bear on the subject the plan gained effectiveness from this process, so that the physical object was modified in accordance with the evolutionary development of the plan. At work today faulty plans and faulty documents are handed on and people accept such things without checking them, and when faults or accidents result the people who have handled such things all blame each other for the faults and disasters resulting from their own careless attitudes. This is all part of the view that life has to become faster and people have to undertake everything they do at a faster pace. They react to this by believing that there is no time for checking and exercising responsibility in the area where they ought to be exercising it, or where they are paid to do that.

In a world where everyone else is to blame except the individual concerned, the power of the ego is so strongly entrenched in everybody that it is believed that an individual has a right to defend what they believe to be true instead of dealing with reality as it is encountered in their experience of projects, people and encounters.

The Sufi recognises what solely concerns him or her when it is encountered. He or she does not wander outside this area of influence. In order to do this it has to be recognised where in one's daily life one can [exercise] responsibility. Most people allow their minds to dwell on concerns completely outside their power of control, and as a result they feel frustrated by the negative attitude they acquire in the process, which in turn causes them to neglect things which they can do within the sphere of influence they can control. In many cases people feel that their sphere of influence is so small that it is worthless to make any effort that might be necessary to bring about improvement when it is required. Consequently, they allow themselves to indulge mentally in broader issues and continually contemplate these in their minds, instead of playing the small part that is essential to being effective in their own life and livelihood.

This can only be altered by character building. Previous generations, in the century before this one, did attempt to build in this way, in that they made certain commitments in their daily lives to each other which enabled them to build an inner strength and accept more commitments and more responsibility. For example, keeping a promise or keeping the correct time of an appointment can become popular enough to be adopted as a fashion, and when the benefits of the habit are generally recognised, society could be persuaded to operate public transport more efficiently by adhering to the times scheduled.

This has become of such little consequence in the modern world that Mr [Boris] Yeltsin on his way back home from the USA had an appointment with the Prime Minister of the Republic of Ireland and was fast asleep in his aircraft when the time of the appointment arrived, causing the members of the Irish party, who kept to the time of the scheduled meeting, to be shocked, embarrassed and disappointed.

The Sufis know that the world interacts in a collective sense and individuals are dependent on collective activity, and that collective activity is dependent on individual responsibility. They lay greater emphasis on collective units such as the family, the workplace, the city [and] the nation, and the interaction of all these with the rest of the world, than on the rights of an individual to do as he or she pleases while trumpeting about individual human rights and ignoring individual duty and responsibility to society.

Today's attitudes have brought about false sympathy for what we believe to be victims of circumstances. More often than not, such victims are products of failing to see that things cannot happen as people wish them to happen when they have a passive and reactive attitude to everything they experience. Such people become entrapped in worlds where they believe they cannot alter any of the events.

The intractable attitudes which operated until recently in Arab-Israeli relations and in Protestant and Catholic Northern Ireland and in Muslim and Serbian Bosnia are all results of thinking in terms of fixed beliefs. The strategy of the First World War was an even more tragic example of fixed beliefs, which kept opposing armies in static positions fighting over a few yards of mud. When people confuse fixed beliefs in their minds with reality in any situation it produces inflexibility in outlook, and can lead to antagonism individually and collectively, to such an extent that when such people encounter their opposite numbers the foundation for destruction and tragedy is immediately laid.

Individuals who continually think about themselves and value their own opinions to such an extent that they are never prepared to listen to others are the product of a habit from which most modern individuals suffer, in that they have never learned the skill of listening attentively to other people in order to weigh up in their own minds what the other person is trying to communicate. In the average individual, the ego has ingrained this habit so deeply that when engaged in conversation the individual may have stopped speaking physically, but his or her mind goes on functioning in relation to what he or she wishes to say, and is thus totally deaf in relation to what the other person is saying vocally.

When the ego becomes so strong and the belief in an idea is emotionally held, or when an individual believes that society in general endorses the view that is strongly held by the individual, the person concerned will be prepared to rob or murder in defence of the notion so vehemently and emotionally held in the mind.

Sufism teaches that if the attention is consistently alert this will produce in the observer an alertness capable of observing everything that occurs from moment to moment. Accordingly the individual is distanced from the event encountered or the problem concerned, and does not therefore become identified with it in a mechanically dreamlike attachment. This distancing of the mind from objects or encounters in the initial stages enables a close objective observation to take place which will, if practised consistently, allow the mind to become more distant with practice; and in becoming more distant from the immediate event, the view of the situation becomes wider and takes in more detail as the distance increases.

This is the acquisition of an eagle-eyed view of life, where all the aspects within the circle of observation can be seen at the same time so that the mind can home in on a particular aspect in order to gain detailed information. This ability can be applied in turn to all the aspects, so that they are seen in context as well as in the variety of specific details comprising the whole situation. As this process becomes enhanced by practising the habit, the circle of observation becomes wider in its circumference and operates together with the circle of influence, so that a person is capable of operating effectively to really influence a situation. Together with the development of commitment, integrity develops to such a degree that a person becomes trusted by others, and through trust gains responsibility. The sphere of the circle of that person's influence naturally becomes greater, and thus the responsibility is also made greater and calls for even more alertness, more care and more attention.

In this way consciousness is expanded at the expense of the unconscious rambling normally undertaken in the minds of people who allow themselves to be rushed thoughtlessly along by the tide of life. Such people consistently blame others as well as circumstances and events, which they claim have distressed them or frustrated them during the course of their lives.

In other words, the Sufis are actively and consciously aware and are therefore in a position to learn how to control their lives and gain more trust and responsibility within any community than those who disregard everybody and everything they encounter and live indulgently as slaves of their whims as they become more and more reactive to all encounters in their mechanically lived experiences, where what they think they believe and see and hear and do are all mistaken for reality.

Sufis become aware of the wide range of other people's perceptions because they have learned to listen, receive and understand the communications of others. In this way they can see where other people's emotions carry them in relation to their motivating forces. For example, some people are seekers of power, others are motivated by money, others are concerned with promoting their children. The way in which people perceive things is directly determined by these attachments. These emotional and instinctual attachments are formed at a fairly early stage in life and are not necessarily soundly constructed because they are built on habitual reactions, where whims formed the initial attachment.

When people listen attentively to what another person is saying, they gain an empathetic understanding of how the other person's view has been formed in relation to any subject under discussion. This empathy is necessary in order to estimate the emotional maturity of the person with whom one is conversing, and enables the observer to construct a logical representation favourable to the other person in the discussion. The logical aspect has to be tailored to the level of the other person's emotional development, and therefore shrewd observation has to be developed before this technique can be adroitly applied, in order to communicate at levels of understanding acceptable to both parties.

Sufis do not use their technique to deceive or manipulate another person: they are only intent on setting up a level of communication with another individual where information of a logical or emotional nature can be exchanged for the mutual benefit of both parties concerned. Before this can be satisfactorily applied in dealing with other people, the Sufi pupil is taught how to sum up his own being by close observation combined with subsequent reflection about all experience encountered each day. The impact of the experiences reviewed in this way can be understood objectively as facets of reality for constructing insights which, when collectively assembled, constitute a continuous thread of wisdom capable of guiding any individual using the process through even the darkest labyrinth that might be encountered.

Jesus of Nazareth said, 'If a house is divided against itself it cannot hope to stand,' and when all the parts of the mind are motivated to work towards one goal for an overall purpose, the effect can be astonishing and gratifying because one's house gains a solid foundation. When this is done within the individual mind, the ability to sum up how another person's mind operates has also to be learned through observation and experience of humanity in general as well as in particular individuals encountered. There is a tremendous variety of difference in how individuals use their thinking ability, and in order to communicate in an acceptable way the Sufi has to learn to sum up quickly and effectively how another person is likely to react in a situation, or in particular circumstances, and yet be able to communicate at an acceptable level with that person.

This cannot be done through the cult of personality which is relied on so heavily today. It can only be done through building trust in the other person's mind and in one's ability to understand the other person's point of view, without judging or condemning, preaching or converting. In other words, the nuances of developing acceptable communication, where an understanding is achieved even between enemies, [are] the result of intuitively sensing what is in the mind of another individual and catering sensitively to deal with that person's point of view at any one time, so that understanding is achieved and further trust in the relationship is built up.

Sufism is, therefore, a consistent task of alert awareness designed to enable the individual to deal collectively, not only with human life, but with the whole of life. Many people who have dealt with the taming of wild animals or animals that have to be controlled, such as horses and dogs, for certain activities useful in life for man and beast, find that the same intuition is necessary in order to promote the development of trust and convey a sense of mutual responsibility. Understanding can come about as the result of love and patience, and this is ultimately necessary when taming wild animals such as African elephants to do work in forests or in road-building.

The development of patience, love and understanding all come[s] about from these initial steps . . . and eventually they prove that love is not something which can be demanded, but is freely given when trust and understanding [are] brought to a mutually satisfactory state in all parties, and where communication of an acceptable nature is taking place between all who take part in a project or encounter.

The domination of the Christian view of history and social behaviour over Western culture was reflected in nineteenth-century philosophical views that the noblest qualities that could be incorporated into the character of individuals were produced by adopting Christian principles. In England, for example, Dr Arnold of Rugby public school was esteemed by the establishment of his day because he insisted on incorporating these 'high' principles in building the character of the boys in his charge. Since such people were destined to become leaders in English society their influence was felt on its major institutions including the church, the civil service, business and the military. In this way people felt that these 'high-minded' ideals would be assimilated into the whole fabric of society.

Newspapers, magazines and church sermons also disseminated the same ideals, so that they became popular throughout society. Books portrayed Christianity as a religion that was superior to all others, and missionaries were sent throughout the British Empire to convert 'heathens' to the one 'true' faith. It was popularly believed that if such people behaved according to the imposed beliefs of Christian culture it would not only raise the quality of their daily lives but would also produce aspirations that would lead to advances in civilisation throughout the world.

Religious teachings of this kind incorporate intellectual principles as axioms designed to improve the quality of human behaviour within society. Because they are axiomatic they are regarded as having permanent worth and not subject to transient, fashionable trends.

Sufis do not share this view because they know that, since all activity is first conceived in the mind before it becomes a reality, intellectual education inevitably produces inconsistent and transitory thought patterns in both an individual and society. Principles of this kind are either read or conveyed orally by religious teachers and philosophers, and the attention of the individual receiving them is only concentrated on them in a momentary way. A few more serious-minded people may think about them from time to time, but few, if any, exercise great concentration when confronted with them or in subsequent thought about them. The thoughts are separated from each other by periods of time when the individual's attention is directed to totally different thoughts and activities.

The spasmodic nature of this activity means that the quality of indelibility is not secured. At the time of their initial assimilation no more emphasis was given them than that which was applied to every other thought passing through the mind. With the passage of time new ideas become more prominent and are discussed collectively, and ideas which once might have been considered axiomatic fall into disfavour or are completely abandoned.

Sufis also observe that such forms of indoctrination are in competition with a whole range of other information which is more attractive to the individual's judgment at any given moment. Because the assimilation process is itself weak, so is its impact on the mind and subsequent behaviour. Character building can therefore be just as easily based on opposite characteristics (such as self-esteem, greed, deceit, etc.) since these often have greater appeal because they are more closely related to deeper, emotional and instinctual, levels of the mind. The internal divisions resulting from this haphazard process meant that the strong moral beliefs about behaviour that prevailed in the nineteenth century were contradicted by the variety of personalities assumed by individuals to deal with their daily experiences.

In other words, most individuals show no consistency in their behaviour patterns. For instance, in Ireland it can easily be observed that people leaving church, where they have displayed a 'Christian mood' and where they believe their attitudes are acceptable to God, will, having left the church, go straight across the road to the nearest public house and change from that mood into one that fits in with the loose social atmosphere of the premises.

Sufism is concerned with unifying the whole being which people have compartmented.

Much guilt can result from this division of the individual's being. In society today much time and effort goes into expurgating this. Just as the intellectual assimilation in an individual's mind is subject to easy forgetfulness because little attention is given to intellectual information in general, the collective view in society is subject to similar transience, and new ideas are quickly adopted and with equal facility discarded. This leads to inconsistent behaviour and an inability to maintain commitments and to carry out responsibility at both an individual and collective level.

Conflict within the mind, coupled with the inability to maintain behaviour in accordance with one's intentions or to live by standards regarded by society as effective for maintaining civilisation at the level of its highest aspirations, soon produces decline and degeneracy in the behaviour of society's role models. Role models who act only on whims and impulses which are freshly conceived and acted upon from moment to moment in a disjointed manner encourage society in general to do the same. Society has chosen to follow such role models today and as a result [they] have not only brought degeneracy but in addition have caused great confusion in a multitude of ways in nearly every sector of the world's affairs. The Sufis believe that this is clearly apparent in the way society is drifting towards economic, social and political disruption. They see it as largely due to the influence of role models who have transmitted a chaotic and hedonistic view to all who care to follow their example; and the example has been followed because it is so easy to flow with the trend.

The Sufi way is quite different from popular trends of this kind, and embodies the imposition of a disciplined self-control resulting in self-knowledge which enables the practitioner to abandon the chaotically constructed habit patterns which form the entity that people in general mistakenly consider to be a stable and unified personality [and] which they present to the world as a complete being.

Although the march of science has done much to undermine Christian belief as it was understood in the previous century, a residual belief in the need to develop character according to high principles of an intellectual kind still exists—despite many influences encouraging freewheeling cultural behaviour which permits individuals to do as they please, so that when a choice in life is presented the easiest or most pleasurable option prevails. Despite the fact that society now teaches people to expurgate feelings of guilt, intellectual notions of high-minded idealism still remain. Nevertheless, there are fewer constraints placed on excessive self-seeking. Consequently a sense of individual and collective responsibility is becoming increasingly redundant [*i.e.* rare] within society.

The intellectual foundations of Christian-based culture and knowledge are quite different from the forms of practice and experience conveyed by Sufis, who use methods which accord with the composition and operation of the universe. Sufi methods incorporate a range of repetitive practices which become deeply engraved on the mind so that the being of an individual becomes unified through the abandonment of all the divisions and divisive habits which have accumulated from childhood onwards.

There is a marked difference between the conception held about 'principles' in the Western world and 'principles' as understood in Sufism. In the version of the Bible authorised by King James it is written that Jesus said 'unto every one that hath shall be given . . . but from him that hath not shall be taken away even that which he hath'. Much speculation can be entered into in relation to the meaning of this sentence. The Sufis know very well that this is one of the great axioms of life, and it is simply saying that, if concentration is placed upon anything, the aspect on which it is placed gains in measure and stature to the detriment of other aspects, which are neglected because no emphasis of concentration is placed upon them.

For example, the human brain is not like a computer, although many people believe that in its construction the operation of the brain works similarly. When the brain is faced with something entirely new the process of learning to deal with the encounter enables a state of recognition to be established. When the encounter is repeated, the recognition is recalled and the process is strengthened and made easier by being made quicker. Each time [an] encounter is observed which is similar to the original one, the recognition becomes engraved more deeply in the mind, and the nerve mechanisms which were potentially available to provide a range of different recognitions fall into disuse and become weakened.

Sufis work entirely using such principles, and when they build character into a pupil they use such methods for building the character and for making it strong enough yet flexible enough to be linked like the strands of a thread to other strands built up in a similar fashion in order to make a guideline for carrying the pupil through life. When Western principles are conceived and imparted to society they are like isolated milestones in the mind, designed to take people from one point to the next on their journey through life. In the average life the path is not always straight, and the milestones can't be seen in advance on a twisting, turning route.

If the classical story of Theseus and Ariadne is recalled, Ariadne, it will be remembered, provided a thread which enabled Theseus to find his way through the twists and turns of the maze which he had to travel in darkness to deal with the Minotaur. It also enabled him to return to the daylight at the entrance to the maze, and it saved his life. Sufi principles are based on this continuously flexible weaving together of principles which enable the pupil's consciousness to operate at many levels and to communicate with others at the level at which they are capable of receiving any message that is being conveyed through the process of communication.

6

OUR NEGLECTED PSYCHOLOGICAL HERITAGE

This essay dates from around 1994. It was composed in reply to a pupil in the UK who had written to the Sheikh mentioning a proposal by some associates of hers that Istanbul should be designated the 'City of Mary' in effort to build a bridge between the West and the world of Islam. The title is the Sheikh's own.

MYSTICISM seeks to introduce humanity to the intuitive factor through sensory feeling of what is within the mind and the body coupled with their responses to the universe around.

Intellect can describe this if it is used in warm emotional ways, dealing with human encounter and the sharing of experience. Symbols and their impact at an emotional or intellectual level can only be truly understood if they lead to what is unseen but which is of the food of love for a real mystic, who encounters that unseen factor in a spirit of ecstasy. For example, a Gothic cathedral is full of symbolic meaning; the rose windows, the soaring arches and the individual geometric analysis of each cathedral can appeal to the emotions and to the intellect in turn, but what it is conveying is at the heart of the cathedral in the depth of its crypt, where it exists unseen and cannot be encountered unless a personal course of development has been undertaken by a pilgrim with the aim in mind that he or she should, during that encounter in the crypt, understand momentarily the meaning of the drop meeting with the ocean.

When I read works by Ibn Arabi such as the *Bezels of Wisdom* I can understand his intellectual description of the development of the levels of comprehension within the experience of humanity as evidenced by the great prophets he uses as examples, and how he describes Muhammad (may God honour him and grant him peace) as the perfect example of the peak of development possible for the human soul in the sense that Sufis understand the expression *insan i-kamil* [perfect man, or whole man]. [But] when I read *Sufis of Andalusia* by Ibn Arabi I saw that he uses a totally different style. His descriptions of encounters with the Sufis of his own time, and some of the lessons he learned from them, are conveyed intellectually, but with a warmth, and contain teaching hints that are far more valuable, in my view, than the long, interminable dissertations and the intellectual conclusions contained in the medieval style of his other works.

For example, Ibn Arabi, in describing what he learned in terms of concentration from an old lady with whom he consorted at an early stage in his life, is of greater real guidance than a mere intellectual description. He says that this early teacher of his pointed out that she regarded him highly because when he sat down with her the whole of him sat down. This of course means that his full presence and all of his concentration was given in complete attention to her and to what she was saying, and the implication was as true then as it is now—that the average individual may sit down in a chair to be in the presence of another, [but] although the body might be there, the mind through inattention can drift off into a million different realms while giving the false impression that it is present with the body or in companionship with the person beside whom the body is sitting.

My purpose in saying all this is [to convey] that writing at length about the symbols and their intellectual meaning, together with the places where these symbols can be found, is of interest in the way that a travel book may or may not encourage the reader to encounter the places and the scenes described. It will remain only as an encounter undertaken at an intellectual, or at best at an emotional level, if the person actually making the encounter is not equipped to experience at other levels of consciousness any impacts which dissolve the barriers during the encounter between what is physical and what is beyond the comprehension of the physical senses, as constituted in the average individual.

Humans base their arguments and deductions entirely on what they have been conditioned to perceive and not on what is actually observable. One of the elements which gives rise to their confusion is the passage of time as it is experienced by the physical senses.

A whole sequence of events which may take place in a short or prolonged space of time, in terms of human measurement, can contain a cohesive experience [which would be] capable of providing understanding about the total experience observed if the events were to be seen as a patterned whole entity. As the constituent parts are unrolled they are experienced under intellectual conditions, and the mind interprets the portion of the totality as a whole entity, instead of understanding that in order to comprehend the real meaning the experience has . . . to be assessed in the future ([that is, the future] from the standpoint of the observer at the time it is seen). This [immediate] interpretation may be quite different from the meaning of the totality capable of being understood when the portion witnessed by itself is placed in the context of the whole experience once observers are able to see all the other parts at a point in time where all constituent parts, which they failed to place within a single context, have manifested in terms of a totality.

Humans use their thought processes in analysing and reasoning in order to break down the constituent parts of an experience; and, in attempting to understand the experience as a whole, speculation and reasoning are used to synthesise a result which is looked upon as an answer or a description of what has been encountered. With regard to history, people are led astray in this way because their hindsight is confused by the fact that they are locked within the cultural outlook of their own time warp. Intellectually they can never experience events of the past because the events themselves were brought about in a different way by the influences of the culture of that time. Because people learn much more by experience than by processes of hearsay, their conclusions are limited in this way.

When another level of consciousness is attained through mystical practice, time and space are seen in a totally different way. For example, places can be seen simultaneously by a mystic who at the same time has the capacity to appear himself at different times at the same place or in a number of other places at exactly the same time.

This capability of experiencing events outside time, as it is observed by the physical senses in the ordinary way, is achievable by any human individual because the power so to do has been provided in a latent sense within each human body at birth. Mystics become aware of this different visioning process, which is enhanced by inner auditory experience in the way that a sound track is attached to a film in a cinema. Professor Henri Corbin, who taught at the Sorbonne, described this in his work on Sufi mysticism as the creative imagination, in contradistinction to what is normally experienced at the intellectual level of understanding, which is poorly equipped because cultural indoctrination prevents any further advance beyond the intellectual level.

Some people are born with the intuitive element more highly developed within themselves than the people around them. They are regarded as being at best an embarrassment to themselves or to those with whom they may communicate about their extra-sensory experiences. Sometimes they have been regarded as anti-social, and during the time of the Inquisition of the Roman Catholic Church intuitive displays were regarded as motivated by the associates of the Devil, and the people exhibiting any form of extra-sensory perception were

The School of Celestial Fire

burned at the stake. At this time, which is described as the modern age, such people are designated as being clairvoyant or looked upon as mystics. Their extra-sensory abilities when displayed still produce a wide range of reaction in the public mind, ranging from sympathetic curiosity to stout opposition with regard to the expression of these abilities.

Sometimes the experiences of such people are recorded, and I will use an illustration from the recorded experience of Emanuel Swedenborg to illustrate this point. This account is contained in a letter from Immanuel Kant (the German philosopher) to Charlotte von Knobloch dated Königsberg, 10 August 1738. He writes: 'The following occurrence appears to me to have the greatest weight of proof, and to place the assertion respecting Swedenborg's extraordinary gift beyond all possibility of doubt. In the year 1759, towards the end of September, on Saturday at 4 o'clock p.m. Swedenborg arrived at Gothenburg from England, when Mr William Castel invited him to his house, together with a party of 15 persons. About 6 o'clock, Swedenborg went out, and returned to the company quite pale and alarmed. He said that a dangerous fire had just broken out in Stockholm, at the Södermalm (Gothenburg is about 50 German miles—about 300 English—from Stockholm), and that it was spreading very fast. He was restless and went out often. He said that the house of one of his friends, whom he named, was already in ashes, and that his own was in danger. At 4 o'clock, after he had been out again, he joyfully exclaimed, "Thank God! The fire is extinguished, the third door from my house." The news occasioned great commotion throughout the whole city, but particularly amongst the company in which he was. It was announced to the governor the same evening. On Sunday morning, Swedenborg was summoned to the governor, who questioned him concerning the disaster.

'Swedenborg described the fire precisely, how it had begun, and in what manner it had ceased, and how long it had continued. On the same day the news spread through the city, and as the governor had thought it worthy of attention, the consternation was considerably increased; because many were in trouble on account of their friends and property, which might have been involved in the disaster. On Monday evening a messenger arrived at Gothenburg, who was dispatched by the Board of Trade during the time of the fire. In the letters brought by him, the fire was described precisely in the manner stated by Swedenborg.

'On Tuesday morning the royal courier arrived at the governor's with the melancholy intelligence of the fire, of the loss which it had occasioned, and of the houses it had damaged and ruined, not in the least differing from that which Swedenborg had given at the very time when it happened; for the fire was extinguished at 8 o'clock.'

When Shams-i-Din Tabrizi accosted Jalaluddin Rumi in Konya he asked Rumi who was the greater—Bayazid al-Bistami or the Prophet Muhammad (may God honour him and grant him peace). Rumi answered correctly that Muhammad (may God honour him and grant him peace) was the greater, because he knew that Muhammad (may God honour him and grant him peace) understood the whole path of spiritual evolution in far greater depth than Bayazid, who was but a wandering dervish by comparison. Nevertheless Bayazid al-Bistami in his own time demonstrated his ability to manifest his being in six different situations simultaneously and at the same time took an active part in each of the events experienced by his contemporaries, who saw him do this while he was still alive in a physical body.

Scientists and intellectuals dismiss such accounts by describing them as myths, legends, or figments of overwrought imagination in the way that all such accounts of similar experiences are dismissed today. A master who is capable of exhibiting an ability of this kind has travelled in a different way to the rest of humanity during the course of his spiritual development, where the ability to demonstrate paranormal activity has come about as side-effects of the evolutionary process to which he has been subjected by a tutor, who [has] passed on the same knowledge and [has] taught him through the medium of experience in terms of a transmission, which all trained mystics undergo.

Such experiences cannot be truly conveyed by written accounts seeking to describe the process through the medium of second-hand experience, and therefore I agree with Solomon, who is recorded in the Bible as having said, 'of making many books there is no end; and much knowledge' (of an intellectual kind) 'is a weariness of the flesh.'

'Get thee wisdom' (*sophia* in Byzantine understanding) 'with all thine understanding.' People who lived in cultures before the present time, who are referred to as ancient, understood perfectly that wisdom was quite different from intellectual information and that the process by which wisdom was obtained was entirely different to the way in which argument, logic and reasoning were used in an intellectual way to arrive at what in the intellectual community are regarded as answers or solutions. Plato wrote an essay illustrating this point, in which he showed that Socrates was always capable of using the arguments of the Sophists (his intellectual contemporaries) to confuse them and to turn their arguments in the direction that he wished to take, and to convince them that what he was saying [was in the end] much more correct than what they themselves had the ability to say.

The School of Celestial Fire

The Byzantine culture inherited all the learning of Pythagoras, Socrates and Plato, and it was known that they in turn had received most of the wisdom that they had acquired from Egyptian priests. They also knew that this wisdom resulted from a course of conditioning which took the pupils of the Egyptian priests, by means of an expansion of their consciousness, through many levels of understanding to that which they were capable of attaining within themselves. The Egyptian priests knew that one pupil would differ from another by attaining a different level of understanding because people all limit themselves in one way or another by believing that they have completed the journey at any one point in time and at a level of development of their own choosing. I am saying here that different people set different limits on the ultimate point which they regard as the level of attainment they desire.

Every Greek scholar who returned from Egypt to enlighten the native culture of the time gave different accounts of Egyptian learning, but in general their accounts agreed about what had been seen and how their tutors interpreted the Egyptian view of the universe. Symbols were used in Egypt to incorporate a whole range of thoughts, and foreign scholars who sought to benefit from symbols incorporated in the teaching were shown how to use these symbols in relation to their own religious beliefs and cultural understanding. They were also taught the art of meditation, where concentration on a symbol for long periods of time could be used to introduce into the conscious level of the mind a whole range of inspirational thought material which came from deeper areas of the mind, not normally concerned with this form of mental stimulation. By this means the symbols were used in a contemplative way to stimulate the emergence of a flow of related visual and auditory experience, which in the case of vision can be described in our modern understanding as eidetic imagery.

In case you do not understand what I mean by eidetic imagery, it can be seen by staring at an object in a relaxed but concentrated way, without thinking of anything else. After a certain amount of time has elapsed, if the gaze is shifted to an adjoining wall, an after-image appears on the wall. Sometimes it is a mere shadow of the object, but at other times and in the experience of different individuals it can be seen as clearly as a photographic image, developed from a photographic negative. A quick way of ascertaining this to be true is to look at an electric light bulb in a room where the light is burning and look away after a short time. A faint image of the light will appear on the wall in the way I have described, and sometimes an image of the electric light bulb can be clearly seen.

Symbols therefore are used as media for stimulating the mind, and the knowledge does not come from the symbol itself but from within the mind which is being stimulated. This is all part of the long, disciplined journey which is described in the Holy Koran as Allah revealing Himself to Himself. The layers within the mind which have been stimulated were described by Jalaluddin Rumi in the *Mathnawi* when he wrote, 'First we were stone, then we became vegetable but forgot we had been stone, and when we became animal we forgot that we had been vegetable, and finally when we became human we forgot that we had been animal.'

Symbols of course incorporate the meaning given them by the culture which uses them, and sometimes creates them, if they have not been borrowed from elsewhere. These meanings can be lost with the passage of time, so that in another culture—subsequent to the original one, where the symbols were initially used—observers are capable of seeing the symbol as a photographer would depict it, but because they are conditioned by the processes operating in the culture in which they live they have no means of interpreting it in the way in which the culture which created or originally used the symbol could gain from its use.

Intellectuals still attempt to provide meaning in relation to the use of symbols, and this is possible at an anthropological level where the same symbols are used by different people in different parts of the physical world who have no contact with each other. Despite the lack of contact, the symbols are the same, and the simple meanings attached to them are largely the same.

When any culture begins to develop on intellectual lines instead of remaining based at an instinctual level of development, its symbols are changed in order to reflect the new intellectual content which has been introduced. With this introduction of a new and more complicated method of abstract thinking, the old cultural symbols are displaced by new ones, to reflect the greater complexity attained in the area of abstract thinking. Conservative use is still made of the old symbols until their meaning becomes more integrated with the new symbols in the use of a composite form, which attempts to incorporate the meaning in abstract terms of [both] the old and newly developed understanding about the religious subject matter or meaning of life.

Collective settlement and the resultant community effort to achieve greater wealth and possessions brings about leisure. Time is then available for abstract thinking, in a more detailed way, about the meaning of life, and for speculating about the part an individual plays in the environment or in the universe itself. As a result of such speculation, myths and legends become merged in religious forms, and dogmatic theories are used to mould beliefs about such concepts in a much more ordered form. Intellectuals vie with each other in doing this in order to gain status in a community by providing explanations that they intend to be believed by people with lesser ability to argue and reason about such things.

Belief results from a process of cultural indoctrination and, unlike faith, is intellectually based. As an example of belief I would point out that people believed in the Christian Dark Ages and early medieval time that the earth was flat, until Galileo read Greek documents written about the time of the last Ptolemy in Egypt together with the works of Aristotle setting out that the earth was round. With the use of his telescope he claimed that the earth was in fact round. He was condemned by the Inquisition for his heretical statements and made to retract them, but his claim was true and was subsequently proved to be true.

In religious matters belief and faith can be confused with each other, and this has occurred more especially in modern times. Ancient people made a clear distinction, because their faith was proved constantly at religious assemblies by means of mystical demonstrations. Modern people are guided only by what religious priests or scientists tell them. In their case, faith is incorporated in belief. Faith in religious matters in the ancient world was concerned with what an individual hoped for, and was created only when these hopes were endorsed by evidence of areas considered to be beyond the reach of the physical senses. For example, oracular divination from areas such as Delphi in Greece satisfied the masses of people in the ancient world when the words of the oracle given in prophetic utterances were subsequently proved to be correct. In Greece, as in Egypt, many miracles were performed in the temples of the gods and goddesses to create faith in the spiritual ideas expressed by the psychic reality—witnessed in the miracles that gave consistency of expression unaffected by time, and that convinced every generation collectively witnessing the religious ceremonies, during which paranormal phenomena occurred, that a psychic reality existed beyond the senses.

In our modern age miracles of healing which occur at Lourdes, or manifestations incorporating a collective human encounter with the Virgin Mary, are reported and quickly dismissed. Not so very long ago, a monk named Padre Pio in southern Italy was seen during Mass to rise high in the air, in the way that the Bible has reported that Jesus was elevated in a similar fashion at his transfiguration. The Christian church ignored Padre Pio when the Pope who was contemporary with him visited the area in which Padre Pio worked. Church authorities tend to take the view that demonstrations of this nature are mysteries of the church and should be accepted as such, and that it is more important for believers in Christianity to accept the dogmatic teaching endorsed through the centuries by the Popes and prelates by whom it was issued.

The point that I am making here is that in the ancient world religious belief was founded on the faith which was created by mystical demonstration. Christian attitudes at a later time regarded such things as trickery like that performed by modern stage illusionists. I do not doubt that certain of these things occurred in ancient times, but ancient people were not as naive as modern people imagine, and they themselves were just as capable then as we are today in our ability to distinguish the difference between a stage magician cutting a woman in half and the manifestation of the Virgin Mary at Fatima in Portugal. In the ceremony of the Kore at Eleusis, the mystery of the mother and daughter sharing a common experience contained the same idea as the myth [of] Isis and her sister Nephthys in Egypt conveyed about the duality of their roles, while being one in unity as sisters in experience. In the Song of Solomon the same theme occurs where the feminine manifestation says, 'I have a little sister.' In the ceremony of the Kore a range of aspects of femininity were depicted in a variety of forms, which described their psychic characteristics within the overall mantle of femininity. References to these aspects were incorporated within the Homeric Hymns, which were chanted during the ceremony. The ideas of sexual impregnation, gestation and birth, together with a comparison of the womb with the underworld and the act of rape with death, are all experiences of the feminine. The ceremony demonstrated the need for arriving at spiritual understanding through femininity, depicted in such a way that gestation itself was shown as a period of passivity, leading to birth and a renewal of life.

In the ceremony of the Kore, in addition to the common experience in the underworld shared by Demeter and her daughter Anodymine, other aspects of femininity were touched upon. In Egyptian mythology Nephthys does not play a prominent part in the activity related to the death of Osiris, nor in the conception of Horus. Set, the jealous brother of Osiris, had scattered the body of Osiris about the land after murdering him. This was then painstakingly reassembled by the wife of Osiris, the goddess Isis, who was pregnant with Horus at the time. Isis, in an archetypal sense, represented the use of femininity to connect areas in the mind which have been forgotten through aeons of human and living existence. (I have referred to what Jalaluddin Rumi said about human evolution—that, as each successive stage was developed, the knowledge gained at an earlier stage was forgotten.) Professor Jung could perhaps have described Isis, in his terminology, as a connector of archetypal material within the mind!

Nephthys was always shown in association with Isis, and was portrayed as one of the forces in the underworld protecting the dead. The Golden-Rectangular compartments which contain the sarcophagi of the pharaohs always had Isis in winged form in one corner and Nephthys in winged form in the other corner. (When the Ark of the Covenant was constructed in the time of Moses, it replicated this Egyptian construction. The two angels were representations that had been seen by Moses in the original constructions in Egypt.) Nephthys herself represented collective feminine character and behaviour in society. Her role domestically reflected the cultural context of everyday life in which the average ancient-Egyptian woman took part. In this role she represented everyday conscious activity, but she and her sister Isis shared a commonality of experience. Femininity is composed of their united characteristics—the conscious and the unconscious. Isis represented the whole unconscious history encompassing humanity's psychic development. Nephthys represented conscious feminine activity at the everyday intellectual and emotional level.

In Sufism, when writers describe the composition of the *nafs* they are describing the impulses, motivations and processes to which humans are subjected by their reaction to the events they experience. These motivations result from cultural indoctrination and transmission, as well as the learning which arises from their instincts, [and] guide them in constructive or destructive ways according to how their character develops. Isis and Nephthys represent the operation of the *nafs* and the behavioural patterns in femininity.

Isis represents the connecting role that femininity plays, in that through passivity the mind is silenced to enable voices from deeper levels to come echoing to the surface, where they can be distinguished and understood in order to make a closer connection between the surface areas and the deeper levels of consciousness. Women collectively experience this heavy state of passivity during menstruation. They understand the feelings that hormonal activity brings about in every individual female in a way that men can never understand, and physical and mental nuances which can range through a wide spectrum, from pain to pleasure.

This experience of sisterhood has been lost to the modern world because great emphasis has been placed upon individual development. In the ancient world and in Islamic culture this sisterhood was a bonding mechanism which took the individual woman into the area of collective experience of femininity. The Sufis describe this by referring to the way an individual soul is absorbed into the soul of humanity. The analogy they generally use is that a tiny spring becomes a river which grows bigger before merging with the ocean.

The point I am making here is that in the modern world individuals develop their own self-centred conceptions about their role in society, and their relationship with society, in a haphazard way. In the ancient world, the mother guided her daughter to create a psychic continuum, which travelled from individual conceptualising to [a stage] of collective feminine conceptualising. This acted as an important step towards conceptualising, in human terms, the unity within the whole of life in order to be able to conceptualise, as far as possible, in relation to the universe as a whole.

Femininity therefore played an important role in this revelation of collective experience. This revelation takes place in contemplation when it is undertaken in a disciplined way. When it is not, it takes place individually in a haphazard and confused manner in dreaming. In Sufism dreaming, which generally takes place at night, is always distinguished from the 'true dream', which takes place in contemplation. This is what Professor Corbin describes as the 'visionary recital' in the Sufism of Sheikh Suhrawardi.

The Golden Ass by Lucius Apuleius describes the tale of a stupid man who knows nothing of femininity and is guided through life by lustful impulses. He brings tremendous hurt and misfortune upon himself because of the way in which he has programmed his development. In the end, however, after he has been beaten down into the uttermost depths of misery and desolation as a result of degradation, Isis appears in a vision to him in all her glorious beauty, arrayed in the majesty of her power as the Queen of Heaven. At that time he is given instruction in the mysteries relating to an understanding of the goddess. He is told . . . that these mysteries are only one half of the process and can only be completed when he is instructed in the mysteries of Osiris.

In Lucius Apuleius' sequels to the book, *The Apologia* and *The Florida,* the results of contemplating in the way I have described are made clear. When the mysteries of Osiris are understood the developed individual is given the ability to draw from the Source of Wisdom in order to deal wisely with every situation encountered in life. This developed process is something that has to be transmitted through the generations of humanity, in the same way that it is necessary to transmit understanding of the role of femininity in bringing about this capability. The life force which unifies individual femininity with individual masculinity links archetypal femininity with archetypal masculinity in a spiritual result which provides a totally different way from acting and thinking in the intellectual sense.

Osiris represented resurrection, in that life continued after physical death because he returned to the underworld as its king and overlord after his consort Isis had 're-membered' his body by bringing the parts of it together again after they had been scattered abroad by Set. Horus lived in the upper world and possessed the ability to be at home in both the upper and lower worlds. His symbol was a royal hawk, which indicated that he could see both far and near and thus was equipped to deal wisely and effectively with every situation he encountered. Osiris was associated with the constellation of Orion and he was closely accompanied by his son, the Dog Star, named Anpu (Anubis). His mother was Nephthys, the sister of Isis.

The three pyramids at Giza south of Cairo in Egypt represent the belt of Orion, where the first two are aligned together. The pyramid of Men Kau Ra is slightly out from their alignment in the way that the third star in Orion's Belt is out of alignment with the other two. The Milky Way, known in ancient Egypt as the Divine Nile, is on Orion's left. On the other side of Orion the star Sirius can be seen, and [it] was used by the Egyptians to mark the beginning of a new calendar year. This took place on the day of its heliacal rising (the day when it rose immediately before the sun appeared on the horizon). This star was always associated with Isis, the goddess of light, brightness and goodness. Her sister Nephthys is a dark star, [what] modern astronomers call a black dwarf pulsar (giving off particle energy similar to x-rays). The ancient Egyptians knew of the existence of this dark star although it cannot be seen through the naked eye or through a telescope because its emissions are not in the wavelength of light. They knew not only of its existence but also that its orbit around the white star of Isis took between forty-nine and fifty years to accomplish. The ability to detect the star was lost after the decline of Egypt's influence in the world, and its existence was only recently discovered in our own time.

In the period which archaeologists call the Old Kingdom, one of the greatest mystical teachers who ever lived in the ancient world was born in Egypt and named Imhotep. His fame spread abroad well beyond the boundaries of his own country. He was regarded in late Egyptian times and during the Graeco-Roman period as a demigod. The people of the Old Kingdom were quite different in their culture, character and appearance from the people who followed them, after a foreign invasion of combined peoples (recorded as the Hyksos) [had] overwhelmed Egypt. The greatest cultural development in the Old Kingdom took place from the third dynasty, that of King Zoser (the Pharaoh of Imhotep), who built the step pyramid at Saqqara near where the main pyramids were subsequently built.

Egyptologists have often wondered why the pyramids of Egypt, of which there are approximately 117 in all, are largely confined to a fairly small area of the country. The reason is that these pyramids are all representative of the complex of stars in and around Orion. The time of the orbit of the dwarf pulsar around Sirius could be looked upon numerically as seven times seven, and because the figure was more than 49 it was rounded off to 50. Numerically seven represents the unity of the number four with the number three[, which represent] the finite and the infinite respectively. The number four in geometry is represented as a square and the number three as a triangle, and the circle represents time in all its phases.

The earth travels around the sun in 365¼ days, and the sun in its path through the heavens, from any point where it is seen to begin on its journey, will return to that point after approximately 25,000 years. This is known as the precession of the equinoxes. From observation of the heliacal rising of the star Sirius the ancient Egyptians were able to calculate the variation in time between the solar day and sidereal time. The circle is therefore a measure of variances in terms of the distance travelled in space. Modern scientists use a light year as their measurement for time in astronomy (a light year is the distance that light travels in one earthly year). The Great Pyramid was known in Egypt as Khuti (The Light) and it was erected on the geometrical juxtaposition of squares and circles around a central circle which also contained a square. That sacred square formed the base of the pyramid, and the tip of the pyramid was aligned on the star Alpha Draconis, which was the pole star of the time when the pyramid was built.

During the precession of the equinoxes a circular shift takes place so that other stars become the pole star and, over time, appear to form a small circle in the heavens. That circle represents the amount of time of the precession of the equinoxes itself. For every year of earthly time observed, the Egyptians saw that Sirius rose one day later than it had the previous year. In this way it travelled backward in the precession of the equinoxes. The ancient Egyptians were able to calculate what has been termed a phoenix cycle, in which it took 1500 years for Sirius (the star of Isis) to return to the same day on which it was first observed as the start of the new calendar year. They also calculated the precession of the equinoxes using highly developed mathematical calculations.

You can see therefore that the ancient Egyptians had tremendous mathematical knowledge and knew much more about astronomy than any of the scholars produced within the Christian era.

The Great Pyramid was built in terms of the divine proportions of the universe (our bodies contain this proportion, and an even better example can be seen by studying a cross-section of the nautilus shell). Herodotus recorded that the surface of each face of the pyramid was equal to the square of its height. Thus informed, we can tell that it contained a factor which is known as the Golden Section (denoted by Ø.) The pyramid was used to calculate latitude and longitude. Using the centre of the pyramid as the centre of a circle, an arc can be drawn which passes through the present site of Suez and stretches to Alexandria. The Egyptians took the centre of this arc as their base measure of longitude in the way that the Greenwich meridian is used today. About eleven miles east of Alexandria the Egyptians had a city called Behdet. This city [had] existed from pre-dynastic times. The Greeks called [it] Canopus, and when Alexander the Great founded the city which was called after him it was sited at Canopus. This is also a star in the constellation Argo, and in the ancient stories this constellation represented a ship and the star Canopus was at the helm of that ship.

Recently solar boats have been discovered buried at the pyramids. These boats were carried in procession at certain ceremonies performed during the reigns of the pharaohs of the Old Kingdom. A similar ceremony took place at the Temple of Apollo at Delphi in Greece, where it has been recorded that a huge boat was also carried in procession. These ceremonies relate very closely to the story of Jason and his journey to Colchis, where there was an Egyptian settlement.

The Egyptians also knew that Nephthys, circling around Sirius, affected life on earth at particular times of the year, and the reason why the heliacal rising of Sirius was closely observed was that the surge of energy on the earth at that time increased rapidly. This flush of energy we know as spring. In Egypt it began in early October, the same as further south in Africa. The Egyptians knew that this surge of energy within the earth itself was of a kind that takes place within the sympathetic nervous system of humans when occurrences such as shock, anger, fear and lust are all felt. The feeling of this surge of energy is overlaid by emotion in the average person's experience. Nevertheless, there is such a surge, which mystics are taught to arouse independently of emotions and to control and develop within themselves.

Where I mention the ability of the Chinese masters of *chi* elsewhere, the feat which I [describe] is accomplished by the emission of particle energy from the master and is of a similar kind to the x-ray emissions from the dark star beside Sirius. When energy such as stellar energy, or electrical energy as we transmit it along power lines, is used, both magnetic and particle energy are involved. A human being has the latent ability to use magnetic and particle energy within the body (and outside it when control over that energy is learned by the mind).

In ancient Egypt, when the mummy was placed in the tomb, grains of corn representing Osiris were placed in a little dish full of fresh earth, which had been watered. These were placed in the graves with the mummy to grow up in the way that corn grows up in the field. The representation was generally understood throughout the ancient world. The message conveyed was that this was a continuum which was not only concerned with the reproduction of life

[but] also represented the role of repetition in the remembrance (reassembling) of the psychic representations in the true dream of contemplation which Corbin described as the visionary recital.

This is the process which Muhammad encountered in the *miraj*, the journey to heaven, up to the point of the lote tree. In [the Koranic chapter] Surat an-Nur there is a reference to a great olive tree from which light springs forth. This is the Light of Life. At the lote tree the visionary recital ends, and we enter the area of the vast forces of energy which motivate our conceptions of the universe as human beings. This energy that is within ourselves and in all life is of the same range of energies that create, motivate, destroy and recreate everything in the universe within harmonious unity under the all-embracing Will of the Source.

Those who undertake the journey in full, and come forth like Horus operating at a higher octave than normal intellectual human experiencing, also know that their individuality is not lost when merged within the soul of humanity, and that humanity itself does not lose its collective individuality when it is absorbed within the ocean of life. This again is Allah Almighty revealing Himself to Himself.

When the freshly harvested grain of corn was held aloft at Eleusis in utter silence at the end of the ceremony, all who were present understood the meaning without the need for a word to be uttered. The life force latent within the grain, in a state of dormant passivity, could sprout when the sacred water was poured upon it. This energy, [which] operated as a living element in the growing of crops, was known to be the same force that gave life to the people themselves and operated to maintain life at a different level in the world of spirits, or the underworld. They also understood that a renewal came about by visiting the underworld, where communication with spirits of the departed could be made in exactly the same way that Emanuel Swedenborg consistently demonstrated throughout his life that he could communicate with those whom his contemporaries considered to be dead—proving again and again that they were living at another level of existence, by giving accurate information that they had conveyed to him.

Dante concentrated in the manner of the troubadours on the beautiful Beatrice, and in contemplation was able to enter the underworld, where he was shown various levels which have been described as hell and other levels contained in heaven. This is the ability of the conscious mind by means of alert concentration to penetrate deeper levels of understanding in a process of recall, where communication takes place via extra-sensory perception in the way that Sheikh Suhrawardi experienced the visionary recital. The layers of mineral, vegetable and animal consciousness are at various levels within our body, and the life force that is in us is capable of uniting the mind in such a way that mind and body are 're-membered' like Osiris.

Because normal consciousness is consistently afflicted by a stream of confused thoughts rushing through that area of the mind, concentration to enable proper contemplation to take place requires a mechanism to block the stream. The Sufis use the name of Allah Almighty repeated with every breath taken in order to still the mind so that deeper penetration can be undertaken—in such a way that communication similar to telepathy enables contact to be made in an extra-sensory way in areas which function at a different vibrational range from that of the light and sound to which our eyes and ears are attuned.

There are many recorded accounts of travellers in the countryside falling asleep and entering a hillside where they encounter realms which have been described as fairyland. Sometimes when people fall asleep in a cave, similar accounts have been recorded. Sometimes in these accounts a traveller is described as being unable to return because the heaviness that they have felt either imprisons them in these realms or puts them into a deep sleep so that they remain lost to the world until time itself releases them.

The cave of the Seven Sleepers, which is mentioned in the Holy Koran, was just such a place, and does in fact exist near the ancient site of Ephesus. In such a cave the energy of the earth acts upon the body and the mind of a person at certain times of the year when the place is visited, to produce a heavy drowsiness which results in deep sleep, which enables extra-sensory perception to take place. This is of a similar nature to what Shakespeare said when he wrote 'to sleep: perchance to dream'. The Mithraic mysteries were conducted in such caves, and early Christian ceremonies were conducted in the caves of the Seven Sleepers, near where Mary the mother of Jesus resided at Ephesus close to the Apostle John. When I visited the cave of the Seven Sleepers there was evidence of early Christian occupation in the area, and names were written in Greek on the tombs of people buried there. The sites of ancient religious ceremonies such as those conducted at Eleusis and Delphi are all areas where strong earth energies operate, unseen by physical eyes. Such energy currents can be experienced throughout the world, and in England there existed at one time a vast network. In modern times people have described them as ley lines, and remnants of the original network are still in operation in some rural areas, long after the Stone Age ceremonies which took place in centres connected with them [have been] forgotten. Energy of this kind forms a bridge between our physical world and unseen realms.

The mythology of Osiris, Isis and Horus was an allegory which illustrated the processes of mystical development undergone by temple initiates. Modern [free]masonry is designed as an allegory on similar lines. Unfortunately it is now only a ritual which is understood entirely at an intellectual level. The mysteries at Eleusis illustrated collective experience of femininity in greater detail than the story about Isis. However, in her role as the earth mother, Isis was comparable with Demeter, who demonstrated at Eleusis a relationship with her daughter like that between Isis and her sister Nephthys.

During one of my visits to Turkey I took pupils to a beautiful and correctly sited temple of Artemis, contained in a lovely valley beside which a sparkling river flowed. At that place the wild force of the hunt can still be felt. The virginal desire for protection of modesty which Artemis displayed is in the atmosphere of the site, and it is easy to imagine her bathing where the river bent around away from her temple. It is also easy to imagine the scene when she was disturbed by a youth looking at her, and the embarrassment that created the angry reaction in which the youth was turned into a stag which was ruthlessly hunted down by her.

At another time, on a visit to a friend's estate in the Tyrol, I found that the terrain there offered similar feelings. The estate was in a valley bordered by high mountains on either side, with a series of gentle little hills running down the middle. I noticed that some of the smaller hills were left in a wild and uncultivated way and appeared in sharp contrast to the meticulously cultivated vineyards surrounding these hills, like islands in a green sea. I pointed out the difference, and my friend told me that the peasants he employed on the estate could never be persuaded to cultivate the overgrown hills and that his ancestors had not been successful either in their attempts at persuasion. To illustrate the point he added that on certain wild and stormy nights, at particular times of the year, the peasants swore that *die wilde Jagd* [the wild hunt] took place, and that people could be heard running and the noise of hunting could be heard. I noted that the type of energy running through that valley in the Tyrol was very similar to the energy running through the isolated valley in Turkey where the Temple of Artemis was sited, and that the energy in the cave of the Seven Sleepers was of a totally different kind, very similar to that at Delphi where the famous oracles were uttered, there in the temple of Apollo. (His mysteries had associations with those of the Egyptian Osiris.)

Paradoxically, isolation results when a particular culture becomes more advanced and developed than others. This isolation is a result of complexity of understanding, and the more complex [the understanding] and the greater the concentration in a self-centred way, in a culture or in an individual, the greater the sense of isolation becomes. In ancient Egypt, for instance, the view of the world remained largely the same throughout many centuries because great concentration on it, together with a consistent maintenance of the lore and understanding about it, isolated the culture from neighbouring nations because Egypt's neighbours regarded the learning of its priests as being at a higher level than their own, as well as looking upon the customs and way of life in Egypt as being uniquely strange and mysterious.

An ethnic group of people can splinter with the passage of time and go to different areas where each sub-group in turn develops its own cultural independence. Social or economic events bring these splintered groups together again in friendship or as enemies in war. If the time lapse is great enough in relation to the separation from their origins, the people appear to have little or nothing in common, because their cultural differences have made the people forget their origins and influence them to believe that they are totally separate from these origins and have a distinctive national development of their own. This form of confusion, which arises in the thought processes, recalls what I was saying about the difference between actual experience of a culture and written accounts of it—either accounts written at the time and later interpreted in a different culture, or accounts written later in an attempt to interpret what the culture under observation was experiencing.

Mysticism is a process which is a development of latent faculties within the whole of life. It has been said by the Sufis that the whole of life is on a journey and that mankind has the ability to complete that journey, by developing the latent faculties which we have inherited through exposure to evolutionary processes which took place throughout aeons of time and are stamped within our being. We can only gain access to these different levels of experience by using the energy of life within ourselves to regenerate the memory in our body in such a way that the mind and the body develop another method of comprehending the experience dwelling within our being in an endeavour to understand what we have stored within ourselves through a process of remembering.

The Sufis remember their Creator, who is the Source of all knowledge, and in this way recover what humanity has forgotten in the passage of time covered by its evolution. The same remembering was undertaken when Isis re-assembled the body of her husband Osiris. Isis represented the passive element within our being, which has been more closely associated with feminine than with masculine activity (the nine months of gestation of the child within the womb [are] an example of development [taking] place in a passive climate).

The process of contemplation is therefore one in which sacred repetition of phrases stops the flow of conscious confused thinking in the mind so that information from subliminal levels within ourselves can arise from the depths to appear within our consciousness, where it can be assimilated and reassembled. Symbols can help the process, and there are slow methods and quick methods available for bringing this about.

In the Qadiri *dhikr* the beating of drums and symbols and gongs in certain rhythmic ways prevents normal conscious thought, because the noise made is so loud that it prevents any train of thought from being continued for any length of time. The pauses, which are made in an intermittent way, form a certain rhythmic pattern which affects the central nervous system in such a way that it is easy for the listener to pass into a state of light trance similar to that in which a hypnotist first gains control over a subject. In this trance a feeling of mental heaviness is experienced which inhibits activity in the mind and body of the listener, and as the process continues the desire to sleep becomes imperative. On the other hand, however, the attention of the mind is retained in such a way that a great clarity within an emptiness keeps the subject from falling into the state which is normally experienced in sleep.

In some ways the experience in the beginning is like falling asleep in a room where a bright electric light has been left burning. In such circumstances the body can feel heavy and desire for sleep is overwhelmingly strong. Although the eyes can be closed, light can still be seen opaquely by the eyes, and this focuses attention on a feeling of light still being on in the mind, which is quite distinct from the blackness encountered when the eyes are closed in darkness.

The energy of the Sufi master and the combination of the energy of his pupils who are taking part in the *dhikr* begin to have their own impact on the sensitivity of a person in this entranced state, so that further inner experience like dreaming begins to be represented within the mind of the entranced subject. A lot of this process of remembering in most *dhikr*s is due to the rhythm of the singing or of the music, where the sound functions at acoustic levels and at wavelengths to which the sympathetic nervous system is sensitive.

In Islamic mysticism the spaciousness of mosques and similar buildings which the Sufis have erected and decorated with flowing Arabic script all have their impact; they produce a cool calm feeling within the mind and produce similar states, in the experience of prayer, to that which the Sufis induce their followers to experience while taking part in a *dhikr*. Buildings therefore have to give the impression of spaciousness and harmony in order that symbols can be used to stimulate the deeper layers of the mind to give up forgotten and secret elements and allow them to come to the attention at the surface of the mind in the area where we consciously see and experience everyday events.

Mysticism has always been misunderstood even although its development has remained uniquely the same, and although a variety of methods can be used to bring about the same process. Intellectuals, who are locked in the one way of thinking and behaving, cannot bring themselves to think in any other way, and therefore they have a fanatical faith in their own assumptions just as fanatical religious people have a complete dependence on, and a burning faith in relation to, the religion they believe in and adhere to with such a desperate sense of insecurity.

When Jesus was asked why the scribes and Pharisees and similar religious teachers of his time did not automatically follow him and agree with what he was teaching, he said: 'They have Moses and the prophets and they know them not.' In other words, they had no understanding of the mysticism in terms of which Moses and the prophets operated. Jesus indicated that his contemporaries acting as intellectual teachers could not understand what he was trying to do. He knew well that they would not understand that he was doing exactly the same thing in his time, using the same or similar methods as Moses and the Hebrew prophets—methods which linked him with the Source in the way that they had been linked with the Source. He was therefore explaining that mystical methods do not vary, and that they form the same links to produce the same result that people [have] achieved in the past, because space and time are not hindrances in relation to mystical development. In the end, what results in an individual through the development of the mystical process is a capability which transcends both time and space.

Professor Corbin wrote extensively in the way the French write, with the same prolixity as evidenced in the medieval style I referred to earlier. After long introductory argument the reader is at last brought to the point where Corbin provides conclusions about the teaching of the great Sheikh Suhrawardi. At that point he demonstrates that, in what Corbin describes as visionary experience, Suhrawardi during this contemplative state was taken on a series of journeys by an angel who pointed to scenes where events were taking place, and the angel explained that each experience had a specific meaning. The Sufis know that all experience is meaningful, and that unless the meaning is grasped from the context, in order to be properly understood, the impact of the experience is nullified in terms of the individual profiting from [it]. Should this experience not be understood, it is presented once again at a subsequent time; the observing individual in question has no control over the time and the place where the same type of experience or a very similar one is presented in a similar context. Such experiences are encountered either while the observer is awake or in a visionary way.

Sufis are taught to review all that has occurred during the hours of daytime when they have been awake in the ordinary everyday sense dealing with what is encountered in everyday life. The memory of each action and [their] reaction to it is reviewed very thoroughly. An individual's behaviour patterns can then be seen during this operation in such a way that he becomes clearly aware of these patterns and how his reactions to these encounters mould and modify his ability to learn from experience.

Dreams which take place when an individual is asleep are used by the mind for the same purpose, but the average person takes little notice of them today. In the ancient world they were given much more credence, and much more time was spent in interpreting them. Nowadays Jungian psychiatrists deal with this type of imagery in order to enable their patients to gain an understanding of how they behaved in the past, and how their character and experience of events shaped their behaviour into patterns used in daily life to cope with their encounters in society.

Sufi masters act much in the same way in relation to their pupils. They know that when a child arrives on earth its mind is entirely free from the mental burdens with which it is loaded in later life where it is conditioned by family, social, national and contemporary cultural thinking. In intellectual consciousness most encounters in daily life are quickly dismissed from the mind and the experience never becomes meaningful because it is not understood, and no change is made to the processes in the mind which are used to deal with an individual's everyday experience.

Dreams and the mystic's visionary experience in the area entered into in contemplation are described by Corbin as the 'creative imagination', which operates in contradistinction to everyday use of the imaginative faculty as a means used by the average individual to express himself or herself. This area of creative imagination is where the visionary recital takes place during a passive state when contemplating, and this state is experienced in an area which lies between waking consciousness and sleeping. Disciplined concentration has to be developed in order that the visionary recital can run smoothly, in the way that a film is seen or where activity has been taped by a video camera for subsequent showing on a screen.

The Sufis know that this concentration can only be developed through a disciplined process. They call this 'remembering' and they use sacred phrases taken from the Koran or repeat sacred aspects connected with the being of Allah Almighty. One of the most common is *La ilaha illa'llah* ('There is no god other than Allah'). The Sufis call this *dhikr* or *dhikr Allah*, in which they repeat the name of Allah as every breath is taken. This form of concentration, as well as remembering the Source of their being, is designed to free the mind from intellectual, emotional and instinctual conceptions which imprison it in a state of chaotic and constant confusion. When the mind and soul are freed by this process after continuous application of it for long periods of time, the contemplative pupil is ready to see the inner film, which I have described in Corbin's terms as the visionary recital. This process enables the mind to see visions in a steady and continuous manner because the confusion, together with opposing thoughts and wilful inattention, has been overcome.

Perhaps I should say that when a film has been run at the wrong speed in a cinema, or it has been made by unskilled amateurs, its reproduction on a screen can be chaotically out of focus, and interruptions such as ineffective lighting prevent the film from being seen smoothly in the way that a properly made film, produced by professionals, is efficiently reproduced in machinery that functions correctly and is controlled by a skilled projectionist. In this way pupils are taught to exercise powers lying latent within the human body in conjunction with a mind which is trained in disciplined ways to transcend the level of everyday consciousness, which is consistently displayed in a poor, underdeveloped way by humanity in general.

In order to do this the teacher of mysticism takes the pupil on a hard, self-disciplined journey back to a state of inner peace in which the pupil's acquired conceptions about life, which imprison the mind in a state of constant confusion, are transformed. During this transformation process the mind and the soul are freed from their misconceptions as more and more enlightenment is gained in relation to the pupil's behaviour while living in the world into which he was born. Eventually this enlightenment brings a state of peace which grows in the being with increasingly greater intensity. During that time many examples of conceptualising are studied and many realms are visited where sections of humanity share similar beliefs, conceptions and behaviour patterns.

The ultimate destination of this journey is a state in which all conceptualising ceases and realms are entered into, when in contemplation, where the pupil encounters the myriad aspects of force or energy which lie behind the form of everything in the universe. The Sufis know that the intensified peace becomes so overwhelming that those who encounter it yearn to be bathed in it with a constant yearning. This is the state of encountering divine love (*agape* [in Greek]). Certain Oriental beliefs have described this state as nirvana. In it, the infinite ocean of energy absorbs what is now the cleansed energy of an individual, so that the drop represented by the individual can return to the ocean which is represented by that all-powerful attraction which holds the whole of the universe within unified activity. Today in the Western world, where great emphasis is placed on the ability to think and reason in an intellectual way, and where catch-phrases about human rights, democracy and freedom of the individual go hand-in-hand with notions that science provides the only truth that can be proved, and where ideas of a Creator ruling the universe are regarded as archaic, the whole atmosphere operates in direct opposition to the promotion of disciplined mystical endeavour. Such endeavour seeks to develop the mind by taking the soul on a journey, with the aim in view to reach the end of the journey by returning to the Source of our creation to operate in complete harmony as an intrinsic part of creation, under the will and direction of the Mind behind creation.

Mysticism therefore is concerned with inducing the expansion of consciousness to develop the latent possibilities within the physical body and to teach the mind in that body to lead the soul, or (as some would have it) the psyche, into changing its conceptions about life through a method of experiencing and understanding experience so that a complete transformation of a spiritual quality takes place in the way that the Source of all life has intended it to evolve.

It is recorded in a *hadith qudsi* [sacred tradition]: 'My whole creation cannot contain me, but I am to be found in the heart of my faithful servant who loves me.' Ibn Arabi illustrates in the *Bezels of Wisdom* that the soul of Adam becomes the soul of Muhammad (may God honour him and grant him peace) in this progression through stages of enlightenment, revealed to humanity at various stages by the great prophets sent from the Source to teach humanity, and that the teaching was crowned by the advent of the last prophet, Muhammad (may God honour him and grant him peace). For example, when Aisha, the beloved wife of our Prophet, was asked about him, she said that he was a living reflection embodying the whole of Koranic teaching within his character and way of behaving during his lifetime.

When I referred just now to pupils in contemplation encountering, during the 'visionary recital', realms where groups of people were gathered together in terms of similar belief and having similar characteristics and patterns of behaviour, I was referring to what Ibn Arabi described in the *Bezels of Wisdom*—an encounter with the whole passage of human spiritual development towards the state of reality, with ultimate wisdom.

I was also thinking about the journey of our Prophet which he undertook from Jerusalem to heaven. That journey, known as the *miraj*, describes the passage of the Prophet accompanied by the archangel Jibril through all the realms until the lote tree was reached, where Jibril indicated to Muhammad (may

God honour him and grant him peace) that he (the archangel) could not go beyond the lote tree, beyond which the realm of pure force operated and where no conceptualising ever took place. The realm is the area referred to as the *logos*. In Greek mythology Zeus held thunderbolts in his hand. They represented energy and force. In Tibetan Buddhist art and sculpture, certain *bodhisattvas* are depicted holding a thunderbolt in one hand. The meaning is the same.

Femininity as an aspect of collective human understanding is an agent of a passive kind, which is necessary for undertaking contemplation. In ancient cults various goddesses were depicted as representations of different aspects of femininity. In mystical contemplation or in true dreaming, a guide accompanies the traveller through various realms, to experience in conceptual ways emotional and instinctual experience designed to test an individual's reaction to this experience and to explain the meaning of the experience so that a comprehensive understanding is built up in the mind of the mystic undertaking the journey. Such figures are often female companions who appeal to the emotions in certain individuals, or voluptuous female figures who appeal to the instincts.

At a later stage other figures such as Khidr appear, in the way that Khidr is described in the Koran as journeying with Moses, who had met him and implored him to continue that journey. The Sufi Sheikh al-Hariri of Basra illustrates the operation of this part of the learning process in *The Assemblies of al-Hariri*, where he describes a whole series of problems during events in which he uses the encounters of Sheikh Abu Zaid of Seruj to illustrate the antics of the human mind and to teach others in a way that shocked and confused, and in which *malamati*[59] behaviour is subtly illustrated.

During the journey of the *miraj* of the Prophet Muhammad (may God honour him and grant him peace), Jibril acted as the Prophet's companion. Although Jibril was not a female figure, he was described as having great beauty and had an aura of tremendous attractiveness. In the account of his visit to Lot at the time when Sodom and Gomorrah were destroyed, it has been recorded in the Koran that when the inhabitants of Sodom saw him there they invaded Lot's house in an endeavour to sodomise him because he appeared to them to be so beautiful. In the traditions of the Prophet Muhammad (may God honour him and grant him peace) one of the Companions recalls that he was present when Muhammad (may God honour him and grant him peace) was giving *sohbet* (association with the teacher) and, in the presence of a number of the Companions, a man of most handsome appearance, who was dressed in a pure white robe, suddenly appeared as if from nowhere, passed among them

---

59 See pp. 261–5.

and disappeared as quickly and silently as he had come. In response to queries from Companions, Muhammad (may God honour him and grant him peace) indicated that the individual was the archangel Jibril.

This figure of passivity was known in the Byzantine culture as the *sophia*, or wisdom (crowned femininity). The face, in the most striking mosaic placed in the conch of the apse in the Hagia Sophia (Aya Sofya), is that of the Virgin Mary with the baby Jesus in her lap. The Byzantines regarded her as emblematic of the *sophia*. The mosaic was of course placed in the building with all the other mosaics long after the first church [had been] erected by the Emperor Theodosius (on occasions when I was there a few pieces of this original building could be seen lying in the garden of the present building, where they were laid out after being excavated). The present building is the third and last erected in Byzantine times. Even when this building was built, the mosaics were not incorporated in it, and they represent ideas which were not part of original Christian thinking because imagery was banned for a long time as being idolatrous and unnecessary. When the Ottomans turned the church into a mosque the mosaics were either curtained off or whitewashed over. One of them, representing the archangel Michael (Melchizedek—traditionally known in Hebrew esotericism as the archangel behind the Face, in the way that Gabriel was known as the archangel before the Face), was destroyed after the Ottoman conquest.

The point I am emphasising here is that depicting Mary in this way is a late-Gnostic development which took place as one set of ideas supplanted the previous set of ideas within Eastern Orthodox Christianity.

If I had companions with me at any time when I visited the Hagia Sophia, I always drew their attention to the depiction, on some of the pillars of the building, of what looked like a living flame. The representation is stylised and can be interpreted as a tongue of flame, and I have always looked upon it as representative of energy which embraces the universe and lies latent within each of us, capable of being developed as a light within ourselves, in the manner described in Surat an-Nur in the Koran. In Christian accounts of the descent of the Holy Ghost upon the apostles of Jesus at the day of Pentecost shortly after it is recorded that Jesus had ascended to heaven, tongues of flame were seen to descend upon them with a mighty rushing wind. Although these symbols appear in the Hagia Sophia I have never been able to obtain an adequate description from any Christian regarding the meaning, understanding or anything about what the Holy Ghost is supposed to be.

Although I digress here, it should be interesting to note that the psychiatrist Carl Jung experienced a mighty rushing wind in his house in a physical sense at the time when he received his most numinous experience and wrote the *Seven Sermons to the Dead* (the whole work has a Byzantine Gnostic flavour in its content). The force to which I have been referring has always been regarded as being within the control of the *logos* (please refer to my description about the thunderbolts of Zeus and Buddhist *bodhisattvas*. My account of the masters of *chi* in China is also relevant, and I would refer you also to the traditions of the Prophet Muhammad (may God honour him and grant him peace), who was reported to have said: 'Seek knowledge even unto China').'

I took a group of people to Ephesus to see the tomb ascribed to St John who is described by the Christians as 'the Divine' and to the house built on the spot where Mary resided. I also took this group to the cave of the Seven Sleepers, which in fact is like all the earliest Christian churches and is exactly like the caves where the Mithraic mysteries were celebrated. Areas like this were used by the early Christians as well as the followers of Mithras because they produce, either continuously or at specific times, phenomena similar to those experienced by pilgrims in the crypts of Gothic cathedrals, or by Egyptian initiates in sanctuaries of a god or goddess in the hidden dark depths of an Egyptian temple.

Such a temple sanctuary is housed in the base of the Louvre in Paris. Unfortunately its physical appearance only is constructed there, and no mystical experience can be gained from it, because the temple as a whole has to be sited in an area where the unseen can be manifested in the same way as a Gothic cathedral was sited to provide experiences of the unseen in accordance with the level of mystical development attained by pilgrims visiting the cathedral. During the initial stages of such mystical development the manifestation of the unseen to which I am referring is gained at the emotional level of the mind together with the ability to sense, through bodily feeling, energy moving through the sympathetic nervous system. At that stage, an initial fleeting feeling of an ecstasy can be glimpsed. When further development is undertaken these feelings are intensified, and when [the mystic is] fully developed they are known as divine love or *agape*. Some individuals, such as Teresa of Avila and John of the Cross, who were Christian mystics, experienced such constant divine love and received other accompanying divine gifts. The love itself has the character of an overwhelming bliss that gives a sense of all-pervading peace that obliterates ordinary human consciousness, to bring about a change in everyday experiencing where analysing by the mind ceases and the desire to compare one thing with another withers away. In this state everything encountered is seen in terms of complete equality, but the seeing is intensified so that greater clarity is conveyed in the contemplation than is experienced in the daily intellectual operation of the mind.

The Sufis, like all mystics, know that there is no such thing as truth in the way that humans seek ultimate information by using their reasoning powers. Sufis know from experience that love is the ultimate cohesive force in the universe. When they experience the ecstatic harmony I have been trying to describe, their soul is bathed in that harmony to such an extent that all else is extinguished, to the point where there is no room for anything else to enter upon or to disturb the blessed inner peace being experienced in that state of harmony. The mystic knows that the light that is the life of the universe has penetrated to enlighten the soul; and, in penetrating, the light within has become the same as the light responsible for the existence of the universe outside.

In the Holy Koran at Surat an-Nur a description of this light is given in a beautiful poetic analogy. The meaning of this analogy was transmitted by Muhammad (may God honour him and grant him peace) to his first caliph, Abu Bakr, and to his cousin Ali, the fourth caliph. This transmission is received in an unbroken line of succession by means of a living spiritual pedigree, and every sheikh, in all the orders, conveys its meaning by a variety of methods embodying both old and new techniques. Some of these, like others contained in Zen Buddhism, produce rapid enlightenment, while other methods are used in a slower way to produce the same result. The teacher selects the way which meets the specific need of an individual pupil. For example, the way of *malamat*, which is generally very much misunderstood even by most Sufis, is a teaching technique which occurs in states of inner contemplation and is also used by Sufi sheikhs for the enlightenment of their pupils.

Ahmed Ghazali, who was the brother of the great Abu Hamid Muhammad al-Ghazali, said that 'love has an advance and a retreat: an increase, a decrease, and a perfection. And the lover has different states in it. In the beginning he may deny it, and then come to agree with it. Thereafter, he may become vexed and then, once more, begin to deny it. These states change from one person to another, and from one time to another: sometimes love increases and the lover denies it, and sometimes it decreases and the lover denies the decrease. (In order to put an end to all these denials and agreements) love must open the self-protecting castle of the lover so that he becomes obedient and surrenders himself.

> 'I said to my heart, "Do not tell (your) secret to the Friend;
> Take care, do not tell the tale of love any more."
> The heart replied: "Do not say such a thing again,
> Surrender yourself to affliction and do not talk so much."'

He [says]: 'There is also the blame (*malamat*) brought about by love's realisation, and that happens when love departs—leaving the lover ashamed before himself, the creatures, and the beloved. Thus, he feels regretful because of love's disappearance. As a result of this, a pain takes love's place as its substitute for a while. Then this pain will penetrate as far as it may. However, it too will vanish (at one point) in order that a new thing may begin. (What has just been mentioned does not happen only once.) It happens quite frequently that love covers its face, avoiding amorous display, and pain makes its appearance, because love is a chameleon; it changes colour every moment. Sometimes it says, "I have gone away," when in fact it has not.'[60]

In the *Kashf al-Mahjub* of al-Hujwiri, the way of *malamat* is described thus: 'Blame has a great effect in making love sincere. The followers of the truth are distinguished by their being the objects of vulgar blame, especially the eminent ones of this community. . . . Therefore He hath set the vulgar over them to loose the tongues of blame against them, and hath made [the] *nafs i-lawwama* (blaming soul), which is part of the composition of humanity, in order that they may be blamed by others for whatever they do, and by themselves for doing evil or for doing good imperfectly.

'Now this is a firm principle in the way to Allah Almighty, for in this path there is no taint or veil more difficult to remove than self-conceit. Allah in His kindness hath barred the way of error against His friends. Their actions, however good, are not approved by the vulgar, who do not see them as they really are: and they themselves do not regard their works of mortification, however numerous, as proceeding from their own strength and power: consequently they are not pleased with themselves and are protected from self-conceit.

'Whoever is approved [of] by Allah is disapproved [of] by the vulgar, and whoever is elected by himself is not among the elect of Allah. . . . Hence the blame of mankind is the food of the friends of Allah, because it is a token of divine approval; it is the delight of the saints of Allah, because it is a sign of nearness to Him: they rejoice in it even as other men rejoice in popularity. There is a tradition [*hadith*], which the Apostle [Muhammad] received from Jibril, that Allah said: "My friends (saints) are under My cloak: beside Myself, none knoweth them except My friends."

Shams-i-Din Tabrizi was sent from the Source to enlighten Jalaluddin Rumi in Konya, who before his enlightenment did not fully comprehend the true nature of reality. Although Rumi's father had associated with sheikhs who knew the way of *malamat*, Rumi did not understand the process of the apportionment of blame. Shams, on the other hand, knew exactly what would occur

---

60 Translated by Nasrollah Pourjavady. The parentheses are in the original.

in the events which would unroll when he began to apply this technique to transform the thought processes of the great imam who had begged to be his pupil.

Shams began the process by sending Jalaluddin to the Jewish quarter, where he obtained wine for Shams, who had requested it. This request was soon followed by Shams' demanding that Rumi should supply him with the services of his own wife for the sexual needs of Shams. Such requests were designed to set up a loathing within the mind of Rumi so that a tremendous inner conflict could begin there. His desire to learn from Shams was brought into conflict with all that he had been taught by his cultural environment and his religion, i.e. a lifetime of complete abstinence from alcohol and a pattern of relating his love and sexual requirements entirely in a close relationship with his wife on the lines advocated by strict adherence to Islamic teaching and principles.

The force of energy within Shams and the mercurial and unorthodox attitudes in relation to what Rumi regarded as the correct standards for living in Islam confused Rumi to such an extent that his mind verged on madness. At the same time, the force of energy which Shams emanated from his being enslaved Rumi in the way that two lovers become enslaved with each other when they fall in love and concentrate entirely on each other to the exclusion of all else. Such a state is similar in its impact to that which a hypnotist exerts on his subjects, once the hypnotist has been able to prove that the subject has come under the force of his will.

When I use the word 'will' here, it should not be understood in the intellectual sense, but in the sense that Sufis and other real mystics understand it—that is, that an emanation of physical energy is emitted from a hypnotist or a Sufi master. In the latter case the energy is much stronger than that of a hypnotist and can affect objects and people outside the person who emits it. As it is emitted it is controlled by the mind of the Sufi sheikh. Although hypnotists have demonstrated this effect in a weaker way throughout the West, people in the modern world tend to dismiss it as a hoax or something to file in the back of their minds which they do not understand.

In China, *tai chi* is taught by masters of *chi*, who subject their pupils to between ten and fifteen years of *tai chi* exercises in order that they can feel this force of energy within their physical bodies. A *tai chi* master has learned to control this energy when it is emitted out into the exterior world by using his mind to concentrate it or disperse it. Many heal in this way, but the practice can be used in a great number of other ways. I have seen a karate master possessing a black belt of the quality of eighth *dan* attack such a master of *chi*. A karate expert of this standard is so speedy in his movements that he can catch

The School of Celestial Fire

a fly in flight with a pair of chopsticks. Nevertheless, before the karate expert could lay a hand on the master of *chi* I saw him grovelling on the ground clutching at himself in severe physical pain.

Although I digress here, I should add that in rare cases a similar force is capable of being released naturally and spasmodically in a haphazard manner. In some cases it brings about an onset of madness as it rushes through the sympathetic nervous system up into the brain. In others it produces an ability to perform a variety of other feats. One such is the ability to demonstrate tremendous strength. For example, I have seen a young girl in her early teens tear a telephone book into pieces in the way that a child can shred tissue paper. I have also seen a Russian peasant chain himself to two railway carriages which had been coupled together, before he dragged them along behind him in the way that it would have taken several heavy horses to do the same job.

To return to the way of *malamat*, I would like to point out that the effects which Shams had upon the mind and behaviour of Rumi caused Rumi to appear to have degenerated in the eyes of the people of Konya to such an extent that they felt pity and shame for what had occurred to the great imam whom they had formerly adored and revered. Shams was, of course, [an object] at whom they directed opprobrium, and this led to mob anger and violence as the feelings of loathing and dislike grew greater in the minds of the Konya people. Shams was fully aware, before he even started, of what would occur, and he took upon himself the blame of the people in order that he could reconstitute the mind of his pupil by the method he knew would achieve the task.

This reaction and blame which the process produced in the minds of the people of Konya eventually led to the exile of Shams and separation from his pupil. Rumi went in search of Shams and he was found at Damascus, where many of the great Sufis have their tombs, where he was constantly in communication with them, in a way that people at the ordinary level of comprehension cannot understand. Rumi begged him to return to Konya, and when Shams arrived back there the blame and dislike grew to such a dangerous extent that Shams was driven from the city once again. It was rumoured that he had been murdered, because he never returned. Rumi endured the utter confusion together with a devastating sense of loss. Thereafter he only slowly regained control over his mind as he developed the ability to function at a level well beyond that at which his mind had previously functioned, before the encounter with Shams-i-Din Tabrizi.

In the way of blame, the master accepts this blame in order to accomplish certain constructive processes which he applies to pupils or to events for the benefit of individuals or for humanity in general. Jesus himself used the same method. In the Garden of Gethsemane Peter boasted that he would never deny Jesus, and the master said: 'You will deny me thrice before the cock crows.' Subsequently, during their interrogation by the authorities, Peter did what his master had foretold, and when the cock crowed Jesus looked across at Peter with a sad smile. The smile was enough to make Peter grief-stricken. At a later date, when Peter had joined the Christian community in Rome and the persecution against the new Christian sect had reached a level where fear had entered into the hearts of the Christians because many were being martyred for their faith, Peter decided to flee from Rome. On the outskirts his master appeared in a vision, and Peter, although he was startled, asked him '*Quo vadis, Domine?*' ['Where are you going, Lord?'] and his master replied, 'I am on the way to Rome to comfort my brethren, who are in great need of me.' Peter, in shame, turned back to Rome, where he was known as the humblest of apostles and where he met his death upside-down on the cross, because he believed that it was not fit that he should be crucified in the way that his master had been.

Unfortunately posterity, guided by priestly speculations which fostered dogmatic notions, was led to believe, within the Christian faith, that Jesus had taken the sins of the world upon his shoulders, and that, as individuals, humanity could be saved from sin if they believed in him. This, of course, is utter nonsense because each individual is solely responsible for every act and deed undertaken in life, and is ultimately his own judge, and the judgment is of such a kind that, if they have been destructive or have hurt or destroyed living creatures, the individuals concerned are destined themselves to undergo the same or similar experiences, from which they may learn. An illustration of this immutable law is contained in allegory form in Buddhist lore, where a butcher is described or is depicted pictorially as killing an ox in one life, and in another life the ox has become the butcher, who is killed in turn as an ox.

Sometimes a Sufi sheikh may act as an *agent provocateur* in order to illustrate the operation of blame to a pupil. A certain Sufi master overheard his pupils discussing what each in turn would do to put the world to right if they had the power of the Qutub (the representative of Allah Almighty on earth). One day as dusk was falling, his favourite pupil saw an old man, bent with age, rush through the city gates as the guards were closing them. This had annoyed them, and they turned and beat the old man and kicked him on the ground, abusing him for causing them annoyance. The Sufi pupil fumed silently in anger and ran back to the *tekke* [*zawiya* or lodge] of his master, who when he was greeted asked him where he had been. The young man panted out the sorry tale and, still in anger, shook his fist, saying, 'If I had had the power of the Qutub I would have struck down these wicked city guards.' The Sufi sheikh smiled and said, 'My son, do not blame and do not judge. Judgment can only be made by Allah Almighty, because He alone possesses all the facts. I was that old man, and I hope from what you have seen that you will learn not to blame without knowledge of the process. When you can understand the process of blame you will be proud to take blame upon yourself, for of such are the friends of the Friend.'

In Graeco-Roman times, there were a range of religious cults teaching the [role] that the aspects of femininity played in [humanity's overall] view of the world which prevailed at the time. One of the most popular cults was that of the Persian Mithras, and it was concerned with male development. The mysteries of Mithras were extremely popular with the Roman legions, and many branches of the cult existed throughout the Roman Empire. This cult appealed to the legions for a number of reasons. On foreign service and particularly in unfriendly areas, men were thrown back on to their own resources in the legions, where they found in their own company intellectual and emotional stimulation.

The cult of Mithras was a disciplined mystical process of concentrated control over character and behaviour in order to help [?arrive] at the stage where contemplation itself could be clear, so that there was consistency within the clarity of the visioned sequences encountered. It was essentially patriarchal, and each Mithraic group was responsible to the one among them who had attained to the level of Pater. The cult of Mithras flourished because the society of the time was essentially patriarchal, although great respect was given to women, and in Roman law if a woman could prove that her husband was adulterous he was punished very severely.

Anthropologists and sociologists believe that prior to about 1500 BC society in many areas was of a matriarchal kind. At that time restless movements of people took place in the Mediterranean area, and wars were fought between rising empires on the development of city cultures, which had changed dependencies on the rural areas to a more collective and stronger trading and manufacturing centre in cities. In these wars the Greeks conquered areas where matriarchal culture had prevailed, and introduced a patriarchal society instead. The Romans followed the Greek pattern, and the military might of the Roman legions depicted the masculine power of the Roman ethos throughout the empire.

In ancient Egypt, the cults of Isis and Osiris enshrined a quality in the eyes of the people there that created equality and a balanced harmony in the relationship between men and women. Egypt remained isolated from its neighbours by the pharaonic armies going out from [its] borders . . . to the south, to the west and to the east in expeditions which were designed to neutralise the possibility of aggressive attack on their homeland. This put a barrier around the country, where foreigners were always treated as strangers [and] never received a very warm welcome. On the other hand, foreigners regarded Egypt as a land of mystery, and it was known as the Black Land, not only because of the colour of the black mud brought down by the Nile, but because foreigners believed that magic and mystery went hand-in-hand in such a way that they could fall under the spell of the magicians who operated there as priests and priestesses in the temples.

Egypt lost its sovereignty for the last time when the fleet of Augustus Caesar destroyed the Egyptian fleet at the battle of Hatim and made it possible for the Roman legions to enter and attack the Egyptian heartland.

As a result of the role of women in a patriarchal culture which was dominated by men, women formed a close bond of sisterhood in such a manner that they took part in female activities and developed a much greater understanding of their role in society, and of the powers that lay within them, by assembling at temples dedicated to various goddesses designed to portray a range of feminine activity. This compensating reaction by women throughout the civilisations of the Mediterranean brought them a very considerable understanding in depth with relation to the feminine side of the human psyche. Many of the most respected soothsayers and seers were priestesses at oracular sites such as Delphi or at temples dedicated to Dionysus, because the ecstatic experiences which women had the opportunity to take part in introduced them to areas of ecstatic experience where many became entranced, while others underwent a stage of madness and confusion from which they recovered and were seen to be much wiser as a result of the experiences which they [had] lived through in the entranced state. Many seers and prophetesses emerged from the Bacchic revels and Dionysian experiences to become counsellors of kings and nobility, and were looked upon as having a wisdom which was of the same nature of philosophy that Socrates and Plato taught at a later stage.

In the understanding of the ancient world the *sophia* became intertwined with the notion of wisdom, and at the intellectual level philosophy was conducted as a way of explaining that the mystical experiences gave rise to a balanced cosmic view of the world which had been acquired by visiting realms beyond physical sight which were designated as the all-embodying underworld, which was divided into areas of misery and areas of bliss, to which the dead departed. Philosophy therefore grew from a sense of bewilderment and questioning to gain a world view so that the pantheons of the gods and goddesses could fit the increasing complexity of rising civilisations.

In this way, humanity tried in the midst of a confused world to understand the ultimate nature of the cosmos and their place in relation to other things which existed in it. The goal of philosophy was the attainment of wisdom so that those who had attained it could describe how they had done it, and how humanity in general could tread the same road. The ancients knew that there was a feminine world connected with the soul and its development, and that the dead benefited from understanding this in order to obtain peace after death in the underworld. This became in Gnostic times the Hagia Sophia of the Christians and the Anima Mundi as understood by the alchemists. As these notions developed, that which was understood to be feminine was associated with the earth and the moon. The highest celestial regions were populated by male deities and they were understood to have power and authority over the world and over humanity.

At the time when Paul of Tarsus took what were essentially the teachings of a Hebrew prophet and reconstituted that teaching to make it available to non-Jewish people, there came about a division within Christianity itself in which the original teachings of Jesus were carried on by the Apostle James in Jerusalem, from where they were carried to the Jewish diaspora. Paul of Tarsus, on the other hand, concentrated on converting what subsequent Christians called pagans to Christianity. The Apostle Peter received a vision which permitted him to join Paul in these endeavours, and together they ended up at the centre of the world in Rome, where Christianity developed alongside expatriate Jews who adhered to the traditional teachings of their fathers. Enmity arose between the two religious groups, and where the Jews, through wealth and influence, were able to turn existing authorities against Pauline Christianity they always tried hard in many different ways to denigrate it.

Throughout the period up to the fourth and fifth centuries AD Pauline Christianity was influenced by established religious cults and opinions, some of which were absorbed to produce Gnostic Christianity. This particular form of Christian development went east when Byzantine culture was introduced into the Roman Empire of the East with the foundation of the city of Constantinople. During the 900 years of Byzantine culture Gnosticism had mixed fortunes. In the beginning it flourished and, like everything else in the way of the world, there was a reaction to it in which the church authorities banned it and made edicts which were intended to destroy Gnostic gospels and works incorporating Gnostic philosophy. The turning point of the tide which eventually destroyed Gnostic mysticism was the edicts formulated at the Council of Nicaea.

The last vestiges in western Europe were wiped out when the Pope and the King of France banded together to destroy the Cathars in what was described as the Albigensian Crusade. Subsequently the Knights Templar, who had been introduced as a Christian order to protect Jerusalem, were also destroyed. That particular order had been introduced to the Pope by the saintly St Bernard of Clairvaux and had been given the Pope's seal of approval to establish Christianity in Jerusalem. Their [role] in the subsequent Crusades resulted in a wider view of religious understanding being given them by contact with Islam and the mystical orders of the Sufis. The great Sheikh Suhrawardi lived at this time and was martyred for heresy by the son of Sultan Saladin (Salahuddin Yusuf ibn Ayub), who drove the Christians from Jerusalem in the Second Crusade.

In the west, as Christianity developed when Rome was re-established under the Holy Roman Emperor Charlemagne, mysticism was discouraged. The popes and cardinals, who were drawn from aristocratic families of the time, were at pains to establish their own power and were successful in promoting the idea that the Holy Pontiff, whom they regarded as the representative on earth of their founder Jesus, was accordingly entitled to be the spiritual leader of Christendom with power over all kings, rulers and nations.

By that time the idea had been implanted firmly in the minds of the people that Jesus was part of a trinity of himself and his mother Mary and . . . his father God [with whom both were one]. Although Mary his mother formed part of that trinity, the strongly patriarchal church authorities restricted her role to using her to teach the masses of Christians in Europe good and noble qualities. In this process many stories were disseminated about Mary and her worthiness to be an intermediary between the people and God because she had been the mother of His son.

For centuries the masses were illiterate and all learning remained within the hands of the church and controlled by the clergy. The masses comprising the laity were therefore manipulated to accept their view of the world and their religious teaching through theology and dogmatic decrees. The medieval passion plays were developed as part of this manipulation of the masses, and the last remnant of them exists in our time as a popular tourist attraction at Oberammergau, where the enactment of the life of Jesus is played out on a stage with local actors taking the parts of Jesus, his mother and the apostles.

In my view, the cult of Mary has been developed by a male priesthood who projected an image of Mary through statues and artistic depictions that were concerned largely with sorrowing as a mother for her son who had taken the sins of the world upon his shoulders. In every Catholic Church a separate sanctuary exists where men and women can use Mary as an intercessor in their pleading. There are sanctuaries set aside in many churches where people have been led to believe that the saints can act as intercessors with the trinity for help to be given to those who use this form of supplication. The name of Mary is invoked in penances which are given out after sins have been confessed to a priest, and in this way a very powerful conception has been created in the minds of Christians that Mary herself can dispense great favours.

In the same way, I consider Christianity to be entirely circumscribed in its activity by intellectual thought and argument, and I consider also that Mary has been projected to the Catholic masses in an entirely intellectual and emotional way. The way in which the conception of Mary has been transmitted is through the process of hearsay, either by intellectual accounts or by artistic depiction. The average Christian has little direct experience of the femininity of Mary and, although she has been seen collectively at times and has been recorded as having spoken to selected individuals, these experiences are minimal.

The whole point that I have been trying to make is that in the ancient world men and women had access to ceremonies where numinous experiences were encountered in the mass, and where femininity in a much wider range of its aspects was portrayed through experience. The role of Mary, on the other hand, in my view has been narrowed down to the point of being stunted in its conception of femininity by a patriarchal clergy, who have used theological arguments and papal edicts to convince people of what they wish them to believe.

The French Revolution and development of the Cult of Nature in the Age of Enlightenment which followed the revolution did little or nothing to enhance the image of Mary in western Europe. Subsequent to that time, Madame Blavatsky wrote *Isis Unveiled* and denigrated Mary's image, together with that of the Catholic Church. In our own time there is a feminine reaction abroad in the Western world among women in an endeavour to free themselves from the yoke of inequality with men. This feminist movement has developed because it has been postulated that humans have rights, and [that women] should be able to demand complete equality with men in Western society. Unfortunately this movement is an intellectual reaction to the plight that women have found themselves in and which was originally exacerbated by the Christian teaching of a patriarchal clergy.

That view still exists among the clergy, and in the Protestant churches opinion has been divided in connection with the desire of women to be priests and to have an equal role with male priests in the church. In the Roman Catholic Church, from which Christianity has been transmitted to the West, clergy have been told by the authorities in Rome and by the Pope himself that the church has no power to authorise women to enter the priesthood. I am using this to show that Christianity has always been patriarchal in its conceptions and in its constitution, and that changes demanded by feminists are meeting with great resistance even in an age when there is very great freedom of thought and opinion and where lobby groups have tremendous influence on society's affairs and direction.

Even before the fall of Constantinople to the Ottoman Turks, at the time of the Crusades the city was attacked and sacked by western Europe's Christian knights and their armies seeking rich booty to finance their fight against the Muslim forces occupying the Holy Land. This shows that western European culture had little respect and certainly no love for Eastern Christianity. The Church of Rome and its clergy did nothing to enhance the image of Eastern Christianity. Today very little is known about Greek and Russian Orthodoxy and even less about the Coptic Church with its offshoot in Ethiopia. [Less still] is known about Ebonites and other fragmentary groups owing their origin to the teaching of Jesus.

In my view, where there exists lack of familiarity with something in a culture, it does not promote interest in the minds of the people. The idea of Constantinople being used as the City of Mary, I believe, would only promote utter horror in the minds of the Turkish people and would certainly arouse hatred and open aggression in the minds and deeds of Islamic fundamentalists wherever they are situated. In this paper I have tried to point out that femininity is not confined to the cult of Mary in Christianity, where the view of it is totally inadequate to bring complete understanding of femininity, in the range and variety of aspects in which humans are capable of understanding this universal archetype.

Christianity in my view is on the wane, and the seeds of its early destruction are now contained within it. I believe, therefore, that it is useless at this stage to try to enhance the image of Mary, when less and less attention is being given in the modern world to the stunted and psychologically crippled notion of Mary which the Catholic Church has presented to the world throughout the history of Christian teaching. I have tried to convey in this paper how femininity was understood in greater depth in the ancient world than ever it has been understood within Christian teaching. The Gnostic ideas about femininity, and their inclusion of Mary as its exemplar, during short periods of time in Byzantine history, still do not contribute a great deal to the corpus of Christian teaching and belief, and any endeavour to alter that situation is, in my view, not only too late[: it will also] cause little stir in a world where humanism and its thought patterns have displaced ideas or concerns about God or His mother in human affairs.

With regard to the part that femininity plays in relation to mystical development, the best analogy I can give is that femininity takes an individual to the well of sweet water; thereafter the individual has to learn how to draw water from that well in order to deal in a balanced and detached way with the problems encountered in daily living. Extra-sensory perception, developed within the intuitive area of the mind as a result of contemplation, enables an individual to gain greater knowledge about a situation or an encounter than a person using only logic and other similar intellectual processes. In this way more facts can be obtained, and the mind is then capable of using instinct, emotion, intuition and rationalising to deal with a problem in a way that produces what is generally described as the wisest solution or result.

At that stage too, mystics know how to operate with the ebb and flow of the tides of force within the universe because they understand how humans react to the impact of such tides on their being, and they also understand the impact that these forces make on the whole of animate life. When a mystic can hear the music of the spheres and the noise of the grass and trees growing in a garden where an intellectual would find only silence, then the mystic has expanded his or her intellectual consciousness beyond the limits of intellect and the restriction of normal sense perception.

In order to illustrate what I am trying to say here I will set down the experience of an Indian Sufi master. This teacher had many pupils and encouraged them to go out into the gardens surrounding the *madrasah* [religious school] where he normally gave *sohbet* and conducted *dhikr* and prayer. He aimed to widen their ability by observing the behaviour of other people and the passage of natural processes as they took place as the changing year advanced. One day he came upon a pupil who was sitting meditating where children were playing and where it could have been concluded that the pupil could have been disturbed by the shouts and laughter of the children at play. The master approached the pupil and suggested that he should move to another area which was shaded by trees and where the grass looked young and green. The pupil looked up into his master's eyes and said, 'O my master, I have tried it there; it is much too noisy.' The master smiled and chided him gently, saying, 'Oh, you boaster!'

People in the modern world hold the view that they are much more civilised and can conduct themselves in a more just and merciful way than the people whom they [consider to have been] barbarous in ancient civilisations. My contention throughout this paper is that people in most of the ancient civilisations had a better understanding of the universe than we have today, and I blame Christianity in the context in which it has been presented by established churches and the splinter groups which were formed from them as the Western world has progressed towards the dawn of the twenty-first century.

Today the ravings about democracy and human rights by world leaders and political lobby groups have darkened the minds of people to such an extent that they can't see when decisions need to be made in connection with international events. World leaders appear to stagger from one weak situation to another in their endeavours to assume the role of the deity by using humanistic concepts and intellectual arguments. When I look back at mass murder committed in the Soviet Union by dictators like Stalin (which makes German atrocities look less by comparison) and when I review mentally the Japanese murder and terror committed in China, I wonder why the next generation believes that the twentieth century can be so proud of its progress and achievements. The pusillanimity of contemporary governments faced with the breakdown of the Republic of Yugoslavia shows their complete inability to deal with such a situation.

Any situation of an even more complex nature, which will definitely arise in the future, will be beyond the ability of present world leaders to resolve because people in certain areas of the world can see by the ineffectual activity of Western rulers that their influence in the world has declined.

The American people shout about democracy and human rights. When it suited them, their military forces went into places like Panama, where their tanks crushed innocent civilians as they were driving along the roads in their private motor cars. This ruthless destruction of human life and property is typical of the behaviour of the American military forces when they are given a free hand and do not have to account to anybody. Ostensibly the operation was intended to capture General Noriega, the Panamanian dictator, who was accused by the Americans of drug running. The real reason, of course, was to maintain American domination in the Canal Zone of Panama.

Led by America, other Western nations went into Somaliland ostensibly to feed starving people who had suffered from war and famine to such an extent that their country was in complete ruin. Instead of the Westerners continuing to feed the inhabitants, the people to whom they were supposed to be giving aid were suddenly made out to be enemies, and the full might of the American military forces was used in trying to crush these people into submitting to American authority, in a land that was not their own, and in a situation where such activity would have been condemned out of hand not so long ago by the world in general as a murderous intrusion into the affairs of another nation.

When the Americans withdrew, together with all the other indiscriminate do-gooders, and the people in Somaliland were left to themselves, they began to agree with each other and took steps to build up their own country in a much more constructive way than the international community had offered to do.

Humanity has been taught to see only with limited vision and poor intelligence. Civilisation in the Western world as it has been known is in great peril of disintegration from within as well as destruction from without, as a direct result of false guidance through the centuries by a church which promoted its own interests while disseminating a form of religious teaching which bore little or no resemblance to what Jesus [had been] trying to teach his Jewish compatriots.

I believe that the leadership that was established after the death of the Prophet Muhammad (may God honour him and grant him peace) by the rule of rightly guided caliphs whom the people chose from among the Prophet's surviving Companions is the kind of leadership which is capable of dealing with the problems of mankind. Unfortunately the people of the world are not yet in a state of mind where they would be prepared to accept such a system. I leave this to the will of Allah Almighty, knowing that His plan will unfold to bring about the necessary changes.

The site and ruins of the city of Aphrodisias, where beauty has been depicted throughout, [were] constructed with the proportions on which the universe is built, to harmonise in the way of all art forms where the Golden Section (Ø) has been incorporated. We appreciate the buildings and the sculptures instinctively because we are placed in immediate harmony with them, since we ourselves contain exactly the same proportions in our human bodies. This experience of beauty is a product of a response mechanism on the energy within our bodies, which translates into emotional pleasure because we see in such beauty a reflection in terms of feeling response that provides a sense of inner wellbeing and a feeling of happiness at the emotional level. Certain areas of natural beauty where positive and negative currents of energy flow together into harmonious unity provide the same pleasure. The same effect can be encountered in buildings like the Gothic cathedrals and in all other buildings and works where the Golden Section (Ø) has been incorporated.

It is possible to distinguish the feelings within the physical body when they respond to positive and negative forces of energy such as can be encountered when visiting the Lady Chapel at Glastonbury. In the summer I have taken people to the Ile de la Cité in Paris, beside the Cathedral of Nôtre Dame, where steps go from the higher level of the road down to the level of the Seine itself, in order to feel the different energies at separate levels which pass through the cathedral. As I explained earlier, the crypts in Gothic cathedrals were designed to introduce people to an area of balance and harmony where these positive and negative currents flow into each other and give a momentary experience of the inner peace and wellbeing which developed mystics experience constantly within themselves.

Christianity absorbed some of the wisdom of the ancient worlds to which it was first introduced, but through self-interest and intellectual thinking and teaching, that was soon lost. Encounters with experience of the type that the Gothic cathedrals were meant to provide were very soon discontinued, and their meaning was lost. When I was young I could see children playing, on the pavements of back streets in cities, a game of hopscotch on a sequence of chalked squares where diagonal movements were made by hopping on one leg from one square to another. The children taking part in this game had no notion that at one time it was an important factor in stirring energy within the central nervous system[s] of pilgrims, who performed a similar type of dance before entering the cathedral, to make themselves more aware at a feeling level of those responses made in their own bodies by the energies that were in harmony outside themselves. By this means the pilgrims were given a fleeting glimpse of the state of ultimate spiritual harmony in which the mystic flows with life, and life heaps abundance upon the mystic.

In the words of Jesus, they place their faith and trust in the beneficence of their Creator and cast their bread upon the waters, and know full well that in His mercy their bread will be returned to them in the fullness of His time.

I have tried to show in this document that I deplore the influence that Christianity has developed at Rome from the Pauline interpretation of the teaching of the Prophet Jesus. The same dogmatism influenced the church of the east, from which the Greek Orthodox liturgy developed in parallel with the Roman Catholic liturgical development in Rome. Before Islam was introduced to the world, a haphazard type of mysticism was carried on in the deserts of Egypt, but apart from scholarly accounts the experiences of this movement have made little or no impact on Western thinking. In the period of Byzantine culture, Gnosticism was popular sometimes, and unpopular and banned at other times.

One of the most important neo-Platonists was the philosopher and teacher Proclus. Proclus was born in Constantinople in the year 410 AD and lived to the age of seventy-five. He was a known initiate of the mystery cults of Egypt and was personally concerned with the rites of the Greek goddess Hecate (this goddess was connected with the occult, fortune telling and witchcraft, and the origins of her cult were connected with the Egyptian mysteries relating to

The School of Celestial Fire

Osiris and Isis being connected with the star Sirius). He was one of the heads of Plato's Academy at Athens, which lasted for about 900 years.

His influence and the influence of his pupils eventually percolated into Europe after the fall of Constantinople to the Ottomans. Men such as Leonardo da Vinci and Dürer studied his works, as well as [those of] other writers whose works in fragmentary form dealt with the teaching of the Pythagoreans and Orphic cult remnants. The works of Aristotle and Plato were part of scholarly learning, and Western thought leant heavily on the ideas that Aristotle conveyed. When the Roman Catholic Church authorised the operation of the Spanish Inquisition, philosophers and seekers of knowledge about the ancient civilisations which had gone before their time were forced to keep any mystical inclination of theirs a close secret in case it was conveyed to the church authorities.

The school that Leonardo da Vinci and his contemporaries had studied in had branched out in Germany under the influence of Dürer, and this school eventually became centred on Prague. Queen Elizabeth I of England, who looked upon herself as the champion of the Protestant faith and was regarded as an enemy of the Roman Catholic Church, sent John Dee to spy in Europe, and he obtained information from Prague of a political kind as well as teachings from the mystical order there. During that time mysticism was brought to England by Giordano Bruno, and at that time men like Francis Bacon, William Shakespeare, Sir Philip Sidney and the Earl of Leicester were all associates of his. Shakespeare's plays [contain] allusions to mystical teaching, and in *The Tempest* a very clear understanding of alchemy is contained.

The secret development of mysticism in western Europe, which developed outside the authority of the Christian church, was influenced by Jewish mysticism. In Spain, during the time of the Moorish rule there, the Jews were permitted freedom of worship and were not discriminated against by the Islamic authorities. When Ferdinand and Isabella drove the last of the Moors from Spain, the Jews fled to Portugal and to Italy, and a few went to the island of Rhodes. These Sephardic Jews had had cultural contact with their brethren in Alexandria, had obtained much of the Gnostic teaching, and had absorbed the learning that was available in the Great Library of Alexandria before it was destroyed by a Christian mob. They claimed that their rabbinical knowledge was a direct transmission from the time of the Essenes, the mystical contemporaries of John the Baptist and Jesus, who were both Essenes (the Romans called the Essenes Therapeutiae or Healers). The Essenes in turn were mystics who [had] inherited their teaching from the Zadokites, with whom all the prophets of Israel were associated. (They lived apart from the activities of the Temple, which were served by the Levites.)

The Sephardic mystical tradition claimed therefore to have received a continuous transmission at least from the days of the Prophet Samuel if not earlier. The Rabbi Shimeon Ben Jochai was responsible for its transmission in Spain, although it was claimed that he had in fact lived in the Holy Land at the time of Saladin and the Knights Templar. One of the great Jewish rabbis[61] who made many commentaries in relation to Jewish religious matters was a physician at the court of Saladin, and since Suhrawardi and other Sufi mystics were contemporary with him, their beliefs and experiences were exchanged in the way that the Knights Templar were also influenced by Sufi teaching.

The method by which Jewish mysticism was introduced in western Europe was through an explanation of the Kabbalah. The theme of the divine man, Adam Kadmon, provided the illustration for the secret writings explaining the mystical processes that went towards his creation. Studies related to the Kabbalah brought about interest in Islamic alchemy, and this influenced Christian alchemy to develop together with cabalistic studies. The story of Christian Rosenkreutz is . . . one of the best-known alchemical legends, of which there are many. These were transmitted down through the various schools teaching mystical knowledge in western Europe. Most were based in Germany and Holland because they were areas of Protestant Christianity.

Freemasonry or Speculative Masonry was very much influenced by remnants of the Knights Templar who escaped from the purge of their order after it had been banned by the Pope just after the time of the Albigensian rebellion. The French Revolution brought about what was considered the Age of Enlightenment because these mystical teachings were brought out into the open after that time. Many schools of mysticism remained secret, but their secrecy was not of the same kind as that imposed by fear when the Inquisition could maim, burn and kill mystics. In the transmission to the West, mysticism of a Gnostic kind was added to and subtracted from as various writers placed their own interpretation upon its development.

None of it, however, can claim purity in its transmission in the way that Islamic Sufis can claim that their transmission goes back in its purity to the Prophet himself and to the caliphs Abu Bakr and Ali. The Western establishment of an intellectual culture tended to follow the same dogmatic attitudes in secular life as the Roman Catholic Church had displayed in relation to religion throughout European history. In the ancient world there was a much purer form of mystical tradition, because it can be demonstrated that, although

---

61 Moses Maimonides.

Proclus lived 700 years after Plato, he was capable of understanding the works of Plato and was able to provide details of an explanatory nature where Plato had not provided them. It is a great pity, therefore, that mysticism should not have been understood in the clear-minded way that Proclus wrote about it. This is the reason that I blame Christianity for the way in which people in the modern world think intellectually and act in such a confused and haphazard way.

In this paper I have tried to convey what I believe is the concern of real mysticism. Although people have become free thinkers, nowadays they still think only in intellectual terms and have closed their minds, using similar mechanisms to those which the Roman Catholic Church introduced centuries ago into western Europe. With regard to my remarks about Christianity, I make no apology for them, because I believe that Jesus was a prophet who taught in the Hebrew mystical tradition, and that what he taught was similar to the teaching of John the Baptist and the Essenes. The teaching given by the Apostle James, who became first Bishop of Jerusalem, is still carried on by an Aramaic-speaking remnant in modern Syria which has been ignored by the main body of Christians today, in the way that the church in the past ignored their existence.

Although the gospels recorded in the New Testament contain much of what Jesus taught, and accounts of his mission, much of the original has been altered during the passage of time. The initial gap between his death and the record which now exists must have taxed the memory of those who dictated from memory to the people who actually recorded the gospels. Subsequent amendments were made to the original written versions in order to agree with various interpretations given them by church councils. (Modern scholars seem still to be anxious to continue this process, and some have even speculated about homosexuality, sexual promiscuity and participation in a mushroom-eating cult. Like the church fathers, modern scholars put no bounds on their desire to indulge in speculation.)

I would say that Christianity as it has been taught, together with the dissemination of Christian notions relating to the cult of Mary, [is] based on an intellectually constructed myth. The idea of Mary was borrowed in the first instance from the Egyptian legend of Isis and Osiris and was subsequently distorted to incorporate Christian ideas during the long period of the church's domination of Western Christian thinking.

The myths and legends of the ancient world were, on the other hand, constructed on facts. As well as being part of the psychological heritage of humanity that Christians have tried so ruthlessly to eradicate throughout the history of western Europe, the legends of the ancient world contained warnings which people need today just as much as the people in the ancient world needed them in their time.

Christians observe All Souls' Day in November each year, when the dead are remembered, but most of them do not understand what this really commemorates. In the ancient world it was known that a cataclysm had occurred in which a great flood had engulfed a continent. Plato refers to this in the *Timaeus*. In the Holy Koran warnings are repeatedly given about disaster overtaking mankind. Similar disasters are recorded in the Book of Revelation in the Bible. These warnings are the latest versions that have come down to us from a tradition contained in most of the ancient legends about a disaster which overtook the world at an earlier period.

Ancient priests and mystical initiates knew that a whole series of disasters had occurred, and that disasters would occur in the future. Modern science now believes that the dinosaurs were destroyed by such a disaster, and the warnings to which I have referred all point to a similar disaster. The ancients were able to pinpoint the source of such disasters and knew when they were due to occur.

The ancient mysteries contain real knowledge based on the observation of the universe itself, and relate to our ongoing development today. I believe that the ancient sages were pointing out that intellectual thought is incapable of arriving at the solutions which humanity requires to understand the warnings which were consistently reiterated. They knew that humanity had to develop the human mind to another level of operation, at an octave higher than that at which Western thinking now operates. This can only be done by a process of mystical development which enables humanity to be guided so that it may avoid similar disasters to those which wiped out previous civilisations, with tremendous loss of life.

7

This is part of a letter to a pupil dated 4 April 1996.

SUFISM is a separation in the mind, between the outer life of the world and the inner life of spirituality, which the Sufi performs as a life of outward activity [while] at the same time, on an inner journey, [attempting] not to distinguish one person, object or experience [from another—in such a way that when] assessing each experience . . . only the same level of enthusiasm in the reaction to the encounter is applied in each case.

In other words, the Western way of analysing produces a whole range of emotional reactions which clutter the mind, do damage to the body through the impact of the negative mental impressions created, and therefore prevent our ability to develop the process which meditation is designed to do by directing the attention to deeper levels of unconsciousness in the mind to make them conscious to ourselves.

When we engage on a life where every task is performed with the alacrity and joy that we pour upon the things which are dearest to our hearts, and we apply that method to everything that we observe or encounter—in observing all our encounters with this similarity of attention and application, these encounters that we experience are understood in an objective [way], so that we begin in the inner life, which is kept private and secret, to understand more about ourselves by observing our reactions to everything we encounter. In this way we can learn to counter the negative reactions which we have grown up with in ourselves quite unconsciously (in our development from the time of our childhood) by reacting in this new-patterned way.

When that is strictly adhered to, and the repetition of the name of the Creator is consistently running through the mind and we hear it like our own voice repeating it, then we are prevented [from] being carried away in our introverted imagination to dream on in an egocentric way where our ego is the hero, and we re-live our belief its brilliant ability to perform wonders or we encounter bitterness and inward tears because we dwell only on the self-inflicted hurts we brought upon ourselves while haphazardly undergoing experience.

Slowly, over the years, by the repetitive application of the exercises prescribed, we gain control over the mind, which was formerly a prisoner of the commanding *nafs*. Because we are able to find in this control an inner calm and acceptance which is the submission to our lord, who enters into our being to bring about a change to the negative, chaotic and melancholic life the average individual leads and thinks is freedom, [we enter] one of consistent wonder and praise for the blessings of our lord.

Only when you achieve an inner balance does this come about, and when that inner balance is achieved you will find that deep from within your own being a whole new breadth of vision develops automatically in the form of counselling that seems to come from nowhere and is certainly not the result of the processes of intellect engaged on working on a problem analytically or logically.

When these thoughts come into the mind they tend to be ignored at first because of inner inattention in the process of observing the self and how it operates. When you are fully aware of what you are doing, and the counselling wells up from within and demands your attention, then the words can be heard like conversation or someone directing you.

Unfortunately, many people who have this experience feel that it unhinges their minds because they have not trained themselves by the processes and exercises I have described [earlier in this letter], and which have always been prescribed for disciplining the minds of my *murids* so that they may become capable of entering into other states of consciousness in a balanced way, free from the wiles of the *nafs* and the distorting interpretation which the *nafs* provides to keep an individual in its grip. . . .

Be constantly humble and learn to attribute all your misfortunes to your own doing, and ask Allah Almighty constantly to help you achieve a balance within your mind by discovering that your thoughts and actions condition and bring about everything that occurs to you in life.

8

ON DREAMS

This is part of a letter to a pupil written in January 1975.

I NEED to explain to you a very important aspect of human behaviour. When people think and act in life, they project their view of life on to all objects and people. For example, the affection men have for old clothes and for their cars and tools; pipe smokers for their pipes; the love of a woman for her home, and the sentimental value she attaches to objects which in other eyes could be mere trivia. This leads to close identification with our surroundings and the people we meet and are associated with.

Because we all hold views about life based on our experience and beliefs, we introduce these views to colour all the judgments we make and to affect our conclusions. In discussing abstract things or events or people, we are not as objective as we imagine, because we think intellectually. Part of this pattern-making process involves teaching us the use of analysis and criticism. The most educated and rational humans consider that they are always constructive in their criticism.

Because criticism involves analysis (i.e. breaking down) it is by nature destructive.

When we think, therefore, we project all our notions on to people and objects, and when the rich (for example) think, they project notions about 'them' (other people) which are related to the poor or the communists or the 'gnomes of Zurich' [financiers], etc. Such figures are the bad men and women—the villains in the situation—and therefore not only become popular scapegoats but in dreams take the villainous roles in the scenes portrayed in the 'inner theatre' of the mind.

In many cases we dissociate from our cellars (the instincts) when we live in the attic (the intellect). We do this by dreaming that servants or slaves or people in inferior social states act in a low moral way. We therefore see their actions as inferior in a moral sense, and yet remain cut off from them because we have projected in our dreams as we do in our daily lives. The servants or slaves (our inferiors) are free to express themselves in their low, vulgar fashion and we go on judging them; but what we are really doing in our dreams is seeing aspects of our own being from which we are normally cut off in waking life by our constant analysis and criticism of 'them' by 'us', of 'you' by 'me'.

People, therefore, in dreams are the props on which we hang the projections of our moods, beliefs, ideas and emotions, etc. When you understand this thoroughly you will begin to learn a lot about yourself and the falseness of 'self'.

9

SELF-OBSERVATION

This is a section of the notes given to new pupils of the Sheikh when they were prescribed exercises after having attended his lectures consistently for some time.

THIS EXERCISE is most important. People are a product of their mechanical habit patterns. They have no co-ordination between their bodies, thoughts, feelings or instincts. This exercise helps you to see your real condition and not how you imagine yourself to be. Stated simply, it means being mentally present at whatever you are doing physically. For example, when you get out of bed in the morning, make yourself conscious of your movements precisely and deliberately. Carry them out with an awareness of your whole physical body—sense yourself as you go about your daily activities.

As you get out of bed, know what you do *as* you do it. As you put your feet on the carpet, be clearly aware of it; as you lift yourself off the bed and walk towards the door, maintain that awareness; etc. The aim is to make all your actions *intentional* and not to have mind and body living separate cut-off lives within your being. Most people, for example, tie their shoelaces as they think about what they are going to do next, perhaps with their emotions 'pressured' by worries about getting to work on time. In that example alone, three distinct and fragmented experiences are taking place simultaneously!

Normally when people are doing something they are so deep in the imaginary areas of their mind that they are almost completely oblivious of their surroundings. Such a state of mind can be dangerous because it leads to being accident-prone. The observing exercise leads to a sense of immediacy and gives an alertness by making you live in the 'now'. It is designed to stop you living in an imaginary future or in nostalgic re-runs of the past—both of which detract from the present moment.

It is a difficult exercise to perform. People can usually keep it up for only a few minutes at a time to begin with. However, it is a key exercise in the development of your powers of concentration and the sharpening of your awareness. Good concentration is vital for the exploration of deeper areas of the mind. The secret lies in its ability to teach you to do one thing at a time, and to do that one thing with the whole of you, not just a part of you. It should be done with the highest degree of concentration you can muster.

Another way of looking at it is to say that doing the exercise involves dividing your attention so that you are simultaneously aware of yourself AND whatever it is you are observing. If you are sitting down talking to someone, try to be aware of your body and its posture, together with the position of your arms and legs. At the same time as you mentally register what is being said, take in the entire scene visually presented to you. In this way you absorb 'information' from the total situation and not just certain narrow aspects of it. Normally people forget their own presence and use words in a form of verbal ping-pong.

By doing this exercise you become *observer* and *observed* simultaneously whilst being stabilised by tactile contact with your own body. Inner and outer aspects of life are linked in a new way, and this enables you to stand back from yourself and become an impartial observer of life. This gives you greater objectivity and makes you aware of how your own instincts, emotions and intellect are *automatically* reacting to life's events in a very mechanical way. Eventually—though this has to be verified individually—this exercise shows how in reality people are at the mercy of their habit patterns and emotional and instinctual compulsions at various levels of their minds. These different areas go largely unnoticed in ordinary life but in fact almost totally condition human behaviour.

People's idea of their personal freedom turns out to be an illusion when put to this test. Life goes on in these 'grooves' of behaviour which in effect virtually control a person's reactions to events. Since people do not have sufficiently developed powers of concentration, they do not have *continuity of consciousness*. Continuity of experience is therefore also lost because attention is scattered and fragmented, and experience is chopped up into separate parts.

The result is that often people cannot learn from the experiences that life continually presents to them. Instead, life goes on in a vague, disconnected way like a series of still shots taken with an automatic camera pointed at random in different directions. Without the controlling influence or stability which self-observation provides, this welter of incoming fragmented information assails the senses and often causes people to become confused so that they live in a chaos within themselves.

Automatic responses take place all the time in the mind and body, and it is these mechanical reactions that deprive people of their peace of mind.

Self-observation properly done over a long period helps you to take your reactions into account. It gradually enables you to separate yourself from your unconscious responses so that you can eventually begin to assert a degree of control over your reactions, and later on, over the various states which are encountered in mystical experience. Thus you learn how to 'be' and cease continually to 'do' things automatically. Your mind can then observe your actions at the time they actually occur.

This exercise has many other aims which are not at first apparent. It helps to slowly replace old habit patterns with new sets of more useful patterns conducive to the expansion of consciousness. It helps to slow down the continuous, rambling stream of thoughts that most people are compelled to endure at the surface of their intellect, which in itself is one of the veils between the conscious and subconscious parts of the mind. It straightens out chaotic dream experiences, which are a reflection of the chaos of the ordinary waking state of most people. When certain meditational or contemplative practices are later undertaken and produce visual phenomena, you will be able to study them objectively without reacting in an involuntary way.

The idea behind the exercise is to make you more like a passive cine camera than the automatic still camera mentioned above. You continuously monitor everything going on around you and in you at the same time.

Staring fixedly at the object of observation can help in this process. It enables you to 'absorb' the object seen, which in turn leads to a tactile relationship with it. When doing this, don't pick out analytically any one aspect of a view seen by the field of vision. Try to take in the whole field in its entirety. This way you 'sink in' to yourself and your surroundings and experience a form of unity. Letting the gaze switch to infinity in a panoramic 180-degree way helps.

Coupled with other exercises, self-observation plays an important part in making pupils centred: that is, living within themselves so that there is a clear polarity between 'out there' and 'in here'. Eventually by consistent practice of the exercise you are not dislodged by life's knocks and can maintain your inner peace. You cease to be the plaything of any stray influence. In this way, you eventually reach the 'beam of your own balance' psychologically.

The difficulty of this exercise demonstrates how little real control over their being people actually have. Try to remember that in essence it should be a process of *relaxed alertness*. Try not to make the common mistake of observing yourself so hard that it produces more tensions than it cures. Gradually increase the length of time you can do this exercise until you can practise it all day. This leads to permanent self-consciousness. Remember—at any instant of the day your attention is focused on something. Find out what that something is!

A greater continuity of personal awareness can be gained by using the method of invocation [another word for *dhikr*]—that is, constant repetition of certain words or phrases from the Holy Koran. This helps to keep you more centred within yourself, more objectively internalised and therefore more 'present' or living in the 'now' through stronger awareness of each moment and your existence in it.

The words 'Allah-Hu' are prescribed for this exercise. [They] can be repeated rapidly as a mental technique to screen out stray, associative thoughts from the mind, or more slowly as a meditation technique to link yourself with deeper areas of your being, particularly later on when the mind has settled down and is less prone to wander. If performed assiduously and as prescribed, it prevents intellectual and emotional fantasising from controlling your mind.

You need to be more aware, and in order to be more aware you have to focus your mind more clearly on moment-to-moment occurrences. Awareness is the aim and the technique for self-discovery. It unifies your being and stabilises your consciousness. Invocation correctly used can greatly aid this process and help to take the tedium out of the basic observation practice.

The biggest distraction to the job of stabilising your inner world is the noise and hubbub of the external world. You have to learn to stand at the threshold of both inner and outer aspects of your life (facing inwards and outwards simultaneously, if you like) so that you live your life completely.

To the Seeker

IN THE WORDS of Sheikh Abdullah Sirr-Dan al-Jamal, to find the state of peace achieved by mystics who have reached the ultimate goal, 'it is necessary to seek them out, associate with them and emulate their example'.

Although there are thousands of Sufis, including some in Western countries, there are also pseudo-Sufis and fake Sufis. By no means everyone who is called, or calls themselves, a sheikh (in Persian *pir*) is a Sufi, let alone a real Sufi teacher.

A real Sufi teacher is a Muslim, whether male or female, who has been authorised to give spiritual exercises, guidance and formal instruction by another teacher whose authority in turn reaches back through an unbroken chain of Sufi teachers to the Prophet Muhammad. Full stop.

This chain of transmission, the *silsilah*, is unique to Sufism and thus distinguishes it from other all other mystical traditions. Its existence means that no one can decide to become a sheikh, in the true meaning of the term. Indeed the *khirqa*—the cloak or other garment that betokens spiritual inheritance—is never bestowed on anyone who actually seeks it. Sheikh Abdullah emphasised that his pupil Abdul-Aziz had only been made a sheikh (of the Mevlevi Order, the 'whirling dervishes') because he did not want to be one, unlike what Sheikh Abdullah called 'the ambitious bastards all around me'.

Moreover, as he said, a real Sufi cannot be bought, and by the same token no one can buy 'sheikhhood'.

The great Rumi not only warned the seeker, 'The way has been marked out: if you depart from it you will perish.' He also warned those who would teach: 'If you try to interfere with the signs on the road, you will be an evildoer.' But that evil is only real because there really is a way, and it really has been marked out. It is there to be followed.

Sheikh Abdullah himself knew that he would leave no direct successor, having said long ago, 'No one will ever wear my *khirqa*.' If you find a genuine teacher in these difficult times, you will face no easy task in observing their behaviour, and thus verifying their sincerity, without using their imagined faults as excuses to protect your own.

Meanwhile we hope you will find something in this book that you can use on the journey: perhaps illumination, perhaps encouragement, or at least overwhelming reason to pursue the straight path—and a resolve never to be content with words; for as Bahauddin Naqshband himself said, 'If you keep these teachings in action, new words will come to you all the time. A person who works only to know is like someone accumulating more and more food they never eat.'

And if all you find here is comfort, you have got the wrong end of the stick.

www.ingramcontent.com/pod-product-compliance
Lightning Source LLC
Chambersburg PA
CBHW022105150426
43195CB00008B/276